**Land Tenure
and Land Taxation
in America**

Land Tenure and Land Taxation in America

By Aaron M. Sakolski, Ph. D.

[handwritten correction: "orton" inserted, making "Morton"]

ROBERT SCHALKENBACH FOUNDATION
NEW YORK

333.3
Sa291

COPYRIGHT © 1957 BY ROBERT SCHALKENBACH FOUNDATION, INC.
50 EAST 69TH STREET, NEW YORK, N.Y.

PRINTED IN U.S.A.

Foreword

The task to which this book is dedicated is primarily historical. The author sought first to show how land was settled in the United States from early colonial times onward, and against this background to trace the evolution of our present land-tenure system. In pursuing this objective, however, he overstepped the essential bounds of the historian. The story that emerges is faithfully documented, but in the telling, it is enriched by an understanding of economics and philosophy. An example of this is the author's discussion of the various proposals that have been made for the taxation of land, and the probable effect of these proposals upon land use and social development. Much, therefore, of what the reader will find helps to illuminate the larger problem of land tenure throughout the world.

In all history land, as distinct from other property, has played a significant and singular role in human progress. In its evolutionary process landownership has changed from a collective concept wherein absolute title rested with no one individual or group, to a legal status whereby individuals or groups obtained the power to hold, use, transfer and transmit its use and tenure for personal benefit, without regard to public welfare. This upheaval, almost universal in the history of mankind, has been one of the principal sources of the strife, the discontent, the political corruption and the economic ruin which have marked the course of great nations. That the problem has been less serious in the United States than in most other countries of the world is due not only to the comparative youth of our nation, but also to the fact that until recently there has been an abundance of "free land" to be had. The country, however, is now thoroughly populated. "Free land" is at an end. As Dr. Sakolski emphasizes, "The history of this process, including an understanding of the 'regard' for land and the evolution of the institution of landownership and use in the United States . . . is worthy of study, if for no other reason than that it forms a basis for future trends and may give indications of the need for a new quest for economic justice."

The land question, as yet unsolved even in this blessed nation of ours, still calls for more than passing thought on the part of our leaders, and today Thomas Jefferson's sage dictum, "The small holders are the most precious part of a state," is the inspiration for enlightened legislation in many of our forty-eight states. Marshall Harris, in his excellent work, *The Origin of the Land Tenure System in the United States* (Iowa State College Press, 1953), points out that ". . . more than a dozen states have endeavored to foster home ownership for the common man by exempting small homesteads from a variety of taxes. Intense interest is found in at least one state and among liberal thinkers as to the advisability of following Jefferson's suggestion by increasing real estate taxes on large landholdings, probably in geometrical progression as they become larger." And these examples could be multiplied.

Another illustrious American, Henry George, expounded Jefferson's thought in his classic volume, *Progress and Poverty*. In prose of remarkable power and beauty, he explained the relationship of man to the land, the ownership of which ". . . is the great fundamental fact which ultimately determines the social, the political, and consequently the intellectual and moral condition of a people." And who will challenge him when he says, "And it must be so. For land is the habitation of man, the storehouse upon which he must draw for all his needs, the material to which his labor must be applied for the supply of all his desires. . . . On the land we are born, from it we live, to it we return again—children of the soil as truly as is the blade of grass or the flower of the field."

Reverting again to the current scene, we may cite a resolution (370-1951) adopted by the Economic and Social Council of the United Nations. This resolution strongly urges its member governments to institute appropriate measures of land reform in the interest of the landless, as well as the small and medium farmers. How reminiscent of the Jeffersonian ideals, and how timeless the good sense!

In many Eastern countries, and some European nations, too, legislation has been enacted that seeks to vest ownership in the man who tills the soil, and to increase the area owned by subsistence farmers. These are the avenues that these nations hope will lead to more adequate food supplies, more decent standards of living, and the more stable economies which are the most potent guarantees of peace.

We deeply regret that the author of this book, Dr. Aaron Morton Sakolski, is not here to write his own foreword. He met his death in an automobile accident on December 29, 1955, while type for this book was being set. Insofar as we have been able, we have tried to accent those thoughts which we believe were uppermost in his mind.

Dr. Sakolski will be remembered for a previous work on the land question, *The Great American Land Bubble*, published in 1932. That memory, we hope, will be etched more deeply as a result of this posthumously published volume, forthrightly titled *Land Tenure and Land Taxation in America*. If our selection of a title is less colorful than the work deserves, it has the simple virtue of underscoring the author's prime intent, uniting the two subjects, land tenure and land taxation as a means of emphasizing their relationship.

Our most grateful thanks go to Dr. Paul W. Gates of Cornell University, himself the author of many outstanding books on land tenure. It was Dr. Gates who assumed the burden of reading proof, of verifying and standardizing quotations, and of checking Bibliography. Without his skillful and painstaking efforts, the book could not appear in its present carefully documented form.

The Publishers

Contents

1. **Landownership—Its Philosophical and Political Aspects** 1
   Landownership among primitive peoples. Land tenure among the American aborigines. Primitive Mexican land tenure. Summary.

2. **The European Background** 11
   The feudal system. The introduction of feudalism in England. The progress of feudal land tenure in England.

3. **Land Systems of the Colonial Era** 18
   The classes of chartered companies. The merchant adventurers. The development of the joint stock company. The Plymouth and Virginia Companies. The early New England and New York land systems. Absentee ownership in New England. The town proprietors of New England. The New England plantation allotments. The New Hampshire grants. The Dutch land system in New York. The Rensselaerwick manor.

4. **Virginia and the Proprietary Colonies** 33
   Land distribution in Virginia. The proprietary colonies. The proprietary grants in New Jersey and Pennsylvania. The Maryland palatinate. The Carolinas. The Georgia colonial land policy. The quitrent system. The motives and methods of colonial land distribution. Summary on colonial land systems. Philosophic conceptions of landed property in the colonial era.

5. The Colonial Land Speculations 46

The early Maine speculation. The early southern land companies. The Indian Line. The Transylvania Company. George Washington's interest in western lands. Franklin's "Vandalia Company." Population pressure as a factor in westward movement. Summary.

6. Land and the American Revolution 59

The abolishment of the law and custom of primogeniture. Jefferson's influence on land-tenure reform. The Continental Congress and land—the Northwest Ordinance. Land in the Constitutional Convention. Landownership proposed as a voting qualification. Land taxation in the Constitutional Convention.

7. Post-Revolutionary State-Land Disposal 69

The disposal of New York state lands. The Phelps and Gorham Purchase. The Wadsworths, lords of the Genesee. The Ogden and Macomb Purchases. Speculation in Pennsylvania and Virginia land warrants. The Georgia "Yazoo" lands. Massachusetts and the Maine lands. Summary.

8. The Early History of the Public Domain 82

The Northwest Ordinance. Sale of land to the Ohio Company. The Symmes Purchase. The Connecticut Company. Summary.

9. The Early Public Land Administration—Town-Jobbing and Land Engrossment 94

Town-jobbing on public land sites. Early public land engrossment. The prairie regions opened up. Early British speculations in western lands. Summary.

10. The Louisiana Territory 106

The antedating of Spanish grants. The squatter claims. Some prominent Spanish land claims. Summary.

Contents

11. **The Public Domain under the Pre-emption Acts** **124**
    The impact of the "Specie Circular." The passage of the Pre-emption Acts. The Swamp Land Acts. Landlordism and land engrossment in the pre-emption period. Land companies in land engrossment. Summary.

12. **The Public Domain Since the Homestead Act** **136**
    The "opening up" of new lands. Frauds and abuses in the Homestead era. The California and New Mexico land grants. Mexican land grants in New Mexico. Summation of land-disposal policies.

13. **Texas Land Disposal** **148**
    Galveston Bay and Texas Land Company.

14. **The Early Railroad Land Grants** **156**
    Early grants to railroads. Illinois Central Railroad—the first large railroad land grant. Summary.

15. **The Transcontinental Land Grants** **165**
    The Northern Pacific Railroad. The origin of the "bonanza farms." Summary.

16. **Political Repercussions of Public Land Policy** **175**
    The early conflict of opinions. Followers of George Henry Evans. The "safety-valve" theory.

17. **Landownership and Land Disposal in Local Politics** **185**
    Land reforms in New York State and New England. Land politics in the former proprietary states. Summary.

18. **Forest and Mineral Lands Developments** **199**
    The forests and their exploitation. Government timber-land disposal. The Weyerhaeuser timber-land holdings. Why the public should own forest land. The disposition and concentration of mineral lands. Impact of the California gold discoveries. The engrossment and concentration of mineral lands. The engrossment of coal-bearing lands. The engrossment of iron-ore-bearing lands. Exploitation of oil-bearing lands.

19. Farm Tenancy and Its Problems 217

Farm tenancy before the Civil War. Farm tenancy after the Civil War. The evils of farm tenancy. The Bankhead-Jones Farm Tenant Act. European policy on farm tenancy. Tenancy and leased-land statistics.

20. The Rise of Urban Real Estate Values 230

Post-Revolutionary boom towns. Washington, the Federal City. Rise of real estate values in the City of New York. The story of Chicago real estate. San Francisco and Los Angeles real estate. Corporation urban engrossment. Summary.

21. The Land and Taxes 248

The European precedents. Early colonial land taxation. Land taxation in the early federal period. Land taxation merges into the general property tax. Taxation of improvements. The incidence of land taxation. Proposals for taxation as remedies for the land question.

22. The Progress of Land Reform in the United States 262

The pioneers in land reform. Early American land reformers. The land question and early American economists. Labor and the land question. The coming of Henry George. The influence of George on land reform and taxation.

23. Landownership: What of the Future? 277

Bungling administration of the public domain. Land reform and international problems. Should we have land reform? The dangers confronting us. What are the remedies? Absorption of the economic rent of land and untaxing improvements. The progressive tax on land. Limitations to landownership. Social control of land use. Land nationalization not necessary.

Chapter 1

Landownership—
Its Philosophical and Political Aspects

There is probably no more controversial question in history than that relating to primitive landownership. For more than two centuries philosophers, historians, sociologists, and anthropologists, as well as others, have conducted research in this subject and each, in the absence of direct or contemporary evidence, has, as a rule, expressed different views or has come to diverse conclusions. Some have held that private ownership of land was a usurpation; that land originally was held in common ownership; that it belonged to the clan or the tribe; that, unlike other forms of property, it was held for the benefit of all and not for a few; that its use was controlled by the ruling authority, whether sovereign, chief, or patriarch; and it was only through some form of usurpation that it was privately engrossed and, in this way, the community or society became separated into landowners, slaves and serfs, or tenants.[1] Thus Sir Henry Maine, the renowned British historian and anthropologist, holds:

> We have the strongest reason for thinking that property once belonged not to individuals nor even to isolated families, but to

[1] When we speak of ownership of land *in common,* we do not imply common occupation of land. From the very beginning of human society, it was undoubtedly the practice of individuals or families to occupy exclusively a tract of land on which they settled and which they used for pasturage or cultivation. But this does not mean that the land was considered their private property or that there was a right of absolute or fee ownership. It can be assumed, as historical studies reveal, that the title to the land, as property, was in the community as a whole, though its occupancy and use were by individuals or groups.

larger societies composed on the patriarchal model. . . . It is more than likely that joint ownership and not separate ownership is the really archaic institution.[2]

This view is supported by E. B. Tylor,[3] another British authority, along with L. H. Morgan[4] and, in approximately the same form, by Herbert Spencer and Lord Avebury, by the Belgian economist, Emile de Laveleye,[5] and the German historian, G. L. von Maurer,[6] as well as other writers of lesser note.

The thesis of these exponents of primitive society, however, has not met with general approval—but in most cases the criticism is based on skepticism rather than outright opposition. Thus the French scholar, Fustel de Coulanges, in his classic work, *The Origin of Property in Land,* takes to task the theories put forth by several of the proponents of the communal land of primitive society, but he does not refute the thesis—he merely points out errors in the historical evidence and even admits that in very early times among certain peoples communal landownership existed. Thus Fustel de Coulanges writes:

> I do not wish to combat the theory. What I want to do is only to examine the authorities on which it is based. I intend simply to take all these authorities, as they are presented to us by the authors of the system, and to verify them. The object of this cold and tedious procedure is not that of proving whether the theory is true or false; it is only to discover whether the authorities that have been quoted can be fairly regarded as appropriate.[7]

Another skeptic of the nature of primitive landownership is the German economic historian, Max Weber, who, in his *General Economic History,* edited by Hellman and Palyr, New York, 1927, stated that "nothing definite can be said in general terms about the economic life of primitive man," and he supports the idea that, as far as German

---

[2] *Ancient Law,* 4th American ed., p. 251.
[3] *Anthropology,* p. 419.
[4] *Ancient Society,* pp. 527-28, 541-42.
[5] *Primitive Property.*
[6] *Einleitung in die Geschichte der Mark-Hof-Dorf-und Stadtverfassung.*
[7] *The Origin of Property in Land,* p. 3.

economic organization is concerned, it was probable that it had its basis in private property in land and not agrarian communism. And so the controversy in "conjectural history" continues!

Landownership among Primitive Peoples

In the arguments pro and con regarding primitive landownership, recent writers are resorting largely to anthropological studies of uncivilized tribes and peoples living under current primitive cultures. Here again we get a diversity of facts and opinions. But as pointed out by Professor George Raymond Geiger, "There is one type of generalization that the anthropologist permits himself to make in handling primitive property, and that is a distinction between property in land and property in movable chattels—a distinction that seems most impressive. This generalization tends to point out that private property in movables is much more clearly defined than property in land. Whereas with land there is ordinarily the emphasis upon joint ownership, the personal titles to chattels, on the contrary, are rather strictly individualized, and a collective treatment of land may go hand in hand with the private ownership of goods and implements. . . . This does not mean that a decisive and single system of collective land tenure is set up as against the private control of movables; it is simply that there seems to be a *general* difference in emphasis in the disposition of these two forms of primitive property."[8]

What Professor Geiger refers to is the restrictions regarding the holding, use, and transmission (i.e., transfer) of land, existing among primitive peoples, which has persisted among more highly civilized cultures, as contrasted with the indifference applied to the right of possession of movables. This may be the evolutionary basis of the feudal system, which has been so widely prevalent throughout the world and which, both in its political and economic aspects, has had a significant impact on the development of modern civilization.

The fact that land, even among primitive and aboriginal peoples, had a different property status than movables is clear evidence that land, whether privately held or collectively owned and used, is a category of realty that is distinctive in its political, economic, and social

[8] *The Theory of the Land Question*, p. 115.

importance. Land has been universally proclaimed as essential to existence, as air and water, but, unlike most other forms of property, it is not reproducible and is not created by human effort. It has a definite and immutable status, which by nature makes it a monopoly. Its transfer of ownership cannot be made by passing possession, but must be attested by some formal means. Even among the most aboriginal tribes where private holding or ownership exists, land transfer or allotment is conducted by ceremonial procedures. And in this process it is manifest that the interest of the community as a whole is involved. Thus land laws have developed from the earliest times, and it is clear from the character of these laws that land, as a species of property, is not only distinctive but has specialized social, political, and economic significance.[9]

It is on this philosophical background that the land question is of such paramount importance in human progress. The problem of landownership and control; the systems of land tenure, past and present; the exploitation of slaves and serfs; the revolts of peasants and other political upheavals; the poverty of peoples; the hierarchy of classes; and many other inequalities and disturbances, past and present, have their roots in the land question.

In earlier times the question was largely political, though it shaped the economic life of the people. Today it is both an economic and a political, as well as a moral, question—a question of economic justice. In the words of Francis Nielson: "It is essential in our inquiry, therefore, that we couple the tracing of the economic basis of early communities with a clear understanding of what we mean by this term justice, and it is necessary for us to inquire whether the early laws of land settlement were just."[10]

Perhaps it might be well here, as a support of this statement, to quote Charles Letourneau, the French anthropologist. In the preface of his book, *Property, Its Origin and Development,* he states:

[9] See *In Quest of Justice,* by Francis Neilson, The Robert Schalkenbach Foundation, New York, 1944, pp. 6–7.

[10] As an illustration, see the recent British Government publication, *Land Tenure in Basutoland,* by V. Sheddick.

In all civilised societies which have preceded our own, the absolute supremacy of the unrestrained and selfish right of private property has been the forerunner of decadence, the main cause of ruin. A more enlightened humanity, having . . . succeeded in creating sociological science, may . . . avoid the rock whereon Athens and Rome were shipwrecked. . . . It will perceive that, for the sake of the common safety, it is urgent to idealise the right of property; not . . . by slavishly copying institutions which their own imperfections have destroyed, but by replacing the license of the selfish right of property by an organisation which, whilst it is altruistic, is also reasonable, scientific, upholding without annihilating the individual, leaving his freedom and his initiative unfettered.[11]

It was this concept of justice that was well illustrated in traditions and laws of the ancient Hebrews, among whom land was regarded as a heritage of God, and whoever was forced to part with his holding had the right of its redemption, and in every fifty years—the year of Jubilee—land acquired by purchase or otherwise was to be returned to the original holders.

And there was an admonition against land engrossment! In the words of the prophet: "Woe unto them that join house to house, that lay field to field until there be no place." The story of Ahab, King of Samaria, who desired to extend his landholdings, and thus "lay field to field," by seeking to acquire the vineyard of Naboth by offering him a better vineyard or "the worth of it in money," and the refusal of Naboth to give up "the inheritance of my fathers," is typical of the tradition that existed regarding landholding under an assumed theocracy. Concerning this tradition, Dean Milman, in his classic work, *The History of the Jews*, says:

> The great principle of this law was the inalienability of estates. Houses in walled towns might be sold in perpetuity, if unredeemed within the year; land only for a limited period. At the Jubilee, every estate reverted, without repurchase, to the original proprietor. Even during this period it might be redeemed, should the proprietor become rich enough, at the value which the estate would produce during the years unelapsed before the Jubilee. This remarkable Agrarian law secured the political equality of

[11]Pp. xi–xii.

the people, and anticipated all the mischiefs so fatal to the early republics of Greece and Italy, the appropriation of the whole territory of the state by a rich and powerful landed oligarchy, with the consequent convulsions of the community from the deadly struggle between the patrician and plebeian orders. In the Hebrew state, the improvident individual might reduce himself and his family to penury or servitude, but he could not perpetuate a race of slaves or paupers. Every fifty years God, the King and Lord of the soil, as it were, resumed the whole territory, and granted it back in the same portions to the descendants of the original possessors. . . . Thus the body of the people were an independent yeomanry, residing on their hereditary farms, the boundaries of which remained forever of the same extent; for the removal of a neighbour's landmark was among the crimes against which the law uttered its severest malediction: an invasion of family property, that of Naboth's vineyard, is selected as the worst crime of a most tyrannical king; and in the decline of the state, the prophets denounce, with their sternest energy, this violation of the very basis of the commonwealth.[12]

The early Christian church fathers were imbued with the ancient Hebrew traditions, and their concept of justice as related to landownership followed along the same lines. Thus St. Cyrian declared:

> No man may come into our commune who sayeth that the land may be sold. God's footstool is not property!

And, similarly, St. Chrysostom:

> God gave the same earth to be cultivated by all. Since, therefore, His bounty is common, how comes it that you have so many fields and your neighbor not even a clod of earth?

Another early church father proclaimed: "The soil was given to the rich and poor in common. The pagans hold earth as property. They do blaspheme God."[13]

---

[12] Quoted from Francis Neilson, *The Eleventh Commandment*, p. 25. For an exposition of the ancient Hebrew conceptions of landownership, see Frederick Verinder, *My Neighbour's Landmark*.

[13] Francis Neilson, *op. cit.*, p. 90.

Land Tenure among the American Aborigines

Despite the interest of scholars in the culture of the North American Indian, little attention has been given to the systems of land tenure that prevailed among the various Indian tribes. It is generally assumed, however, that the pre-Columbian inhabitants of the eastern coastal regions, who practiced agriculture, as well as those migratory tribes of the prairie region, held their lands in common. Yet, as stated by Philip Alexander Bruce in his *Economic History of Virginia,* "There is some doubt as to the character of the tenure; each tribe possessed an absolute title to the division of country in which it was immediately seated, subject only to the general proprietorship of the king, to whom an annual tribute was paid in the form of a certain proportion of maize, beasts, fish, fowl, hides, fur, copper, and beads, but the relation of each family to the different plats of cultivated ground is not so clearly defined."

John Smith, the Virginia colonizer, "declared that each household knew its own fields and gardens, while [Robert] Beverley [the Virginia historian] asserted that no special property in land was claimed by individual Indians, but was held in common by the members of a whole tribe. . . . The statement of Smith seems to be confirmed by the relation which the Indian householder bore to other forms of property; thus he could devise his wigwam to his widow, and after her death to his favorite child. Again, a theft of maize was regarded as so heinous an act that it was punished with death, an evidence that separate ownership in this grain was strictly recognized when it had been gathered. Furthermore, there is no record that after the annual harvest the crops were divided among the householders of the town. Being held for all practical purposes in separate tenure, the ground must have been cleared very largely by individual energy without special regard to the common interests, . . ."[14]

Among the Six Nations of the Iroquois Indians it is generally assumed that the land was held and cultivated in common, since each clan of the tribe occupied a common dwelling. The celebrated "long houses," as these dwellings were called, were eighty or one hundred feet long by twenty or thirty feet broad. Each of these long houses sheltered

[14]Philip Alexander Bruce, *Economic History of Virginia in the Seventeenth Century,* Vol. I, pp. 149-50.

from ten to twenty families. It is thus contended that this communism in the use of dwellings entailed a communism in other forms of property. However, there is some evidence that there were among the Iroquois separate fields, cleared and sowed and harvested by individual families.[15]

Like the Indians of the eastern seaboard, some of the midwestern tribes, such as the Omahas, were also subdivided into clans or social units, sharing the game and fish killed by the members of the group. "Each of these large families possessed a certain portion of tillable land and cultivated it, but without having any right to alienate it. The families of the same tribe, however, might exchange with one another. As for the unoccupied land, each could cultivate this or that portion at his convenience."[16]

Among the Pueblo Indians of New Mexico and Arizona, agriculture was the chief source of sustenance, and since they, like the Iroquois Indians, lived in common dwellings, it seems logical to assume that at the time of the Spanish Conquest they held and cultivated their lands in common. That this may not be the system in all cases among these Indian groups today is undoubtedly due to the contact with Europeans, which has altered to some degree their social organization and their views of property rights.

Primitive Mexican Land Tenure

The inhabitants of Mexico and Central America are reputed to have had a more advanced civilization than that of most tribes of North American Indians. Moreover, they were, in the main, sedentary and depended largely on agriculture for sustenance. Their system of land tenure is accordingly of a more developed and complex nature and is of historical interest as illustrating the theory and character of primitive land use and ownership. Considerable data on this topic have been uncovered by historians, among whom, aside from the early Spanish writ-

---

[15]See Letourneau, *op. cit.*, pp. 46–47.

[16]*Ibid.*, p. 47. Letourneau bases this statement on a study by O. Dorsey, "Omaha Sociology," published in the *Report of the Smithsonian Institution*, 1886.

ers, are William Prescott and Herbert Howe Bancroft. Both of these authorities indicate that, notwithstanding the existence of a feudal hierarchy, land, though cultivated in part individually, was not held in individual absolute ownership. Concerning this, Charles Letourneau, basing his statements largely on Prescott and Bancroft, writes:

> The survival of the ancient communal system . . . was more marked in the management and ownership of the folklands. These lands, called Calpulli, were measured and registered in such a way as clearly to determine the rights of clans and even those of the wards and streets of towns. The Mexican register was a painted picture, whereon was figured each domain with its boundaries, every description of land being indicated by a separate color. . . . Plebeian tenures were perpetual, inalienable possessions in mortmain, and, what is especially noteworthy, were never owned by individual title. They were common estates, the usufruct of which was distributed according to fixed rules. Without ever owning the soil itself, every member of the community had a right to the usufruct of a portion of the communal domain, proportionate to his personal importance. This part he could not sell, but was allowed to let for a few years; for the community were specially desirous that no field should remain uncultivated. Thus, when the holder of an allotment let his ground lie fallow for two years running, he received a notice from the chief of his "Calpulli" admonishing him of his carelessness. If he took no heed, the following year his lot was taken from him and adjudged to a more diligent tenant. . . . If the tenant died childless, . . . his share was declared vacant and conferred upon another member of the community. To sum up, in these plebeian tenures the community took uncontested advantage of its superior rights, and it had in nowise bent its neck beneath the yoke of private property.[17]

[17]*Ibid.*, pp. 130–31. It is interesting to note that the aboriginal collective land system of Mexico was only partially disturbed by the Spanish conquerors. According to the United Nations publication, *Progress in Land Reform,* p. 38: "Land [in Mexico] held in *ejido* tenure is the property of a town or village either for collective use or distribution among the inhabitants for cultivation in small plots, to which each individual has a right of occupancy and use so long as he keeps the land under cultivation. In colonial times villages had received grants of land of this kind, but during the Nineteenth Century had lost their landholdings to the owners of large estates. The restitution or grant of *ejido* land has thus involved the splitting up of the large *latifundia* and the return of the land to village ownership."

Summary

It may be gathered from the preceding pages that, throughout the course of history, land as a species of property has played a distinctive and important role in human progress. In general, it may be said that in the evolution of civilizations landownership changed from a collective concept, wherein absolute title to the soil was held by no individual or group (but was regarded as a necessity available for general use of society or the community), to a legal status, whereby individuals or groups, through political or economic power, were able to hold, use, transfer, and transmit its use and tenure for their own benefit or aggression, without any necessary regard for public welfare. This evolution, almost universal in the history of mankind, may be regarded as one of the principal sources of political upheavals and agrarian discontent, accompanied by political corruption and economic ruin, which have marked the course of great nations and empires both past and present. It is for this reason that the study of the land question assumes a paramount importance in solving the ever-recurring problems of human welfare. That the land problem has been only less serious in the United States than in most other countries of the world is due not only to the fact that our nation is still comparatively young but also to the fact that until more recent years it was blessed with an abundance of practically uninhabited land area. The disposition of this area has been unusually rapid and erratic. The country, however, is now thoroughly populated. "Free land" is at an end. Large areas are engrossed in private ownership. The history of this process, including an understanding of the "regard" for land and the evolution of the institution of landownership and use in the United States, therefore, is worthy of study, if for no other reason than that it forms a basis for future trends and may give indications of the need for a new quest for economic justice. The history of the cultures of the world indicates that land has been used under many different types of control and under restrictions as to landownership and use. How did it happen that private ownership of land in fee came to be the typical land institution of the New World? Let us see!

Chapter 2

The European Background

When the early colonists came to America, they brought with them the burden of European laws, traditions, and customs that existed at the time in their former localities. These constituted a maze of legal and technical entanglements regarding landownership and land tenure that had come down through the centuries. Despite changes in political and economic conditions, many obsolete and harassing restrictions, inherited from the feudal era, were still observed and enforced.

Yet it was a time of revolutionary changes. For the colonists, coming as they did to a territory of primeval environment, where individual ownership and exploitation of the soil were largely unknown, there existed opportunities to cast aside the old laws and traditions and reconstruct new systems of property allotments, ownership, and transfer. How these opportunities were utilized or were almost completely ignored will be told in following chapters, but in order to understand fully the underlying conditions which influenced and activated the early settlers in establishing their institutions of landownership and land distribution, a brief survey will be made of the development of land tenure in Europe, particularly as it relates to the island of Great Britain.

The Feudal System

Despite the scholarly researches that have been made on the development of primitive property ownership, particularly as it relates to land, there is, as already stated, considerable controversy as to both its origin and nature. The growth of feudalism during the Middle Ages and the conditions that laid its foundations have already been told in numerous studies during the last two centuries and need not be recounted here. But as stated by Professor Hawtrey,[1] "Feudalism is in principle the identification of sovereignty with landownership. To own a region and to rule over it are indeed not easily differentiated."

This accounts for the widespread prevalence of feudalism throughout the world in different areas and at varying periods, and in such isolated and distinct regions as Japan and Ethiopia. The basis of feudalism is a hierarchy of ownership and control. Its fundamental concept is political rather than economic. It is for this reason that feudalism involved not only proprietorship of the soil but also of the inhabitants living on it. Political power could be maintained only by control of the population and by attaching the population to the soil and thus making them part and parcel of the land on which they resided. This created a species of slavery as a means for sustaining the political power of the sovereign.

All this does not mean that economic factors in the system were not present and did not play an important role in its development. Military power, the prime support of political power, can be sustained only by economic resources, and as feudalism was primarily a means of marshaling military forces, it had an economic as well as a political foundation. As time went on, the economic foundation became stronger than the political foundation.

The Introduction of Feudalism in England

The origin and causes of the growth of feudalism in Great Britain have been a field of scholarly controversy. Some authorities ascribe it to the Norman Conquest. Others contend it existed in the Roman era, which lasted for several centuries, and, already firmly established, was strengthened after the Anglo-Saxon invasion of Britain. As an English economic historian states it: "The great mass of the population [in the Saxon era] was engaged in agriculture, and every man had, so to speak, a stake in the land and belonged to a manor or an overlord. A landless man was altogether outside the pale of social life. Land, in fact, was the

---

[1] R. G. Hawtrey, *Economic Aspects of Sovereignty*, pp. 4–5.

European Background

basis of everything and it is for this reason that it is so important to understand the conditions of tenure and the whole land system of that age."[2]

The boldness of this statement of the universal prevalence of feudalism in Britain in the Anglo-Saxon era is, however, refuted by other authorities, notably the Russian economist, P. Vinogradoff,[3] and notably by Sir Henry Maine,[4] who states in his work, *Ancient Law,* that "property once belonged not to individuals, not even to isolated families, but to larger societies."

Whatever the situation actually was regarding land tenure in the Anglo-Saxon era, it is generally agreed that the feudal system became predominant in the period following the Norman Conquest. As stated by Sir Frederick Pollock in his concise treatise, *The Land Laws:* "The Norman Conquest was the means of introducing great and systematic changes in the government and laws of England, and not least in the law governing the tenure of land." And he follows this up by the statement, "And to this day, though the really characteristic incidents of the feudal tenures have disappeared or left only the faintest of traces, the scheme of our land laws can, as to its form, be described only as a modified feudalism."[5]

The Progress of Feudal Land Tenure in England

It has been said that the changes in the system of land tenure in Britain have been so gradual that, as important as they have been, they have passed largely unnoticed, and only patient research has brought their true nature to light. Sir Frederick Pollock remarks in his study of the English land laws that by the first half of the thirteenth century feudalism was at its most perfect stage in England, and from the latter part of that century onward the system underwent a series of grave modifications, but "the main lines of the feudal theory were always ostensibly preserved."[6]

[2] H. B. Gibbins, *Industry in England*, p. 46.
[3] *Villainage in England, passim.*
[4] *Ancient Law,* 4th American ed., p. 261.
[5] *The Land Laws,* 3rd ed., London, Vol. I, p. 53.
[6] *Ibid.,* p. 53.

Among the features that persisted were the laws and customs pertaining to rents and inheritance. The features that were relegated or abandoned were the military requirements and the menial services of the lords and tenants. Primogeniture and its corollary, the entail, inherent in the military phase of feudalism, were preserved and retained, and continued to be a tradition in English land tenure almost until the present day. It was a legal and customary harassment which perplexed the population and, as shall be pointed out later, was rather speedily repealed by the American colonists when they were given the liberty to do so.

Following the Peasants' Revolt of 1381 in England, villeinage, meaning serfdom, gradually declined and through several centuries became extinct. This was accomplished through the commutation of labor services of the tenants into money rents. It did not give the serfs, bondsmen, or tenants a right of ownership in the land, but it released them from attachment to the soil and enabled them to become free men and move from place to place. But this, in itself, created the problem of "the landless man" and led to the evils of vagabondage, which, when further intensified in the period of "inclosures" of the sixteenth and seventeenth centuries, became a harassing social problem in Great Britain and ultimately led to enactment of the notorious English Poor Laws, a series of legislation that has been universally condemned by most British economists and historians during two centuries.

The advantage of feudalism was that it gave every capable person some right to the use of some land. Thus the basis of subsistence was present. The individual was thus protected against starvation, vagrancy, and even poverty. Contrast this with our existing institution of fee land-ownership, under which the privilege of land use and occupation can be denied the individual and forces him to seek other means of subsistence or become a "dispossessed freeman." The renowned British economic historian, Thorold Rogers, in his notable work, *Six Centuries of Work and Wages*, contends that the "golden age" of the British laborer was in the fifteenth and the early sixteenth centuries, when the feudalistic system of land tenure still persisted. This could reasonably be ascribed to the automatic right of the individual, whether as serf or peasant, to the use of some land by means of which he was assured both employment and a domicile.

Perhaps the most potent cause of the breakdown of the old feudalism was the growth of cities and towns during the Middle Ages and the rise of manufactures and trading. Feudalism, with its essential characteristic of attaching the individual to a specific piece of land, could not be applied to city or town residence. Moreover, the cities and towns received royal charters and privileges, which were outside the scope and jurisdiction of lords and overlords. Thus a class of "freemen" was formed, and landownership or land tenancy relieved from feudal dues and services was created or later enlarged. It is mainly from this class that the great political leaders of Great Britain from the time of Elizabeth were drawn. Not only did they assume political power, but in time they became the potent promoters of British colonization throughout the world. Though they created for themselves a dominant influence in political affairs, they were not particularly interested in changing the systems of land tenure or the laws relating thereto. In many cases, because of affluence and the desire for social and political prestige, they themselves became large landowners and sought to maintain the position of their families by receiving titles of nobility and by building up landed estates for their posterity. Thus they assented to the traditions underlying primogeniture and entail.

This may be one of the reasons why land reform made such slow progress in Great Britain. It was not until the reign of Charles II that the original character of the old feudal system in England was changed by statute, and the theory of the feudal hierarchy, based upon military service and the adage that "title to all land lies in the Crown," was ostensibly abolished. This act, abolishing the military tenures and their incidents, was passed in 1660, although a previous act of the Commonwealth, passed in 1656, enacted the same provisions "in a rather more elaborate form."[7]

According to the statute of 1660, all freehold tenures were reduced to the one type of "free and common socage"—socage was land held by free tenure but without military service. Although this did not abolish

[7] Pollock, *op. cit.*, p. 130.

the tenant system that long prevailed, it enabled tenants in fee simple to dispose by will of their lands; and thus, as stated by Sir Frederick Pollock, the whole of the fee-simple land in the British Kingdom became disposable by will. Nevertheless, primogeniture and entail still prevailed, and thus land cultivated by free tenants who paid quitrents became the predominant system of landholding during the period of colonization of America. It continues in Great Britain until this day. It is a system of "landlordism"—an evil that has hindered the economic progress of agriculture and urban development on the British Isles for the last three centuries.

Speaking of this English "landlordism," George Brodrick, writing in 1881, states:[8]

> The law of Primogeniture and the custom of Entail have erected great landowners into a privileged caste, admission to which is the highest aspiration of the English plutocracy, while the disappearance of a true middle class from English counties has removed the main counterpoise to their undue weight. They hold in their gift that social promotion which is the most seductive of bribes to English minds of the common order, and they are treated with a deference out of all proportion to their merit by men, and still more by women, eagerly struggling for this promotion.
>
> This inordinate respect for great landowners, as such, was not equally characteristic of rural England in earlier times and would probably not survive the modernized feudal land system to which it owes its origin. It is wholly distinct from the spirit of clanship and military alliance which attached the feudal retainer to his lord, and enabled the most powerful barons to impose their will on vast tracts of country. Even in those days, a sturdy undergrowth of independent yeomanry and freeholders continued to flourish under the vast shadow of baronial suzerainty. The greatest landowners of all were greater than any now found to be on the roll of the Peerage; but great landowners, as a class, did not tower, as they now do, above the smaller gentry, then a far more numerous body. . . . Even after the institution of the unpaid magistracy had withered the spirit of self-government and consolidated the power of the landed aristocracy within each county, it is

[8] *English Land and English Landlords*, pp. 412–13.

clear that rural society in England presented a much greater equality of fortunes and conditions, with a much greater community of habits, and tastes, than it does in the present day. . . . It was rapidly impaired as the English Land System matured itself under modern conditions, and for the last hundred years the landed aristocracy has approached more nearly to a social oligarchy than it ever did before.

Another English writer of the same period as George Brodrick, T. H. S. Escott, describes the trend toward landownership concentration in Great Britain toward the end of the last century as follows:

The total area of the United Kingdom is 76,300,000 acres, of which 26,300,000 acres consist of mountains, rough pasturage and waste, while 50,000,000 are crops, meadows, permanent pasture, and woods and forests. Most of this land is in the hands of large landowners; excluding the proprietors of less than one acre, one-fourth is held by 1,200 persons, each averaging 16,200 acres; another fourth by 6,200 persons, at an average of 3,150 acres; another fourth by 50,770, at an average of 380 acres; while the remaining fourth is held by 261,830 persons, at an average of 70 acres. The cultivation of this land is mainly in the hands of tenant farmers of whom there are 561,000 in the United Kingdom, each holding an average of 56 acres. The tendency is for land to become concentrated in the hands of large landlords, small proprietors being bought up. Thus the small squire is becoming gradually extinct, while the yeoman, or small landowners farming their own land, have almost entirely disappeared. How rapidly we in England have passed from an agricultural to a manufacturing people may be judged from the fact that whereas fifty years ago a fifth of the working population of England were engaged in agriculture, those now occupied in this manner are less than a tenth.[9]

A logical development of this land concentration was the British land-reform movement, first sponsored by the pioneers of land reform, notably Thomas Spence and William Ogilvie, and taken up by Richard Cobden, John Stuart Mill, Lord Addison, Francis Neilson, and a host of other British statesmen, philosophers, and economists. Their work has been bearing fruit in the recent British legislation relating to land use and ownership, of which we shall speak later in this volume.

[9]*England; Her People, Polity, and Pursuits,* new and revised ed.

Chapter 3

Land Systems of the Colonial Era

In tracing the land history of the American colonies, it should be borne in mind that the first settlements were made by chartered trading companies; i.e., organizations for the purpose of gain rather than political or territorial dominion. Accordingly, to understand properly the background of these settlements, a knowledge of the nature, character, and purposes of these so-called "chartered companies" or corporations is essential.

The Classes of Chartered Companies

There were, in general, two classes of chartered organizations in Great Britain for conducting foreign trade, the so-called regulated companies and the joint stock companies, or, as they are known today, the corporations. Out of the latter developed the colonial companies which comprised the organizations concerned with the American continent. In point of time the "regulated companies" antedate the "chartered companies." The former were organizations of individual merchants banded together in a way that resembled the old craft and mercantile guilds which then prevailed in the cities and towns of England. As stated by John P. Davis, "They were the result of the application to the foreign trade of England of the form of organization evolved from the experience of England in its domestic trade and industry."[1]

In the fourteenth and fifteenth centuries, as British merchants gradually displaced foreigners in the foreign trade of the country, they fol-

---

[1] *Corporations*, Vol. II, p. 66.

lowed, in organization, the structure of the older European groups, which constituted trading oligarchies, such as the Hanseatic League. The earliest associations of English merchants of this nature were known as "merchants of the staple." A staple was the town or place, at home or abroad, to which merchants who were engaged in foreign trade brought their goods to be sold or exported to foreigners. Usually they were grouped together on the basis of a single export or import commodity, such as wool or cloth. In this way they were closely identified with the local merchant guilds dealing in the same products, as, for instance, the Mercers Company of London. There were thus no questions regarding territorial matters or land acquisitions in their rights, privileges, or obligations.

The Merchant Adventurers

The actual forerunners of the later colonial companies were chartered organizations known as "merchant adventurers," organizations of national scope, which joined together the foreign traders into a sort of partnership. These traders, though still conducting their transactions as individuals, maintained a common code and submitted to a common jurisdiction, much in the manner of organized exchanges of modern times. The charters of such organizations originated in 1407, and the first was granted by Henry IV.

An oft-quoted description of such a company is given by John Wheeler, a writer of the Elizabethan era, in his *Treatise on Commerce:*

> The Company of Merchant Adventurers consisteth of a great number of wealthy and well experimented merchants, dwelling in divers cities, great maritime towns, and other parts of the realm.... These men of old time linked and bound themselves together in company for the exercise of merchandise and sea-fare trading in cloth, kersey, and all other, as well English as foreign commodities vendible abroad, by the which they brought into the places where they traded, much wealth, benefit, and commodity, and for that cause have obtained many very excellent and singular privileges, rights, jurisdictions, exemptions, and immunities, all which those of the aforesaid fellowship equally enjoy after a well ordered manner and form, and according to the ordinances, laws, and customs devised and agreed upon by common consent of all the

merchants. . . . The said company hath a governor, or in his absence a deputy, and four and twenty assistants in the mart towns, who have . . . full authority as well from her Majesty as from the princes, states and rulers of the Low Countries, and beyond the seas. . . .[2]

The Development of the Joint Stock Company

In course of time, particularly when British commercial enterprise was carried into lands and countries largely unknown, the joint stock or "colonial company" was developed. The distinction between these organizations and that represented by the merchant adventurers was a pooling of a common purse and the sharing proportionately of the gains and losses. Moreover, it represented the furtherance of the principle of self-government by organizations trading beyond the seas and was fortified by the grant of a trade monopoly. Along with these privileges came the implied powers of land settlement and territorial exploitation.

The outstanding example of a concern of this character was the East India Company. This appears to be an offshoot of an older "regulated company" of Levant merchants. It was given an original charter by Queen Elizabeth I on December 31, 1600. It should be noted that this antedates by six years the granting of the charters to the two earliest companies organized to settle and exploit the North American continent. Though the East India Company was, to all intents and purposes, a trading monopoly, history reveals that it became a governing body with jurisdictional powers that also comprised the ownership, control, and distribution of land.[3]

The Plymouth and Virginia Companies

The first colonial charters for the settlement of the continent of North America, as is well known, were granted to the Plymouth Company and to the (London) Virginia Company. These were "twin charters," granted on the same day, on April 10, 1606, by James I. Both

[2]*Treatise on Commerce,* quoted in Davis, *op. cit.,* pp. 77–78.
[3]Another company having the broad powers and privileges of the East India Company was the Hudson's Bay Company, which has continued its existence for several centuries, but with alterations in its rights and powers.

were joint stock companies having self-governing provisions, to be composed of stockholders consisting of "knights, gentlemen, merchants and other adventurers." Though they were ostensibly trading corporations, similar to the East India Company, they were in effect colonizing companies, and the ownership of or profit from the sale of land was undoubtedly one of the purposes of their organization. This certainly was in the minds of the stockholders.

It was provided in the charters of both companies that the King was to grant land to any person recommended by the council of each colony on its petition, and, as shall be shown later, grants of land became so common, at least in the early period, that the King or his councilors were given little choice or consent in the transactions. The only reservation as to land use was the usual provision, in those days, that 5 per cent of the gold and silver recovered from the lands be reserved for the King.

A noteworthy feature of the charters was the almost entire absence of provisions as to the means, methods, and procedures for land distribution. All that was said in the Plymouth Company charter relating to this matter was, "We [the King] authorize the said Council [of the company] from time to time to distribute and convey such portions of lands hereby granted, respect being had to the proportions [investments of each] of the adventurers [stockholders]." No mention was made in the charters regarding the acquisition of land from the aborigines, and it seems that their title to the territory was ignored. However, it became a quite common practice to make so-called "purchases" from the Indians, both by the companies and the individuals. Such practices continued to provide fraudulent claims to land titles, until finally forbidden by the British Government in 1763.

As a matter of historical fact, in the very early period of settlement, a system of community landownership was followed both in the Plymouth and the Virginia settlements. It was not until after the danger of Indian attacks was lessened and the colonists had increased in numbers sufficiently to warrant a wider area of dispersion that systems of land grants and land allotments were adopted. Thenceforth, "land-grabbing" became the general practice in the colonies and persisted throughout the whole colonial area and long thereafter.

The Early New England and New York Land Systems

The Pilgrim Fathers who came on the *Mayflower* were a tightly knit group, not only because of their strong religious beliefs and their "separatism" from the Church of England, but also because of their sojourn to Holland, where, as foreigners, they naturally formed an isolated colony. But the fact that after their arrival on the New England coast they congregated in single settlements and lived for a while in what has been called "Yankee communism" was a matter of necessity more than of choice. They were confronted by a savage population whose land they appropriated and whose customary ways of life they disturbed. They accordingly deemed it safest to live in "forts," as was done elsewhere in unsettled regions. After a more peaceful environment developed with increase in their number, they were forced to spread out in order to obtain the necessities of survival. That they followed a system of "town settlements" was to be expected, not only because of the nature of the environment and terrain, but also because they, largely "landless" town dwellers in their homeland, set up town organizations such as long existed in England.

Regarding this type of village or community settlement in Britain, Thorold Rogers wrote:

> The houses of the villagers, built of wattles, smeared inside and out with mud or clay, were crowded near the church, in the street of the settlement, though there were in large parishes, outlying homesteads. In all cases the church was the common hall of the parish, and a fortress in time of danger, occupying the site of the stockade which had been built when the first settlers occupied the ground. In the body of the church were frequently stored produce, corn and wool. Here too, I believe, the common feasts of the parish were held, till such time as the proceeds from the local guild enabled the people to erect their own guild-house. The only houses of any pretension in the village were the lord's, the parson's, and the miller's, who by prescription took toll of all the inhabitants, who were bound to grind at his mill, who is a busy, and according to current report, not an over-scrupulous personage in his dealings with his fellow villagers.[4]

[4] James E. Thorold Rogers, *The Economic Interpretation of History*, p. 14.

The New England town, on the basis of historical records, was almost an exact replica of this early English village. The difference was not in the structure of the village but in the system of land tenure. Because the heritage of the feudal system still left its marks, most of the English villagers held their lands either as freeholders or copyholders under fixed rents or services, or both. The most arable lands were still the property of the lord. These conditions, of course, were absent during the era of New England's settlement.

A feature of English feudalism was the allotment of strips of lands to families of the village to be individually cultivated. This we shall see was a basis for land distribution in early New England, but as feudalism was on the decline in Britain, the character of land tenure underwent a legal change. The fee-ownership system instead of the tenant system of ownership became prevalent in New England.

As previously stated, the *Mayflower* colonists, the first to make a permanent settlement in New England, were a group more interested in religious freedom for themselves than in profiting from landownership. Also, as has been already stated, they originally formed a compact association, which was at first intensified by the need of protection against the Indians. Seven years after they arrived, however, in order to substantiate their right to settlement, they bought from the London merchants seven hundred shares of the Plymouth Company stock for £1,800—an amount said to be subscribed by the merchants to send the Pilgrims to America. Through this purchase they were enabled to claim ownership of land, and thus it was possible to free themselves from their early communist organization, which had failed to work satisfactorily. However, they clung to their village type of organization. In the earliest distribution each able-bodied person was allotted a garden plot of one acre, and subsequently an additional twenty acres for each was distributed, while a "commons" of meadow land, as in Britain, was set aside for the general use. Here, again, no respect was paid to the actual ownership title to the lands held by the Indians. Their claim to the land was based entirely on a "juridical" right granted by the King of England, who granted away that which he did not own or have title to.

As the colonists increased in numbers and became self-supporting, they spread out by establishing new and similar village organizations, centered about a church. Thus a "township system" was established in New England, and the town became the basic unit of political organization. However, the methods of distributing land were not uniform, and a number of large grants, most of them originating in England, were made in the early period of New England colonization. These grants were made when the Massachusetts Bay Company, the company which absorbed the early Plymouth Colony, was created. In fact, grants of land were so numerous in the New England territory that their boundaries overlapped and there were constant disputes among the grantees. The charter of the original Plymouth Company was annulled in 1635. It was the practice of the Council of New England (the Plymouth Company) to distribute dividends to shareholders by parceling out territory among them by means of drawings as well as making positive grants.

The first of these drawings was made in 1623 (according to Justin Winsor, *Narrative and Critical History*) to the remaining twenty members of the Council. The region comprised land between Cape Cod and the Bay of Fundy. It appears, however, that few, if any, of those participating in the drawing ever claimed or benefited from their allotment. Five years thereafter (March 19, 1628) a grant of land in the same region, along with a charter, was issued to a new company to be known as the Governor and Company of the Massachusetts Bay in New England. The charter was similar to that of the original London Company, but the bounds of the territory were better defined and form the basis for territory comprised in the present state of Massachusetts. This company, as already has been stated, absorbed the early Plymouth Colony and removed the headquarters to Massachusetts, under the governorship of John Winthrop.

One of the earliest acts of the Massachusetts Bay Company was to appoint a committee to draw up a plan of land distribution. This committee, after a short period of deliberation, recommended that the land be distributed to the adventurers (members) and to others who were willing to settle in the colony. During the same year a number of "settlers," with their families and indentured servants, mostly Puritans, arrived in New England and founded the town of Salem. A plan was soon adopted for allotting land "so as to avoid all contentions among the adventurers." By vote at town meetings or by appointed committees, the surrounding land was distributed on the basis of need or ability to cultivate the soil. Allotments usually ranged under a hundred acres.

Following the example of the earlier Plymouth Colony, a town plan was drawn up and, in addition to outlying allotments, a site within the town of not more than a half acre was given to each settler. Thus the town or unit system of land allotment became the common practice in the Massachusetts Colony. In this way the New England communities, such as Boston, Charleston, Springfield, and a number of others, had their origin. It may be said, therefore, that, unlike the earlier London Company, the Massachusetts Bay Company was not a "land company" or an instrument of speculation in real estate. No profit was sought by the shareholders by obtaining land to rent or to resell. Indeed, much of the success of the Massachusetts Colony, as well as its rapid settlement, may be ascribed to this situation.

Absentee Ownership in New England

It will be noted that, during the early phase of New England settlement, landownership was a form of "absenteeism." This, we have seen, gradually gave way to a policy of settler ownership. Absenteeism was well established in Britain before the era of colonization and became common not only in England but notably in Ireland. The first proprietors of the Plymouth Company had, with very few exceptions, no intention of removing to the territory which they acquired or expected to acquire. The motive of their land hunger was profit and not land settlement. With the growing scarcity of land about them, landlordism became as lucrative and as attractive as commerce and industry. No other investment offered a more certain and steady yield of income than real estate. After the fall of feudalism, large estates, peopled with crowded tenants, each bidding against the other for the use of the soil, gave some assurance of income accretion from ownership of land. "Rack renting" became a general practice in Great Britain and Ireland.

There was reason to believe that it could and would be extended to America.

As already indicated, large land areas were granted or obtained "by purchase" from the Indians in the early period of New England settlement. In many cases these "purchases" were made by individuals or groups and not by the governing authorities. Many of these lapsed or were rendered invalid in the confusion of conflicting land claims. Only a few of the grantees emigrated or sent agents to the country to promote settlements or to divide up the ownership of the region. As time went on, however, pressure of population led to actual settlements and, in many cases, the titles of the original grantees or their heirs and assigns neglected or were unable to assert or enforce their claims.

According to Alfred N. Chandler, a tract printed in Boston in 1716 stated: "Though this country be large, and much good land in it, which for want of people cannot be improved in many generations; yet a shame it is to say, this colony cannot provide themselves necessary food. In the first settling of this country, land was easy to be attained, and at a low price, which was an inducement to multitudes to come over as indented servants; but now the land being so generally taken up, few come over that can live elsewhere. . . . If the country should put a tax upon such tracts of land as lie convenient to settle upon, in order to make the holders willing to throw them up to the country, such yearly tax would be more justifiable, and more equal, than to tax a poor man ten shillings, that has much ado to live; those estates being valued worth hundreds of pounds by the owners thereof, who keep only in hopes that as other places hereafter shall be settled, they may advance upon the price. And in the meantime their poor neighbors must pay perhaps a greater tax than would be put upon him in the most arbitrary kingdom in Europe."[5]

In this we have an early statement of Henry George's philosophy. It is an indication that a "land question" developed early in America; that land engrossment, as in Europe, became a general practice and inequitable taxation in America dates back to early colonial times.

[5]*Land Title Origins, A Tale of Force and Fraud*, pp. 112–13.

The Town Proprietors of New England

The New England practice of creating towns, as a method of land settlement, was by no means a plan to give every inhabitant an allotment of land. Though the Massachusetts Bay colonists were in the main family groups closely connected socially and attached to a church organization, they were controlled and governed by a selected group comprised of shareholders in the company, who, as such, claimed pre-emption of the land. It was this governing body which distributed areas as town or settlement sites to quasi-corporations known as "town proprietors." These proprietors, as shareholders, upon moving to the areas allotted to them, proceeded to divide up the bounds of the town among themselves. The allotment of each was made by several methods, among which, as already indicated, was the drawing of lots. The allottees became the town fathers, the original landlords, whose heirs continued to enjoy this distinction for generations. Their followers or retinues, such as indentured servants, received no land and were deprived of the privilege of a voice in the local government. The ownership of land as a badge of suffrage continued in the New England colonies for many years after the Revolution. Moreover, in the early years of land settlement in New England, it was a policy of the "proprietors" to maintain their land monopoly, since, in some cases, the consent of the governing body was required to a transfer of an "in-lot" and "out-lot" by the owner.

Even in democratic Rhode Island, a "proprietary" was composed of two classes of inhabitants. According to Bicknell, in his *History of Rhode Island,* Roger Williams, after receiving a twenty-mile grant of land from the Indians, formed a proprietary of purchasers and created two classes of citizens, one consisting of landholders and the other of "young men, single persons, who were a landless gentry, with no voice in the affairs of the community."

This restraint on land alienation was probably the most distinctive feature of the New England town-proprietorship land system. The underlying cause of it was obviously the desire to preserve the homogeneity and the religious and political unity of the community. It was feared that the admission of strangers as freeholders would disrupt the social and religious harmony which prevailed among the original settlers and proprietors. So well grounded was this restrictive provision that in 1660 the colonial legislature of Connecticut enacted a law which stated that "no inhabitant shall have power to make sale of his accommodation of house and lands until he has first propounded the sale thereof to the town where it is situated, and they may refuse to accept of the sale tendered."[6] Other New England colonies, however, passed no general law in regard to this matter, but left it to be determined by the proprietors of the individual towns.

Another force which undoubtedly impelled the early New England town settlers to restrict land alienation was opposition to engrossment of real estate by wealthy or absentee owners. Thus the Springfield, Massachusetts, proprietors in 1636 would permit only one allotment of a town lot to an individual. Other early town settlements had similar restrictions. As time went on, however, dissensions arose because of the influx of newcomers, and the restrictions were gradually abandoned.[7]

The New England Plantation Allotments

Though it was a common practice to establish towns by proprietary groups in the early settlement of New England, there were also grants made of outlying areas. These were known as "plantations." For the most part they comprised land along rivers and in the fertile valleys. There is very little history regarding these grants, but in time they became important, since, with the forced withdrawal of the Indian inhabitants and the press of population growth in the face of limited tillable and accessible soil, the lands rose greatly in value. As a consequence, from almost the very earliest period, private land speculation became a feature of New England economy. Speaking of this, Akagi, in his book, *The Town Proprietors of the New England Colonies,* remarks:

> Next to the migratory tendency of the New Englanders, the influence of the speculative proprietors was no less striking. The land speculation opened up a new avenue of activities to the shrewd land jobbers and of investment to capitalists of all sorts. It en-

[6] See *Connecticut Public Records*, Vol. I, p. 351.
[7] For more details regarding this topic, see Marshall Harris, *Origin of the Land Tenure System in the United States*, pp. 282-84.

riched many of the political leaders through their shares in the commercialized land grants. The speculative proprietors or their agents . . . created imaginary wealth and penetrated not only the New England colonies, but also New York and New Jersey, and even England, in their effort to harvest profits from their lands. As against the radical pioneer on the frontiers, the well-to-do and more or less prosperous class on the seaboard and in the old interior towns, disinclined to move away from their homes, became the breeding ground of speculators. But the good lands in the New England colonies were being rapidly occupied and exhausted and, by the close of the colonial period, these speculative proprietors had already fixed their eyes upon the more fertile and expansive western lands.[8]

The New Hampshire Grants

Space does not permit in this study a review of the land policies of methods of land distribution in the separate New England colonies. On the whole, the methods of land distribution were very similar to that already described. In some outlying areas, such as New Hampshire and Maine, some large grants of unsettled areas were made. New Hampshire became a royal province in 1741, with Benning Wentworth as the first governor. This section of New England had been originally granted to John Mason, but the grant was not confirmed by the King. However, Mason's heirs claimed the land and brought suits to confirm it. Much of the land was already taken up through titles granted by the Massachusetts Bay Company. In 1664, the Lord Chief Justices of England decided that the Massachusetts Bay Company had no right to grant these titles, and upheld the "vested rights" of John Mason in the land. This naturally created confusion and local resentment and resistance. Mason was finally bought off by the province.

The largest unsettled area of New Hampshire Province comprised what is now the state of Vermont. When New Hampshire became a separate province, Governor Wentworth, to forestall New York's claim to the area, lavishly granted large tracts to a number of individuals. These became known as the "New Hampshire Grants."[9]

[8] P. 295.
[9] See New York Historical Society Collections, 1869, 1870, Vol. 18, for a list of these grants.

Whole townships were wafted away. The governor, however, reserved for himself a fee, together with 500 acres in each township. In all, about 129 township grants were made of Vermont lands. The grantees proceeded to divide the townships into sections and offer them for sale in a manner similar to that followed later in the distribution of the public domain. At the end of ten years it was required that every landholder should pay an annual rental of one shilling per hundred acres, but there is no evidence that this rental was actually paid or ever claimed. At this period of New England settlement, when wasteland was becoming scarce, the holdings of most of the original grantees were disposed of to actual settlers and others.[10] Thus another era of "absentee ownership" was ended.

However, New York still maintained its claim to the Vermont area, under the grant to the Duke of York, and, declaring the New Hampshire Grants illegal, proceeded to distribute the land on its own account. The dispute was not settled finally until after the admittance of Vermont as a state of the Union.

The Dutch Land System in New York

The Dutch settled New York under the auspices of a chartered colonial company similar to the British chartered colonial companies. As early as 1613, several Dutch merchants petitioned for and received the privilege of forming a company to trade in the region of the Hudson River. This was further amplified into a colonization corporation, the (Dutch) West India Company, in which the States-General of Holland had a financial interest. As is well known, this company made its first settlement on Manhattan Island, which was reputedly purchased from the Indians by trading merchandise valued at twenty-four dollars. The charter granted the right to distribute land to settlers, but large stockholders could be allotted areas under feudal or manorial rights, provided they furnished a retinue of actual settlers. These feudal lords were called "patroons."

Each patroon was to receive as his absolute proprietary a tract of eight miles along both sides of any navigable river as an "eternal

[10] See F. M. Woodard, *The Town Proprietors in Vermont*.

heritage," with additional lateral territory "so far as the situation of the occupier permitted." Settlers on the land were bound to it in a sort of serfdom and could hold land only under a system of quitrents or services. There was no requirement that the patroon reside on the land, and thus there was created a system of absentee ownership. Several such patroonships were established before the British occupation, the most famous of which was that of Killian van Rensselaer, a merchant of Amsterdam, whose landholdings in the neighborhood of Albany were held intact for several generations of his heirs.

In addition to vast areas granted to patroons, small allotments of land were made to independent settlers, particularly in the area around Manhattan. It should be noted, however, that the Dutch, unlike the English, Spanish, French, and Swedes, were not so much interested in land acquisitions as in trade with the Indians, especially in peltries. Instead of tobacco, their currency was beaver skins.

During much of the Dutch period of settlement, Holland was the leading trading nation of Europe. The difficulty experienced by the Dutch patroons in obtaining actual settlers on their domains and the limited areas opened up to settlement are evidence that landownership was not the prime motive of the Dutch adventurers. Landownership appears to have been only incidental, as a means of defense against the Indians and against competing colonizing powers.

The Rensselaerwick Manor

The largest and best known of the Dutch manors was Rensselaerwick. This was located on both sides of the Hudson River in the area around the present site of Albany, and thus included within its limits Fort Orange, set up by the Dutch West India Company as an outpost against the Indians and French. The manor embraced hundreds of thousands of acres. The original "patroon," as already stated, was Killian van Rensselaer, an Amsterdam merchant. He did not come to his domain, and the manor was presided over by an agent. Killian's heirs did come to New York and for generations presided over the vast estate. The patroonship was finally dissolved under the New York laws against primogeniture and the forceful commutation of land rents.

During the period of the Rensselaer patroonship, the domain was only gradually filled up with settlers. A map made in 1767 shows only 148 families on the west side of the Hudson and 133 families on the east side. However, by 1800, when Stephen van Rensselaer, the renowned politician and statesman, presided over the manor, the tenants had increased to 3,000. This was due in large part to Stephen van Rensselaer's activities and his liberal terms offered to new tenants. Nevertheless, in time, opposition to rents developed on the part of the tenants and there was trouble for the Rensselaers! The story of this "antirent war" will be taken up in a later chapter.[11]

Among other manors in New York State which deserve mention, but which space prevents description of, were the Livingston Manor (160,000 acres), now in Columbia County; the Philipse Manor along the Hudson above New York (Yonkers); the Pelham Manor; the Manor of Morrisania (of which Gouverneur Morris became the owner); the Fordham Manor; and the Scarsdale, Cortlandt, and Philipsburg manors.

---

[11] Daniel D. Bainard, *A Discourse of the Life, Services and Character of Stephen Van Rensselaer . . . with an Historical Sketch of the Colony and Manor of Rensselaerwyck* (Albany, 1839). See also S. G. Nissenson, *The Patroon's Domain* (New York, 1937).

Chapter 4

Virginia and the Proprietary Colonies

Land Distribution in Virginia

As already has been noted, the early Virginia settlements were made under the auspices of the London Company, the twin corporation which received its charter from James I on April 10, 1606. The shareholders proceeded almost immediately to exploit their grant, and it was provided that, although all products of labor during the first seven years were to be pooled, each emigrant at the end of the seventh year was to receive a share of stock in the company and a proportionate grant of land.

Though the original motives of the promoters of the London Company were similar to those of the New England (Plymouth) Company, the economic, climatic, and geographical conditions in the area of Virginia were considerably different from those prevailing in New England, and this situation had an important bearing on the policies of land distribution and land settlement.

After severe hardships, verging on collapse, the first settlers began to spread out. They were aided in this move by the successful cultivation of tobacco, which was in great demand in Europe and, as is well known, became the staple product of the region. This development was a potent force in the distribution of the settlers on plantations rather than the congregation type of settlement that prevailed in New England. Hence large tracts were granted to individuals, not with a view to subdivision or resale, but with the object of retention and settlement.

The Virginian, in order to be a gentleman, as in England, had to be the owner of a vast estate. In this capacity he was aided not by tenants or copyholders, but by indented servants and slaves. Land, plantations, tobacco, and slaves were thus the props of the Virginia economy.

Although the Council of the Virginia Company early announced that it was its intention to "allot to every man that hath already adventured his money and person" plots of land, ". . . the holder of which may dispose of his lot, or go there to possess it, or send families to cultivate as he may do for half the clear profits," large grants to officials and individuals, particularly after the revocation of the company's charter in 1624, became the general rule. The aim to attract settlers, however, was an important factor, and land was given to individuals who were instrumental in promoting this immigration.[1]

Grants of land in fee simple rather than in tenancy became the more usual practice, though the quitrent system was not entirely ignored. As in the case of the Plymouth Company, land was allotted as dividends to shareholders. Thus Berkeley's Hundred, 4,500 acres on the upper James River was granted to five prominent men in England as a first dividend on their shareholdings. "In a feudal manner the company held land for its absentee shareholders."[2] In order to obtain cash, the Company borrowed money by issuing "bills of adventure" of the same denomination as the shares (£12,10^s), entitling the holders to allotment of lands of 100 acres for each bill. Some holders of these bills associated together and jointly took up allotments to be held for speculation. Among the settlements resulting from this system are Smith's Hundred and Martin's Hundred.

In 1624, James I finally succeeded in annulling the charter of the London Company but did not disturb its land privileges or those who had received grants under it. For a long time after the revocation of the charter, land was still exchanged for the company's shares. Because allotments were generally made along the navigable rivers and in many

---

[1] For a good account of the policy of land distribution in Virginia, see a pamphlet by Fairfax Harrison entitled *Virginia Land Grants,* Richmond, Old Dominion Press, 1925.

[2] See Chandler, *op. cit.,* p. 85.

cases comprised large tracts, the population of the colony was spread over an extended area containing but few towns or villages. This, as we may see, was in contrast to the New England system of land settlement.

The Proprietary Colonies

In addition to the incorporation of colonial companies to foster the settlement of North America, such as the incorporated companies already mentioned and others that followed later, the King of England assumed the privilege of making personal grants of American territory to individuals of his choice. These grants, in a way, differed very little from the colonial corporations, since the powers, rights, and duties of both bear a strong resemblance to each other. And the purpose of the grants in both cases was the same; namely, the enlargement and settlement of the British dominions.

But in the matter of land distribution and land tenure, there was an important difference. The grants to individuals of large areas connoted a feudalist arrangement, similar, though with important differences, to that which had prevailed until the seventeenth century in Great Britain. In other words, the grants were made under the theory that the land, in essence, still belonged to the King, who held supreme political power over it and its inhabitants and could forfeit the grant on the ground of nonuse in cases of failure to settle it. But despite its feudalistic character, the old theory of attaching the inhabitants to the soil in a condition of serfdom was almost completely absent. This was to be expected in view of the decadence of the tenure theory that had been going on in Great Britain and culminated in 1662 when Charles II signed the act releasing his noble retainers from furnishing military forces to the Crown.

Moreover, the power of the King to demand contributions in the form of taxes or tribute was expressly waived in most proprietary grants, notably those of Maryland and Pennsylvania, though in the case of Pennsylvania it was stipulated that such taxes could be levied "with the consent of the proprietary or Chief Governor and assembly, or by the Act of Parliament in England."

The Proprietary Grants in New Jersey and Pennsylvania

The land now comprising the state of New Jersey was included in the grant made by Charles II to his brother, James, the Duke of York. But James, in 1664, "for and in consideration of the sum of ten shillings," sold to John Lord Berkeley, "one of his majesties most honorable privy council," and to Sir George Carteret, also "one of his majesties most honorable privy council," this territory to be called New Cesarea or New Jersey, reserving a rental of "a peppercorn upon the feast of the Nativity of St. John the Baptist (only if the same be demanded)."

These two "gentlemen," both of unsavory reputation, thus became the absolute owners of New Jersey, later divided into East Jersey and West Jersey, and "all land titles . . . rest upon their signatures and public officials continue to perpetuate their memories by giving their names to streets and school houses."[3] Because of the conflicting claims by the Dutch and other authorities arising from grants of land with undefined boundaries, a period of litigation ensued which continued down almost to the present day. In this way, land titles in New Jersey as well as in other parts of America are based on force and possession rather than on grounds of legitimate descent or transfer.

Berkeley and Carteret, the absentee landlords, proceeded at once to exploit their grants. As absolute lord proprietors, they appointed a resident governor to whom was given the power to sell and to rent the land and to levy taxes and otherwise rule over the territory. As in the case of the other colonies, to induce immigration, land was offered on the basis of "headrights"; i.e., so much acreage for each indentured servant or settler brought into the territory. The allotment of headrights, as usual, was subject to a quitrent. Lords Berkeley and Carteret, having experienced difficulties in collecting rents and facing open revolts by settlers on the land, sought to dispose of their New Jersey grant at wholesale in England. They finally divided the territory between themselves. Carteret received East Jersey, comprising approximately 3,000 square miles, and Berkeley (who had already sold much of his interest in the territory to a group of Quakers, of which William Penn was a member) consented to receive West Jersey, an area of 4,595

[3] *Ibid.*, p. 306.

square miles. In this way the proprietors separated into two groups, one known as the East Jersey Company, and the other the West Jersey Company. These continued to operate for many years, though they lost their governing privileges when New Jersey became a royal province in 1702. However, they still retained their title to the land and gradually disposed of most of it through dividends to shareholders. In the meantime, the disputes regarding land titles and the refusal of settlers to pay their land rents continued.

The land history of colonial Pennsylvania was more orderly and less confusing than that of New Jersey. Like the latter, part of the territory, particularly along the Delaware Bay, had already been open to settlement by the Dutch, Swedes, and others before William Penn received his grant from Charles II in 1681.

Penn, having already been concerned in land deals in New Jersey, proposed to Charles that the £16,000 of back pay due his father as admiral of the British Navy be commuted into a grant of land lying west of the Delaware River. This the King was willing to do, and in a document dated February 28/March 4, 1681, granted to Penn, his heirs and assignees, as absolute proprietor, "all that tract of land in America . . . bounded on the east by the Delaware River from 12 miles northward of New Castle unto the 43° north latitude. On the south by a circle drawn at twelves miles distance from New Castle, northward and westward unto the beginning of the 40° north, then by a straight line west to 5° in longitude from the easterly boundary." The grant had the usual proviso regarding the King's sovereignty over the territory and the payment of 20 per cent royalty on all gold and silver discovered. The territory was to be erected into a province and "seigniorie" to be called "Pennsylvania."

Penn, a pious Quaker, received in his grant the power and privileges of a feudal lord, but his interest appears to have been more in settling the country than in exercising its governmental powers. However, he and his heirs disposed of most of his grant under a quitrent system. He laid out Philadelphia, divided the place into lots, and scoured Europe and Britain for settlers under conditions very similar to those already operative in the other colonies. The Penn family continued to hold their position as proprietors until the Revolution, but they avoided exercise of feudal powers.

The Maryland Palatinate

The grant of a territory north of the Virginia settlements to Cecil Calvert, the first Lord Baltimore, in 1633, was peculiar in several respects. It set up a system of feudal tenure such as was not provided in similar colonial grants. The charter received by Calvert not only granted ownership of all the land, minerals, rivers, and fishing privileges, but it also included the right to confer titles, incorporate cities and towns, levy import and export taxes, erect manors, and exercise other ancient feudal rights, and, in addition, the King bound himself and his successors not to levy taxes upon the people other than customs duties. Thus there was created in America a palatinate similar to that existing on the continent of Europe.

A grant of this nature, comprising feudal privileges, had an important bearing on the nature of ownership and the distribution of land in Maryland. It literally meant a hierarchy of landownership based on a system of rent payments. Thus Calvert, in his initial advertisement for settlers, stated that "every first adventurer, who shall transport five men between 15 and 50 years of age, shall receive for himself and his heirs for ever, a grant of two thousand acres of land at a yearly rent of four hundred pounds of good wheat—twenty pounds rent per hundred acres." The payment of rents in wheat was a rather common practice then existing in England.

When settlements were undertaken in Maryland, manors comprising large acreages were set up, and the system of quitrents was established, which continued in modified form in some localities, as in the case of Baltimore City, almost down to the present day. However, this attempted revival of feudal land tenure met with little success. The manors, where they actually came into existence, were broken up. In the latter part of the seventeenth century land conveyances in Maryland became relatively frequent, and such conveyances were required to be registered. In this way, most of the large original grants and the Baltimore proprietorship were broken up. As a result of the increase of population in the colony, land values rose also. The original practice of granting land warrants under the "headright" system was abandoned in favor of outright purchase. Thus, today, the land-tenure system of Maryland does not differ essentially from that of the New England or other British Crown colonies.[4]

The Carolinas

The grant of the Carolinas to Lord Ashley Cooper, together with the then proprietors of New Jersey, John Berkeley and George Carteret, all favorites of Charles II, was very similar to that of Lord Baltimore in Maryland. Under it, they were to establish a feudal regime, based on landownership or landholding—under a system of sub-infeudation, already outlawed in England. The proprietors adopted the "Fundamental Constitutions in London in 1669"—a charter of government supposedly written by John Locke, but not in accordance with Locke's later ideas set down in his *Essay on Civil Government*. These "Fundamental Constitutions" were amended several times, and it appears that they were never applied strictly in the government of the territory.

The proprietors endeavored to sell the land in large tracts, constituting seigniories and baronies, the purchaser to have feudal powers. Quitrents from tenants were required, but throughout the era of the proprietorship there is evidence that such payments were generally avoided and the proprietors had difficulty in enforcing a governmental system on the settlers or of obtaining revenues sufficient to maintain the government. The whole system finally collapsed and in September 1729, South Carolina (together with North Carolina, which was severed from it) became a royal province.

The land grants previously made were confirmed, however, and quitrents were made payable to the Crown. But large baronies ceased and royal grants of land became limited in quantity. The feudal plan of landholding in time gave way to a fee system, and both large and small holdings persisted.

[4] See V. J. Wyckoff, "The Sizes of Plantations in Seventeenth-Century Maryland," in *Maryland Historical Magazine*, Vol. XXXII, No. 4, and "Land Prices in Seventeenth-Century Maryland," in *American Economic Review*, Vol. XXVIII, March 1938, pp. 82–88.

The Georgia Colonial Land Policy

Unlike the other and earlier colonies, Georgia was not founded under a plan of land exploitation by chartered companies or feudal proprietaries. "A humanitarian motive led to the founding of the colony."[5] General James Oglethorpe and his associates planned the colony as a haven for relief and rehabilitation of unfortunate debtors. The disposal of vacant land, or its retention for personal gain, therefore, was not a motive in the founding of the colony. Toward this end regulations were made in the original charter placing a maximum limitation upon the number of acres that could be granted to one individual. It was stipulated "that no greater quantity of lands be granted, either entirely or in parcels, to or for the use, or in trust for any one person, than five hundred acres."[6]

The trustees of the colony went even farther and ruled that, for military and economic reasons, they would not allot to a settler more than fifty acres "to prevent the accumulation of several lots into one hand lest the garrison should be lessened, and likewise to prevent a division of these lots into smaller parcels lest that which was no more than sufficient for one planter, when entire, should if divided amongst several, be too scanty for their subsistence."

To carry out this policy, land was granted "in tail male." This had the objective that it could neither be mortgaged nor sold—a provision that hampered the success of the colony. Another damper on the land allotments was restrictions against slaveholding. These restrictions, despite their high moral purposes, were not such as would invite settlers to the colony, particularly when in the neighboring territories large tracts of land could be leased on liberal terms and where Negro slaves could be used without limit.

Within five years after the founding of the colony, complaints were made by the settlers to the trustees. The outcome was a relinquishment of the entail provision in land allotments, and by 1750 "the principle of absolute ownership of land was recognized in the colony."[7] Slavery

[5] See Enoch Marvin Banks, *The Economics of Land Tenure in Georgia*, p. 11.
[6] *Ibid*, p. 11.
[7] *Ibid.*, p. 13.

was also permitted. All this gave an impetus to land settlement in Georgia. Between 1750 and the outbreak of the Revolution, the colony's population greatly increased. Land was plentiful and the region enjoyed a period of prosperity and expansion. However, as slaves were included along with members of a family as individuals, for whom 50 acres each were allotted, it was not long before large plantations began to grow in Georgia, as had already developed in the other southern colonies.

The Quitrent System

From the preceding pages covering landownership and distribution in the American colonies, it should be noticed that, with the exception of New England and possibly Virginia, the quitrent system of land tenure was largely in vogue. However, in practice it was a theoretical legalistic concept, since with few exceptions, notably in New York, it was not adhered to in practice, and the payment of rents was largely ignored or refused. Regarding the failure of the system, Professor Beverley Bond, Jr., author of the scholarly work, *The Quit-Rent System in the American Colonies,* writes:

> As a general form of land-tenure in the American colonies the quit-rent system was not wholly successful. This failure resulted from the fundamentally different character of the quit-rent in England and America. In England it had come as a relief from onerous feudal dues. As such it was accepted without question; at first, as a welcome relief, later, as a customary charge. In America the very circumstances attending the introduction of the quit-rent were different from those in England. The lands which the colonists rescued by their own labor from the primeval wilderness had paid no previous feudal dues. The quit-rent constituted, therefore, not a welcome relief, but a tax upon the land. The colonists finally came to look upon it as an imposition upon the land for the benefit of an outside power. Their independence of spirit added fuel to the hostility. Perhaps even then the quit-rent would have been accepted, such is the power of custom, had it prevailed in all the colonies. But when the plans of the New England Council failed, and the land-tenure in all the corporate colonies became free of feudal charges, the doom of the quit-rent

system was sounded. The example of New England soon stirred up opposition in the neighboring colonies. As communication became more frequent, this influence would have made itself felt to a more marked degree in the colonies to the southward, had not the Revolution intervened.

The problems that confronted the crown and the proprietors in establishing the quit-rent system in a new country militated against its success. Separated by long distances from the home government, the colonial governors were at a great disadvantage in carrying out instructions. Their dependence upon the assemblies for measures of enforcement greatly added to their perplexities. In all the colonies, except Maryland, the history of the quit-rent was one of persistent struggles between the governor and the assembly, the former representing the crown or the proprietor, the latter the tenants. Compromises became necessary, but usually it was the overlord who surrendered a large part of his claims in order to secure even a measure of respect for his rights in the soil.[8]

The Motives and Methods of Colonial Land Distribution

The acquisition of land and the pecuniary benefits of its ownership or disposal were undoubtedly prime motives of the shareholders of the colonial trading companies and the holders of land grants in the American colonies. America, from its very beginning as a field of economic exploitation, was a speculation in land and pelts. Though many of the actual settlers emigrated to these shores to escape religious or political persecution, they were merely given the opportunity to do so because of the need for settlers on the land to make it economically valuable. It is doubtful whether any of the grantees of vast areas from the British Crown, even Calvert or Penn, had, as a prime or sole motive for their undertakings, the relief of their brethren from religious persecutions. This, in effect, was merely incidental to other and more persistent motives—the pecuniary benefits of landownership and land disposal.

---

[8] *The American Historical Review*, Vol. XVII (April 1912), p. 514. A more detailed discussion is contained in Professor Bond's complete volume under the same title, published by the Yale University Press, 1919.

The different methods of land disposal and land settlement in the various geographical areas of the British-American dominions were due more largely to differences in climate, soil, terrain, and the presence of unfriendly aborigines than to differences in theories of land tenure or in political and religious beliefs. That the New England colonies adopted, for the most part, a system of relatively small allotments, centered about a community, was not so much the result of a preconceived or definite plan of land settlement as a provision for better defense and for local market and exchange of products among the inhabitants. Nevertheless, the urge for association in common worship by people of strong religious beliefs, which undoubtedly has been a factor in village and town development throughout the world, was a potent force in the decisions leading to methods of land allotments.

Summary on Colonial Land Systems

From the foregoing pages it is apparent that, notwithstanding the differences in the land systems of the various colonies and the distinctions between colonial land companies and proprietary grants, the ownership and profitable disposal of land were, with a few exceptions, the prime objectives. Absentee ownership was the rule, and the spirit of "landlordism" in England and Ireland, which was then taking root, was extended to the vast unsettled areas of America. The privilege of landownership, which was offered to actual settlers, was for the purpose of improving the land and, by increasing population, to make the undisposed portions more valuable. The fact that the original owners and promoters did not, in many cases, obtain their objectives and did not realize the wealth or income expected was primarily due to the abundance of land opened for settlement and the inability to enforce the collections of payments and of rents. Revolt against restricted privileges of landownership and against the governing privileges given to owners of land, whether heads of manors or freeholders, was manifested in the colonies a century before the Revolution and continued long thereafter, particularly as "land hunger" was unabated, and land speculation became a prevalent disease among the colonists. Of this we shall speak more in the next chapter.

Philosophic Conceptions of Landed Property in the Colonial Era

Having reviewed the history of land acquisition and landownership in the colonial era, it might be well and proper at this point to refer to the philosophic and moral concepts of landed property that prevailed in the same period. It should be borne in mind that at this time the theories of "natural rights" and civic freedoms were beginning to emerge and found expressions in the works of such philosophers as Spinoza, John Locke, Judge Blackstone, Harrington, and others. The theories of Locke are particularly noteworthy in this connection, not only because of his genius and influence, but also because he is reputed to be the author of the only constitution set up as a basis for government of an American colony. Moreover, it is generally conceded by most historians that Locke's political doctrines were a powerful force in stimulating the movement which resulted in the American Revolution. But despite all this, Locke's philosophy regarding landed property appears to have been largely bypassed by the political philosophers, statesmen, and leaders of the colonial and Revolutionary eras, and certainly there is little evidence that they were eager or willing to adopt his ideas on the subject at that time.

Locke expressed his views on landed property in Chapter V, Book II, of his two *Treatises on Civil Government,* in the chapter titled "On Property." In this chapter he carefully distinguishes, as other writers have done before and after him, between the bare land as property and the fruits of labor applied to land. He held that the first is the common heritage of all men, and only the second—namely, the labor applied to the land in use—is the legitimate basis for private landownership. Thus Locke, like Henry George, distinguishes land itself as an entity distinct from the improvements made on the land. And he also counseled against concentration of landownership, stating that "as much land as a man tills, plants, improves, cultivates, and can use the product of, so much is his property. . . . The measure of property Nature well set, by the extent of men's labour and the convenience of life," and he also states that as long as the land is put to use there is no injustice in its private ownership, provided "there is enough, and as good, left in common for others." Though Locke's philosophy did not set up a demand for restraint on land concentration in the colonies, it undoubtedly had an influence on some of the fathers of the Revolution as well as on the French physiocrats and classical British economists. Both Thomas Jefferson and John Adams, as shall be shown later, were opposed to large individual landholdings. And Benjamin Franklin, though a participant in colonial land-grabbing, denied that the right to private property was absolute. But it was only after land was well settled and tended to become scarce, as a natural monoply, that property ideas expressed by John Locke and his followers in later years took root on our continent. This development will also be discussed in a later chapter.

Summary

In summing up the role of landownership and land distribution as related to the colonial grants, it may be stated that, in origin, though the colonial charters were based largely on the concept of the trading companies then existing in Britain, they were, in essence, land-speculation ventures. This motive was stimulated by the rise of the British mercantile classes during the period and their gradual assumption of a predominant role in British politics. The absence of any elaborate details regarding land distribution in the colonial charters indicates that landownership, as a political factor, had already lost much of its effect in governmental matters, while its economic aspects, as a factor in providing for human existence and as furnishing a means of social aggrandizement, was becoming more important. The economic conditions in England at the time were such that the new "landless" classes, created by the disintegration of feudalism and the growth of the enclosure movement, led to economic misery and political discontent. The effort to establish colonies was the outcome of this situation. But land-grabbing was also an important motive. As already pointed out, the rising mercantile classes were eager to be landlords. Absentee ownership of large areas was a badge of social prestige.

Chapter 5

The Colonial Land Speculations

The colonial land system was essentially English. Despite subsequent political changes and upheavals, it has been largely maintained and only little modified. Such modifications as have been made were due not so much to a desire or movement for land reform as for adjustment to prevailing political and economic conditions. Thus the development of fee ownership in preference to a tenancy or quitrent system may be ascribed more largely to the early abundance of land rather than to a positive move to do away with the evils of the latter system. As stated by W. A. Phillips, a western congressman, in 1885 in his book, *Labor, Land and Law*, "The essential feature of the land policy seemed to be that in this New World each man should get as much land as he could, and if he did not sell it to some successor, his family should have the exclusive right to use it forever. Escaping from the aristocracy and despotism of Europe, each man hoped he could found an aristocratic family of his own. Tenure was not based on a recognition of human rights, but on privilege. The richer and more aristocratic colonists desired great estates and the spread of an aristocratic landed system. Such institutions met the favor and received the patronage of the home governments. Poor settlers and colonists had little power and were anxious to secure all the land they could."[1]

From the preceding chapters it is apparent that the conveyance of unoccupied lands to chartered companies, private groups and individuals with an agreement to undertake the management, settlement,

[1] P. 319.

and resale was a common practice throughout the colonial era. Practically all of the early English land settlement of America was conducted on this plan. The effect was to originate a process of land speculation and landlordism that persisted throughout the whole period of settlement and continues to this day. Though land speculation fostered land settlement and scattered the population throughout the boundaries of the royal grants and even beyond, the result was not always in the best interest of orderly political and economic development. Indian warfare, disregard for the common rights of mankind, and frontier hardships marred the history of one of the greatest and most important episodes in the movement of human population.

During the first hundred years of North American colonization, economic and political conditions within and without the colonies gave little encouragement to private land schemes. Land was too plentiful. But as population began to fill up the accessible regions within charter grants, and good tillable land became scarcer and more valuable, the move to obtain unsettled regions for pecuniary gain came more into vogue, and land-grabbing, by both fair and foul means, became an occupation as well as an activity of the colonial "adventurer."

Toward the end of the eighteenth century, wealth had accumulated in the colonies. Free land, obtained under crown grants or "headrights," had practically ceased. Cities and channels of trade were established and population had gradually pushed forward to and beyond the Alleghenies. The vast unoccupied tracts beyond became a speculation lure. The main objectives were the large unsettled tracts lying within or adjacent to the charter limits or boundaries of the various colonies.

The Early Maine Speculation

Among the early enterprises undertaken with the motive of land speculation were two companies organized in the Massachusetts Colony to acquire large tracts in Maine. In 1661 the Massachusetts Colony sold to several individuals for £400 a large tract on the Kennebec River. This became known as the Kennebec Purchase. The heirs held this territory, largely unsettled, for nearly a century. In 1753 they incorporated as the Proprietors of the Kennebec Purchase and proceeded to dispose of their holdings. The corporation continued in existence until 1816.[2]

Another early Maine land company was the Pejepscut Company. Neither of these early projects held any promise of profit to proprietors until about a quarter century before the Revolution, and it was not until after the Revolution that actual disposal of these outlying areas was actively put into effect.

The Early Southern Land Companies

We have pointed out that proprietorship of large landed estates was highly regarded by the colonials. As in England, it was an emblem of nobility. It carried with it political as well as pecuniary preferment. This was particularly characteristic of the southern colonies. There during the colonial days the presence of large landed estates, engrossed in comparatively few hands, fostered a landed aristocracy. It was further abetted by the system of Negro slavery and indentured servants. The "plantation system," with emphasis on a single crop, became the rule and crowded out the landless "freeman," who sought refuge in the back country or less accessible regions, or who was forced to reside as a laborer or mechanic in the towns and cities. This gave rise to a class of "poor whites," in contrast with the landowning class, which largely controlled the suffrage and dominated the political life of the period. Landownership was desirable, therefore, for economic and social as well as for political reasons. The Virginian was not much of a "gentleman" unless he lived in the midst of his countless acres. If he was a non-resident owner or a large "patentee" of the Crown, he employed land agents on the spot to look after his estates or to lease or sell his holdings. Grants of land in the southern colonies were a fertile source of political intrigues. The local gentry were frequently in conflict with the Crown-appointed governors regarding land questions. In fact, land-grabbing in the South began before the importance of either Negroes or tobacco was recognized.

As the areas east of the Allegheny Mountains were gradually en-

[2]See *Maine Historical Collections*, Vol. II, pp. 269–94.

Colonial Land Speculations

grossed, and as plantations and towns spread out beyond the piedmont sections, covetous eyes were pointed toward the vast unsettled areas to the westward. It was not until after the French and Indian War that the political sovereignty and administrative control of the territory were established. Various colonies claimed a share of the westward area as parts of their original charter grants, or as claims under the right of "discovery," or through "purchase" from the Indians. As the charter limits of each colony were not definitely fixed, their claims overlapped and there were conflicts, amounting in some cases to open warfare, over the jurisdiction of unsettled areas. Inter-colonial jealousy and territorial greed led the rival claimants to take measures, secretly and openly, to assert their rights by actual occupation or by royal conveyances.

The first definite move to obtain a large grant of western land was made in 1748, when a group of Virginian gentlemen, styling themselves the Ohio Company, obtained a crown grant of 500,000 acres west of the Alleghenies adjacent to Virginia. The next year another group of forty-six Virginians, styling themselves the Loyal Company, received an additional 800,000 acres nearby. Both grants were made by the governor and Council of Virginia. The locations were not surveyed, nor, for that matter, definitely marked out. That of the Ohio Company was to be located "south of the Ohio River," and the Loyal Company's grant was to be "in one or more surveys beginning on the bounds between Virginia and South Carolina and running westward to the North Seas." Both companies were to locate their lands and make return of surveys within four years' time. At this time, it should be noted, the areas in question were under the disputed ownership of the English and the French, while the actual possession was held by the Indians, who acknowledged the suzerainty of neither of the disputing European powers. But such disregard of the rights of others was an insignificant obstacle to the land-grabbers of the period.

The grants undoubtedly had a political significance. Without this western territory, the southern colonies would be confined to the area east of the Alleghenies and without an outlet to the Ohio and Mississippi rivers. The French blocked this by pushing their settlements southward and by establishing Fort Duquesne at the present location of

Pittsburgh. The conflict was finally decided by the treaty of peace which ended the bloody French and Indian War. This treaty recognized the claim of the British to the territory.

Despite the dangers and difficulties involved, both the Ohio and the Loyal companies set about to secure their grants. Christopher Gist, one of the noted surveyors of Virginia, was sent in October 1750 to "search out" and to discover the Ohio Company's lands. He went down the Ohio River as far south as the present site of Louisville, Kentucky. During the journey he made strong overtures of friendship with the Indians. He was enthusiastic about the project. "Nothing," he said, "is wanted but cultivation to make it a most delightful country." In the meantime the Loyal Company group was not idle. Its proprietors sent Dr. Thomas Walker of Albemarle, Virginia, to make a reconnaissance and to discover a proper place of settlement. As might be expected, the two "companies" then became involved in a controversy, and neither made an actual survey or fixed the bounds of their respective grants.

The ease with which they obtained their grants, however, and the glowing accounts of the potential values of the vast area led to other land-settlement schemes and aroused an epidemic of interest in these wild outlying lands. The interest was intensified by the outbreak of the French and Indian War, at which time volunteers were promised land in the new territory, ranging from five thousand acres each for high-ranking officers down to fifty acres for each private. At about the same time, Governor Dinwiddie, who arrived in Virginia in 1751, granted land to applicants in the regions—in all, more than a million acres.

These grants of western lands in large tracts brought protests from the commonalty. The Virginia House of Burgesses expressed their disapproval and requested that in the future the governor make small grants and thus curb the land monopoly of the large companies.[3]

Some of the speculators in these western lands sought not only to acquire the ownership of the land but also to establish new colonies, with separate and distinct governments. They sent lobbyists to London to obtain the Crown's sanction to land-grabbing schemes, and thus the

---

[3] See Kenneth P. Bailey, *The Ohio Company of Virginia*.

question of the disposal of the vast western domain, lately won from the French, infested British politics and induced corruption and favoritism in the colonial governments themselves. One half of England is "Now Land Mad," wrote George Croghan of Philadelphia, one of the land schemers, to Sir William Johnson, British Indian agent for the colonies, on March 30, 1766, "and everybody there has his eyes fixed in this country."[4]

The Indian Line

The British authorities, despite the corruption and greed of its members, who were oppressed with the burdens left by the wars with the French and Indians in America, desired an era of peace in the dominions overseas. They therefore sought to curb the system of landgrabbing. A royal order was issued in 1763 prohibiting the colonial governors from granting land patents beyond the headwaters of the streams running into the Atlantic, and barring land "purchases" by individuals from the Indians in the area. This resulted in the drawing of the "Indian Line," which extended along the Allegheny Mountains through central Pennsylvania and southward along the line of the Blue Ridge Mountains of Virginia and the Carolinas. This decree created serious opposition from the land-hungry colonists, among whom were George Washington and a number of other Revolutionary compatriots. Despite the opposition, however, the order was not rescinded, and to make matters worse for the land engrossers, Parliament in 1774 enacted the Quebec Bill, which annexed the crown lands northwest of the Ohio River to the royal province of Quebec. This measure was among the grievances cited in the Declaration of Independence. The Revolutionary Congress never recognized the Quebec Act as valid.

There were at this time in Virginia many prominent persons engaged in land deals, including George Washington and his brothers. These banded together in groups or in "companies." There were the Lees, the Nicholsons, the Carters, the Masons, and the Byrds, all large landholders. Patrick Henry, along with Peter Jefferson, a surveyor, father of Thomas Jefferson, were also deeply concerned in land deals.

[4]*Sir William Johnson Papers*, Vol. V., p. 129. See also C. W. Aevord, *The Mississippi Valley in British Politics*.

Farther south, in the Carolinas, and to the north, in Pennsylvania, there were also prominent colonists who eagerly grasped for the fertile regions sloping toward the Mississippi.

The Transylvania Company

Judge Richard Henderson of North Carolina, the employer and backer of Daniel Boone, the pioneer, promoted the settlement of the Kentucky region and claimed ownership of a vast unsettled tract there. He organized a group of speculators under the name of the Transylvania Company. Ignoring the British Government's interdiction against Indian land purchases, he "bought" from the Cherokees in 1773 about one half of the present state of Kentucky and immediately began settling the land. He advertised widely for pioneers and "shareholders." In his announcements, Henderson waxed enthusiastic. "The country [Transylvania] might invite," he wrote, "a prince from his palace merely for the pleasure of contemplating its beauty and its excellence, but only add the rapturous idea of property, and what allurements can the world offer for the loss of so glorious a prospect."[5]

Henderson and his associates ran into a noose of inter-colonial conflict regarding the jurisdiction of the region. They endeavored during the Revolution to get the Continental Congress to erect their territory into another state, but Patrick Henry and Thomas Jefferson, in the interest of Virginia, had their Indian purchase declared illegal. The Kentuckians then threatened to fight, and to appease the irate speculators, Virginia made grants to actual settlers and finally closed out the Transylvania claim by giving Henderson's Company 200,000 acres Land-grabbing soon became widespread in this new territory, and the engrossment of large tracts resulted in large importations of slaves into Kentucky, the redundant descendants of which, in later years, had to be "sold down the river."

As Kentucky was settled by zeal for landownership and by the greed of land-grabbers, so also was Tennessee. John Sevier, a hero of the Battle of Kings Mountain, the colonizer of the new "State of Franklin"

[5]See A. Henderson, "A Pre-Revolutionary Revolt in the Old Southwest," in *Mississippi Valley Historical Review*, Vol. 17, p. 198 *et seq*.

(which later became Tennessee), claimed title to immense tracts in that region and, still unsatisfied, continuously grasped for more.

George Washington's Interest in Western Lands

Like many of his compatriots, George Washington, along with his half brothers, Augustine and Lawrence Washington, were concerned in western land speculation. They were participants in the Ohio Company and other land-grabbing ventures. As a surveyor and as land agent for Lord Fairfax, whose estates in northern Virginia comprised 5,000,000 acres, Washington, early in his career, was brought into contact with "absentee landlordism" and at this time appears to have become infected with the "wild land" virus. He, indeed, was one of the most active land speculators of colonial times. He took an active part in pressing the claims of the Ohio Company and, together with his neighbors, the Lees, formed the Mississippi Company and petitioned in 1768 for an additional large land grant. After the French and Indian War, in which he took a prominent part, he entered wholeheartedly into western land acquisitions. He treated as "a scrap of paper" the British edict forbidding the colonial governors from granting patents for land lying beyond the Alleghenies. He was not discouraged by it. He wrote to his friend and agent, Captain William Crawford, whom he employed to seek out and pre-empt the best lands in this region:

> I can never look upon that proclamation in any other light (but this I say between ourselves) than as a temporary expedient to quiet the Minds of the Indians and must fall of course in a few years especially when those Indians are consenting to our Occupying the Lands. Any person therefore who neglects the present opportunity of hunting out good Lands and in some measure marking and distinguishing them for their own (in order to keep others from settling them) will never regain it.[6]

In October 1770, Washington set out on a journey to inspect the lands he was bent on acquiring for himself and others—land which had been set aside by Virginia as bounties to officers and soldiers. He made

[6] John C. Fitzpatrick, *The Writings of George Washington*, Vol. 2, p. 469. See also Herbert Baxter Adams, *Maryland's Influence in Founding a National Commonwealth*, appendix, "Washington's Land Speculations."

notes on the territory, and after acquiring part of these "soldier lands" he inserted the following advertisement in the *Maryland Journal and Baltimore Advertiser,* August 20, 1773:[6a]

> Mount Vernon, in Virginia, July 15, 1773
>
> The subscriber having obtained patents for upwards of twenty thousand acres of land on the Ohio and Great Kanawha (ten thousand of which are situated on the banks of the first-mentioned river, between the mouths of the two Kanawhas, and the remainder on the Great Kanawha, or New River, from the mouth, or near it, upward in one continued survey) proposes to divide the same into any sized tenements that may be desired, and lease them upon moderate terms, allowing a reasonable number of years rent free, provided within the space of two years from next October, three acres for every fifty contained in each lot, and proportionately as above, shall be enclosed and laid down in good grass for meadows, and, moreover, that at least fifty fruit trees for every like quantity of land shall be planted on the premises. . . . To which may be added, that as patents have now actually passed the seals for the several tracts here offered to be leased, settlers on them may cultivate and enjoy the lands in peace and safety notwithstanding the unsettled counsels respecting a new colony on the Ohio; and, as no right-money is to be paid for the lands, and quit rent of two shillings sterling a hundred, demandable some years hence, only, it is highly presumable that they will always be held on a more desirable footing than when both these are laid on with a heavy hand.

It appears from the foregoing announcement that Washington proposed to settle the lands and not to sell them. He wished settlers to clear, fence, and till the tenements. How like the English practice! And how much opposed to democratic principles! In fact, Washington, until he set out to lead the embattled farmers in the struggle for political freedom, was a Virginia landlord. These gentry were fast assuming all the traits, characteristics, and privileges of the landed aristocracy of the mother country. There, land was not only the badge of wealth, it was the emblem of nobility. The first families of Virginia not only sought land, but they sought to retain it. When the King's proclamation re-

[6a] Phillips, *Labor, Land and Law,* p. 323.

stricting settlement of western lands was issued, it created the political resentment of the Virginia aristocracy that led to revolt, but it also gave an opportunity to the common folk, the landless yeomanry, to assert themselves and take a hand in the determination of the popular will. The Revolutionary War eventually resulted in the abolition of landownership as a basis for political prestige and preferment, and to this movement Washington, Jefferson, and other landed associates slowly and calmly yielded. As true patriots they sacrificed personal interests in the common cause. But they continued to hold property in land as a sacred right.

Another of Virginia's "Revolutionary Fathers" who was steeped in western land speculation was Patrick Henry. There is strong historical proof that Henry was engaged in land speculation both before and after the Revolution. Jefferson described Henry as being "insatiable in money," and his participation in the Georgia land frauds (see p. 78) and other western land schemes may bear this out.

Thomas Jefferson, a large landowner on his own account, who later in life frowned upon speculation and land-grabbing, expressed the view in 1774 that the land never belonged to the British King and it was time for the colonies "to declare that he has no right to grant lands of himself," and listed this privilege, when he wrote the Declaration of Independence, among the British King's usurpations, stating, "He has endeavoured to prevent the population of these States; for that purpose obstructing the Laws of Naturalization of Foreigners; refusing to pass others to encourage their migrations hither, *and raising the conditions of new appropriations of Lands."* (Italics inserted.)

Franklin's "Vandalia Company"

Another great American of the colonial era also was a victim of the western land fever. Benjamin Franklin's many-sided occupations included gainful pursuits and desire for pecuniary profit. Be it said of him, however, that he was not the originator of a bold scheme to obtain a vast territory, one of the largest land deals ever concocted on the American continent. He merely aided in its promotion.

When Franklin was in London in 1766 as an agent of Pennsylvania, his enterprising son, William Franklin, then governor of New Jersey, conceived the idea of buying the claims of French settlers to land in Illinois—a scheme later expanded to a proposed purchase of an immense tract lying northwest of the Ohio River. Associated with him were Sir William Johnson, the British Government's Indian agent in the northern colonies, and several wealthy Philadelphians. They wrote Franklin, requesting the use of his influence to get the approval of the British Government.

Franklin was for it. "I like the project of a colony in the Illinois country," he wrote his son, "and will forward it to my utmost here." His reward for his services would be a share in the deal and a limited right to nominate others. Knowing the frailties of politicians, Franklin sought to gain approbation of the project by distributing among them "shares" in the project.

He interested a prominent London banker, Thomas Walpole, who became the nominal head of the affair, and the deal became known as the Walpole Grant. But in Philadelphia it was called the Vandalia Company. While shares were being distributed in the ownership of the "new colony," the petition, which was referred by the British Cabinet to the Board of Trade, was not acted on for six years and was finally disapproved by Lord Hillsborough, the head of the Board, much to the disgust of Franklin. However, Franklin, possibly through his remarkable arguments printed in reply to the Board of Trade's decision, finally won out. The British Cabinet eventually gave its approval to the scheme, but this was undoubtedly due to the belief that the action would appease the revolting colonies. The grant, however, came too late, and when Franklin returned to Philadelphia in 1775, the colonies were already in revolt and the scheme of a "new colony" was dropped.[6b]

There were a number of other land-grabbing schemes in the Northwest, but space does not permit giving the details. Since the Revolu-

---

[6b]Letters of Franklin to his son, William Temple Franklin, of 1766–68, in John Bigelow, editor, *The Complete Works of Benjamin Franklin*, Vol. 4, pp. 136–45. See also Thomas Perkins Abernethy, *Western Lands and the American Revolution*.

tionary War put a curb on them and since those currently in existence were not recognized as valid by the Continental Congress, they, for the most part, lapsed or were later invalidated by Congress or the courts.

Population Pressure as a Factor in Westward Movement

The struggle for the western lands, with the accompanying speculation fever, was undoubtedly caused by the pressure of population and the consequent rise in land values in the settled areas. Several decades before the Revolutionary War, the settled portions of New England had already become overcrowded. Connecticut, in particular, felt the need for an outlet for surplus population. Packed within narrow limits and confined to rocky hills, the sturdy Yankee farmers looked with envious eyes upon the rich unoccupied lands to the westward. As already noted, this adventuresome pioneer spirit was fostered by the fever of land speculation as well as by need and desire for new land. Silas Deane, who as a young man collected material for a history of his native state of Connecticut, repeatedly urged an outlet for her people and pointed to the need of western lands for this purpose. The Susquehannah Company, organized in 1753 by a group of Connecticut capitalists, purchased from the Indians a tract of land in western Pennsylvania (the Wyoming region) and, despite the armed opposition of Governor Penn, made settlements in what now constitutes the anthracite region of the United States. The disputed area was held, notwithstanding the invalidity of Indian purchases and the terrors of the French and Indian War, though its development was greatly retarded by an attack of the Indians in 1778, known as the Wyoming Massacre.

There were other and similar movements by local population groups in New England and elsewhere which sought to establish actual settlements beyond the "Indian Line."

Summary

From the foregoing brief account of land schemes and land engrossment in the early westward movement, it should be noted that land hunger and the desire to reap the profits of the unearned increment arising from landownership through population growth were manifest among early colonists. These characteristics have never been lost or discarded. They have continued throughout the whole period of our national history. The colonial precedents enumerated herein formed the background for movements along the same lines, but of somewhat different character, as shall be shown later in these pages.

Chapter 6

Land and the American Revolution

In 1835, the French philosopher, Alexis de Tocqueville, wrote in his historic work, *Democracy in America:* "Laws and customs are frequently to be met with in the United States, which contrast strongly with all that surrounds them. These laws seem to be drawn up in a spirit contrary to the prevailing tenor of American legislation; and these customs are no less opposed to the general tone of society. If the English colonies had been founded in an age of darkness, or if their origin was already lost in the lapse of years, the problem would be insoluble."[1]

Though it is not definitely known, De Tocqueville might have had in mind the retention and acceptance of the antiquated English land laws. Land tenure as initiated in the colonies, albeit with some modifications, was continued during and after the Revolution. In some areas it was the persistence of a power and privilege which left an aristocratic trace in the veins of the nation's body politic, which, despite democratic gains, it has never been able to eliminate.

We have already seen in the previous chapters that the attempts to introduce a feudal system of land tenure in the American colonies largely resulted in failure, and quitrents demanded of settlers were ignored or evaded through general connivance or open revolt. Yet in some areas, particularly in the South and Southwest, ownership of large estates, supported by some of the laws relating to land tenure transferred from the old countries of Europe, was an emblem of political

[1] Vol. I, pp. 44–45.

prestige and preference. In fact, in several of the states, years after the Revolution, real estate ownership was a requirement of political suffrage, as originally set down in the colonial laws.[2] Moreover, landownership was restricted to citizens and not open to aliens.

Writing on this topic, De Tocqueville remarks:

> In most of the States situated to the southwest of the Hudson, some great English proprietors had settled, who had imported with them aristocratic principles and the English law of inheritance. . . . In the South, one man, aided by slaves, could cultivate a great extent of country; it was therefore common to see rich landed proprietors. But their influence was not altogether aristocratic as the term is understood in Europe, since they possessed no privileges; and the cultivation of their estates being carried on by slaves, they had no tenants depending on them and consequently no patronage. Still, the great proprietors south of the Hudson constituted a superior class, having ideas and tastes of its own, and forming the centre of political action. This kind of aristocracy sympathized with the body of the people, whose passions and interests it easily embraced; but it was too weak and too short-lived to excite either love or hatred for itself. This was the class which headed the insurrection in the South, and furnished the best leaders of the American Revolution.[3]

Perhaps, as De Tocqueville indicates, it was respect for law and customs which, despite the awakened democratic tendencies that followed the Revolution, led to the retention of a system of land tenure not entirely compatible with political and economic equality.

The Abolishment of the Law and Custom of Primogeniture

The laws of inheritance as applied to land, in the case of primogeniture and entail, at the time of the American Revolution were as obnoxious to Britains of liberal thought as they were to many of the American colonists. But the sway of British aristocracy, based on a landed nobility, prevented action for their elimination or moderation. How-

---

[2]For a discussion of property qualifications for voters at the time of the Constitutional Convention, see Charles A. Beard, *An Economic Interpretation of the Constitution of the United States,* Chap. IV.

[3]*Op. cit.,* Vol. I, p. 58.

ever, when the colonies were freed from the yoke of the mother country, they took measures, in some cases without much delay, to be rid of these social evils. Thus Daniel Webster, in an address delivered at Plymouth, Massachusetts, on December 22, 1820, remarked that though "the character of political institutions of New England was determined by the fundamental laws respecting property," the states, by abolishing the right of primogeniture, by curtailing entails, long trusts, and other processes for fettering and tying up lands, and by the enactment of facilities for the alienation of estates for public registries and simplified forms of conveyance, had fixed the future frame and form of government in New England. "The consequence of all these causes," he said, "has been a great subdivision of the soil and a great equality of condition, the true basis, most certainly, of a popular government."

It has been pointed out by John Fiske that the succession to property at the time of the Revolution was regulated in New York and the southern states by the English rule of primogeniture.[4] In New Jersey, Pennsylvania, Delaware, and the four New England states, primogeniture was modified by allowing to the eldest son a double share in the distribution of landed property among heirs. Georgia was the first state to abolish this rule of primogeniture after the Revolution by decreeing the equal distribution to direct heirs of intestate property, and between 1784 and 1796 her example was followed by all the other former colonies. At about the same time, the law and custom of entail was either definitely abolished or the obstacles to their discontinuance were removed. Likewise, in New York, the manorial privileges of the patroons were abolished, and in Maryland and the Carolinas the manorial system, as previously stated, after a slow period of disintegration, was allowed to expire and the unallotted lands of the proprietors forfeited to the state. Pennsylvania, the Carolinas, and Georgia also abolished the colonial proprietorship system after the Revolution, but Pennsylvania indemnified the Penn family to the amount of $500,000.

Jefferson's Influence on Land-Tenure Reform

Thomas Jefferson is given credit for putting through, while governor,

[4] *The Critical Period of American History,* pp. 70–71.

the abolition of primogeniture and entail in Virginia. In view of the large and influential class of large landholders in that state at the time, this undoubtedly was not an easy task.

Jefferson's opposition to primogeniture and entail, along with his dislike of land engrossment, was based on his concept of political equality. He had the examples of France and Britain before him, nations in which the acquisition and accumulation of property, particularly in land, brought about a domination of political power and destroyed the basis of political equality. As stated by Marshall Harris, "He led the fight against entails because the maintenance of large estates in the same family did not meet his standards of equality. He uprooted the practice of primogeniture, or even the Hebrew idea of a double portion for the eldest son, in favor of equal devolution. Then he helped formulate the plans for distributing the public domain, which provided for placing the land in the hands of many persons in units suitable to the typical farm family."[5]

But Jefferson did even more! In a letter to the Reverend James Madison, written from France in 1795, he actually suggested what was in effect both homestead tax exemptions and graduated land taxes. In his letter Jefferson stated:

> The descent of property of every kind . . . to all the children, or to all the brothers, sisters, or other relations in equal degree is a politic measure and a practical one. Another means of silently lessening the inequality of property is to exempt all from taxation below a certain point and to tax the higher portions of property in geometrical progression as they rise. . . . It is not too soon to provide by every possible means that as few as possible shall be without a little portion of land. The small land holders are the most precious part of the state.[6]

The power and individuality of Jefferson's thinking are reflected in the idea of taxing large holdings of land "in geometrical progression." The extent to which the economic rent of land is taxed is fully as important as the type of ownership of land. Moreover, as land taxation

[5]*Origin of the Land Tenure System in the United States*, p. 347.
[6]*Jefferson's Writings*, ed. by Ford, Vol. 7, p. 36.

approaches the full economic rent of land, we come ever closer to the situation of which John Locke wrote when he explained how it is possible "to have a property in several parts of that which God gave to mankind in common, and that without any express compact of all the commoners [i.e., all men]."

As history shows, Jefferson's influence was not strong enough to cause a complete abolition of entails and primogeniture throughout all the American colonies. According to Henry William Spiegel, in Maine, Massachusetts, Delaware, and Rhode Island, entails are still admitted, though the holder is entitled to convey the property in fee simple.[7] Other states do not have any provisions relating to the subject. However, as stated by Dr. Spiegel, there is not much doubt that the courts of these states would decline to recognize entails, though the statute *de Donis* of 1285, whose last relic was abolished in Great Britain in 1925, seems to be in force there. Today, entails and a number of other curiosities of ancient land tenure have merely an historical interest, but we have seen they were planted here in the colonial era, and the continued existence of some large estates in New England and New York until the middle of the nineteenth century could be attributed to them.[8]

The Continental Congress and Land—The Northwest Ordinance

As questions of land tenure were matters of the several states, the Continental Congress, save in connection with the western territory taken from or granted by the British Crown, was not concerned with

[7] *Land Tenure Policies at Home and Abroad*, pp. 25–26.

[8] It may be interesting to know, in view of the general opposition to the relics of feudal land tenure after the Revolution, as represented by primogeniture and entail, that the movement was not altogether by the aristocratic-minded members of certain sections. Thus, as noted by Professor Richard Morris in his book, *Studies in the History of American Law*, a philosopher of the cotton kingdom, George Fitzhugh, published a book in Richmond, Va., in 1854, entitled *Sociology for the South*, in which he advocated the creation of entails and the reintroduction of primogeniture. Also, in later years, because the tendency toward successive division of farms among heirs owing to the equal inheritance laws has led to undersized farms, there have been proposals both in the country and abroad for substitutes of the customs of entail and primogeniture in order to insure the continuation of family-sized farms. For a discussion of this topic, see Henry Spiegel, *Land Tenure Policies at Home and Abroad*, pp. 26–27.

such matters. In the Ordinance of 1787, the first definite legislation that set up a government for the newly acquired Northwest Territory, the Congress, then sitting under the Articles of Confederation, gave its sanction to the abolition of primogeniture on the following terms: [8a]

EXTRACT FROM GENERAL LAWS, UNITED STATES

1. Be it ordained by the United States in Congress assembled, That, &c.
2. Be it ordained by the authority aforesaid, That the estates both of resident and non resident proprietors in the said territory dying intestate shall descend to and be distributed among their children and the descendants of a deceased child in equal parts the descendants of a deceased child or grand-child to take the share of their deceased parent in equal parts among them; and where there shall be no children or descendants, then in equal parts to the next of kin in equal degree and among collateral the children of a deceased brother or sister of the intestate shall have, in equal parts among them, their deceased parent's share; and there shall in no case be a distinction between kindred of the whole and half blood; saving in all cases to the widow of the intestate her third part of the real estate for life.

Land in the Constitutional Convention

The Property Qualifications for Congressmen. It appears that the Constitutional Convention was little concerned with the matter of land-ownership and land distribution. Many of its members were large landowners and men of affluence, and property protection was of great concern to them. But the topic of qualification for voters and for members of the legislature did receive some consideration. At the session of July 26, 1787, George Mason of Virginia, owner of large estates and a speculator in western lands, moved "that the Committee of Detail be instructed to receive a clause requiring certain qualifications of landed property & citizenship of the U. States, in members of the Legislature, and disqualifying persons having unsettled Acc.ts with or being indebted to the U.S., from being members of the Nat.¹ Legislature." The motion

[8a]Worthington C. Ford, *et al,* editors, *Journals of the Continental Congress* (Washington, 1904–1937), Vol. XXXII, pp. 334–35.

was seconded by the delegate from South Carolina, Charles Pinckney, who, like Mason, was a large landowner. But it was opposed by Gouverneur Morris of New York, himself a large landowner, who said that if qualifications were proper he would "prefer them in the electors rather than in the elected."

It should be borne in mind that, in this period, property qualifications for local voters were almost universal, and the practice continued in several states for a number of years following the establishment of the national government. Morris cautioned against "minutious regulations in a Constitution. The parliamentary qualifications quoted by Col. Mason, had been disregarded in practice; and was but a scheme of the landed ag.st the monied interest." Rufus King, of New York, "observed that there might be great danger in requiring landed property as a qualification since it would exclude the monied interest, whose aids may be essential in particular emergencies to the public safety."

James Madison, whose *Journal of the Proceedings of the Constitutional Convention* we are quoting, in commenting on Mason's proposal, "moved to strike out the word *landed,* before the word 'qualifications,' " remarking that "Landed possessions were no certain evidence of real wealth," and adding that

> Many enjoyed them to a great extent who were more in debt than they were worth. The unjust Laws of the States had proceeded more from this class of men, than any others. It had often happened that men who had acquired landed property on credit, got into the Legislatures with a view of promoting an unjust protection ag.st their Creditors. In the next place, if a small quantity of land should be made the standard, it would be no security; if a large one, it would exclude the proper representatives of those classes of Citizens who were not landholders. . . . The three principal classes into which our citizens were divisible, were the landed the commercial, & the manufacturing. The 2.^{d} & 3.^{d} class, bear as yet a small proportion to the first. The proportion however will daily increase. We see in the populous Countries in Europe, now what we shall be hereafter. These classes understand much less of each others interests & affairs, than men of the same class inhabiting different districts. It is particularly requisite therefore that the interests of one or two of them should not be left entirely

to the care, or impartiality of the third. This must be the case if landed qualifications should be required; few of the mercantile, & scarcely any of the manufacturing class chusing whilst they continue in business to turn any part of their Stock into landed property. For these reasons he wished if it were possible that some other criterion than the mere possession of land should be devised. He concurred with Mr Govr Morris in thinking that qualifications in the Electors would be much more effectual than in the elected. The former would discriminate between real & ostensible property in the latter; But he was aware of the difficulty of forming any uniform standard that would suit the different circumstances & opinions prevailing in the different States.[9]

Madison's arguments prevailed and Colonel Mason's motion was rejected unanimously. The outcome of the debate was that the qualifications of the electors were left to be decided by the states, each for itself.[10]

Landownership Proposed as a Voting Qualification

When the time came for the Constitutional Convention to debate the qualifications of voters in national elections (August 7, 1787), there were sharp differences of opinions. The draft of this section of the Constitution, which fixed the qualifications of voters in each state for the House of Representatives as the same as "those of the electors in the several States, of the most numerous branch of their own legislatures," was set before the convention. Gouverneur Morris moved to have it struck out so that some other provision might be substituted which would "restrain the right of suffrage to freeholders," i.e., landowners. This move precipitated a sharp discussion. Morris contended that to give the votes to people who had no property would lead them to sell their votes to the rich, who would be able to buy them and thus foster "aristocracy." Colonel Mason answered this argument, asking: "Does no other kind of property but land evidence a common interest in the

[9] See James Madison, "Journal of the Constitutional Convention of 1787," in Gaillard Hunt, editor, *The Writings of James Madison*, Vol. IV, pp. 73-76.

[10] See George Bancroft, *History of the United States*, Vol. VI, pp. 271-74. According to Bancroft, George Mason and the Pinckneys would have a qualification of landed property for the Executive and the Judicial, as well as members of Congress.

proprietor? . . . Ought the merchant, the monied man, the parent of a number of children whose fortunes are to be pursued in his own Country to be viewed as suspicious characters, and unworthy to be trusted with the common rights of their fellow Citizen?"

Madison, the Virginia gentleman, though expressing the view that "freeholders of the Country would be the safest depositories of Republican liberty," pointed out: "In future times a great majority of the people will not only be without landed, but any other sort of property. (These will either combine, under the influence of their common situation . . . or . . . they will become the tools of opulence & ambition, in which case there will be equal danger on another side.") He saw danger in a restricted franchise based on property as well as in an unrestricted franchise, but favored the unrestricted. Benjamin Franklin, on the other hand, urged that "we sh.^{d} not depress the virtue & public spirit of our common people" who had contributed so much to the success of the Revolution, and recommended a liberal franchise. This and other arguments against limiting the suffrage to landowners won out, and the provision regarding qualifications of electors for members of Congress was to be fixed by each state as applied to the most numerous branch of the state's legislature.[10a] This provision stands today.

Land Taxation in the Constitutional Convention

Land as a subject for federal taxation was not specifically discussed in the Constitutional Convention. But as land and slaves constituted the chief items of wealth in the colonies—and they were items that could be "directly" taxed as wealth—in debating the taxing powers of the federal government, particularly with reference to distributing the burden among the several states, the question arose whether wealth, population, or representation in the Congress should be the basis of "direct taxation." As might be expected, the states in which property values were higher in proportion to population were favorable to direct taxation on the basis of population, whereas those states which were only partially settled and where slaves formed a considerable portion of the inhabitants opposed this basis. On the whole, there was consider-

[10a] *Writings of James Madison,* Vol. IV, pp. 109–29.

able opposition by some delegates to giving any power of direct taxation to the federal government. The controversy was finally settled by apportioning representation and "direct taxation" among the states in accordance with population, but slaves ("all other persons") were to be counted only as three fifths.

Commenting on the outcome of the debates on qualifications of voters and members of Congress in the Constitutional Convention, Charles A. Beard, the American historian, in his well-known study, *An Economic Interpretation of the Constitution of the United States*, remarks:

> Propositions to establish property restrictions were defeated, not because they were believed to be inherently opposed to the genius of American government, but for economic reasons—strange as it may seem. These economic reasons were clearly set forth by Madison in the debate over landed qualifications for legislators ... when he showed, first, that slight property qualifications would not keep out small farmers whose paper money schemes had been so disastrous to personalty; and, secondly, that landed property qualifications would exclude from Congress the representation of "the classes of citizens who were not landholders," *i.e.* the personalty interests. This was true, he thought, because the mercantile and manufacturing classes would hardly be willing to turn their personalty into sufficient quantities of landed property to make them eligible for a seat in Congress.[11]

Beard went on to say: "The fact emerges, therefore, that the personalty interests reflected in the Convention could, in truth, see no safeguard at all in a freehold qualification against the assaults on vested personalty rights which had been made by the agrarians in every state."[11a]

---

[11] Pp. 165–66.
[11a] *Ibid.*

Chapter 7

Post-Revolutionary State-Land Disposal

During and after the Revolution, most of the original states passed legislation validating land titles acquired under the colonial regime, whether in the form of grants made by the colonial companies, or under "headrights" and other methods, or in the nature of crown grants. However, there was still within the claimed territories of the new states considerable areas of unsettled or untenanted land—some, of course, still held by the aborigines—to which the states laid claim as successors of the British Crown.

By the end of the Revolutionary hostilities, all the states were in a bankrupt condition. Their paper currencies were almost worthless and their other forms of indebtedness were at a tremendous discount. Partly to recoup their finances, and partly to create taxable resources, as well as to compensate their soldiers, the states, on the whole, proceeded to dispose of these lands. The scramble to distribute these vacant areas, as well as the eagerness of speculators to purchase them, along with the consequential wastes, fraud, and corruption, forms one of the tragic episodes in the early critical period of our national history.

The Disposal of New York State Lands

New York was one of the states which possessed a vast area of unallotted crown lands. At the end of the Revolutionary War, settlements in New York State were concentrated for the most part along the Hudson Valley, but pioneers had already moved westward along the Mohawk River as far as the German Flats. Here the sturdy Herkimer and his fellow Germans beat back Major St. Leger and his Indian and Tory allies, thus making possible the victory of Saratoga. Beyond these regions, to the west and north, was wilderness. Much of the territory was occupied by the Six Nations of Iroquois Indians. Their jurisdiction of the area had been studiously guarded by Sir William Johnson, the British Indian agent, who did not neglect, however, to pre-empt for himself large tracts as "gifts" from his Indian friends. But the once powerful Six Nations had been decimated and scattered by General Sullivan's expedition and could no longer give any substantial opposition to the oncoming white settler. Though they still were nominally considered owners of the territory, they occupied only small sections of it. Thus the danger of savage warfare, which had retarded the settling of the land, was removed.

But the pre-emption of the unsettled region west of the Mohawk Valley was still in dispute. Both Massachusetts and Connecticut claimed it and contested the right of New York State to take ownership or jurisdiction over it. The fact that the Indians were considered to have legal title to it was not much of an obstacle. A few barrels of rum and a supply of shawls, blankets, and trinkets could buy them off.

The Continental Congress, the only cementing force during the Revolution that held the separate colonies together, was anxious to have the dispute settled. It succeeded in having the sister states, New York and Massachusetts, negotiate a peaceful settlement. On December 16, 1786, New York, in return for political authority over the territory, ceded to Massachusetts the pre-emption right to "all that part of the state lying west of a line beginning at a point in the north line of Pennsylvania, eighty-two miles west of the northeast corner of the state, and running from thence due north through Seneca Lake to Lake Ontario." Within this vast domain, comprising more than six million acres, New York reserved for itself the ownership right of merely a strip of land one mile wide along the Niagara River.[1]

---

[1] In the agreement Massachusetts was also granted 230,000 acres lying along the Susquehanna River, between the Oswego and Chenango rivers. This tract, which became known as the "Boston Ten Towns," was sold by Massachusetts to Samuel Brown and associates of Stockbridge, Mass., in November 1787. Several of the purchasers moved to the region and settled on the land, but the

The Phelps and Gorham Purchase

Massachusetts thus became the possessor—subject to the extinguishment of the Indian title—of a vast western empire, for which she had no earthly need, and which she would gladly dispose of at a price. Impoverished by the war, and with her treasury scrip passing current at about 30 per cent of the par value, the state, in April 1788, eagerly accepted an offer of two of her prominent citizens, Nathaniel Gorham and Oliver Phelps, to purchase the entire tract, payable in Massachusetts "consolidated scrip" in three annual installments. In July 1788, Phelps and Gorham, "by treaty" at Canandaigua, "purchased" from the Indians the easterly portion comprising about 2,600,000 acres, or slightly more than one third of the total region. The owners, by making a payment for this section, obtained title to it. It thus became known as the Phelps and Gorham Purchase.

The Phelps and Gorham Purchase did not pass without rivalry and opposition. Previous to the cession of the territory to Massachusetts, a group of prominent New York land-grabbers formed the New York Genesee Land Company. Among the promoters were John Livingston, Peter Schuyler, Dr. Caleb Benton, Robert Troup, and other wealthy landowners and politicians. They claimed to have leased from the Indians the Massachusetts territory for 999 years at an annual rental of $2,000 in Spanish dollars. In February 1788, just two months before Phelps and Gorham extinguished the Indian title, Benson and Livingston petitioned the New York legislature to recognize the lease. This petition, however, was pre-emptorily rejected, and its validity was denied by Massachusetts.

The promoters, however, would not be downed. They employed agents to go about the state, lavishing presents on politicians and on the Indians to win their favor. They even suggested the formation of a separate state. For this, one of the members was jailed on a charge of treason. Livingston and his associates proposed a settlement by presenting a proposition that New York obtain a direct conveyance of all Indian lands in the state, and that the Genesee Company be rewarded

---

bulk of it got into the hands of William Bingham, the wealthy Philadelphia merchant, of whom we shall hear more later.

by a grant of one million acres. Since Massachusetts had already been granted this pre-emption right, the proposition had to be rejected. However, in 1793 the New York legislature passed an act for the relief of the Genesee Company by conveying to its members certain lands in the northern part of the state, known as the Old Military Tract, but there is no record that the land was ever claimed or a patent to it granted.

Phelps and Gorham were unable to make the required payments to Massachusetts within the required two years and surrendered the unpre-empted portion of their purchase. Robert Morris, the financier and the leading land speculator of the post-Revolutionary period, who was suspected of being an associate of the Massachusetts promoters, stepped into the breach and purchased the unpaid-for portion. This area became known as the Genesee Country.

Morris also bought from Phelps and Gorham 1,200,000 acres for £30,000 in Massachusetts currency, which he resold to Sir William Pulteney and two associates for twice that sum. This section became known as the Pulteney Purchase. It figured as a "land company," exercising strong-arm, high-pressure salesmanship for several decades of New York history. Later Morris succeeded in selling the westerly portion of his vast Genesee tract to a group of Dutchmen who formed themselves into the Holland Land Company, chartered in Holland. It took almost a half century for these Dutchmen to dispose of their holdings at retail. To recount the history of this distributing process would require a volume in itself. In fact, a detailed history of the Holland Land Company, published by the Buffalo Historical Society, appeared in 1924 under the authorship of Paul Demund Evans.

The Dutch financiers thought they had made a good bargain in purchasing one half of western New York. Through the enthusiasm of their agent, Théophile Cazenove, they added to their New York holdings about one million acres of additional land located in Pennsylvania. These, as we shall see later, came largely from Judge James Wilson, a leading lawyer of the day and later a United States Supreme Court Justice, who, in his eagerness to corner the Pennsylvania land warrants granted to Revolutionary soldiers, "bit off more than he could chew."

The Dutch and the Pulteney purchases in New York were remarkable because at the time the New York laws prohibited alien ownership of lands. But in 1798, largely through Aaron Burr's influence, the statute was amended so as to give the Dutch and English owners legal title to their Genesee lands.[2]

The Wadsworths, Lords of the Genesee

Before they gave up part of their purchase of New York wild lands, Phelps and Gorham succeeded in selling to General Jeremiah Wadsworth, the wealthy capitalist of Hartford, Connecticut, about 30,000 acres bordering on the Genesee River. Oliver Phelps, who acted as agent in the transaction, had this area surveyed. To him may be ascribed credit for first employing the method of laying out the lands in rectangular townships of six miles square (later adopted by the federal government), though most authorities ascribe the inauguration of the system to Thomas Jefferson.[3] However, it may be stated authoritatively that it originated in New England during the colonial era, though the six-mile-square unit was not always adhered to there.

The Wadsworth purchase is distinctive in that it was held largely intact by the original purchasers and their heirs for generations. Its chief place of settlement, called by the Indians "Big Tree," but later known as Geneseo, is located not far from the present site of Rochester. Jeremiah Wadsworth conveyed some of the land to his young cousins, James and William Wadsworth, and appointed them his land agents. The tract comprised one of the choice sections of the Phelps and Gorham purchase and was considered the most valuable. It was acquired

[2] It took some time for Robert Morris to extinguish the Indian title to the Genesee lands. The delay was attributed to the Indian wars in Ohio. Finally, in 1787, Thomas Morris, eldest son of Robert Morris, with the aid of the Wadsworths of Genesee, who had purchased a large tract from Phelps and Gorham, gathered the Indians together at the Wadsworth homestead at Big Tree, near the present site of Rochester. Here also assembled representatives of the United States Government, of New York, and of Massachusetts, together with agents of the Holland Land Company. Robert Morris himself could not be present, since at the time he was in a debtor's prison in Philadelphia. The Indians balked at his absence and insisted on dealing only with "the white man with the big belly," but through persuasion and a diligent supply of whiskey, blankets, and feminine trinkets—and promises never fulfilled—the Indians were finally induced to sell their lands for $100,000.

[3] See Payson Jackson Treat, *The National Land System*, p. 180.

by Jeremiah Wadsworth at $1.00 per acre. Today the lands are valued at several hundred times this price. Despite repeated early attempts of the Wadsworths, both in this country and also abroad, to dispose of parts of their lands, they achieved little success in their efforts, owing to the rivalry and competition of other American land-disposing agents. Because of this lack of success, the Wadsworths decided to follow the practice of leasing the lands to tenants. This plan proved profitable and, in time, they added additional tracts to their original holdings. In this way the Wadsworths became the "Lords of Genesee."[4]

The Ogden and Macomb Purchases

In addition to the lands taken over as confiscated properties from the Loyalists, New York State, at the end of the Revolutionary War, became the owner of vast unpatented domains lying north of the upper reaches of the Hudson River and westward to the section ceded to Massachusetts. Along with the other colonies which had struggled for seven years against the mother country, the state government had become impoverished. Cash funds were urgently needed. So when peace returned, the plan of raising money by the sale of the crown lands was favorably received. The state legislature on May 5, 1785, passed "an act for the speedy sale of the unappropriated Lands of the State." It empowered a State Land Commission to dispose of any unsold lands as it might deem proper. This gave a wonderful opportunity to the growing tribe of land speculators of the period.

The first public offerings of the state land commissioners were two ranges of townships on the St. Lawrence River, around the present site of Ogdensburg. The auction commenced on July 10, 1787, for disposal of small tracts in the area, but possibly by collusion with the commissioners no bids were received for these. Moreover, it was agreed by the group that sought to acquire the land that a successful bidder of any tract would immediately convey his purchase to Alexander Macomb, who was designated the agent of the conspiring land jobbers who sought to purchase the entire area intact.

[4] For an illuminating picture of the extensive Wadsworth landholdings, see Neil Adams McNall, *The First Half Century of Wadsworth Tenancy*, and the same author's *An Agricultural History of the Genesee Valley, 1790—1860*.

The plan was successful. For £3,200 Samuel Ogden, in association with Macomb, obtained the entire area, which became known as the Ogden Purchase. The group subsequently divided the acreage among themselves.

Following the Ogden deal, the New York land commissioners passed out to bidders for nominal payments other tracts in the same region. By 1792, for a sum of about $1,500,000, they disposed of 5,542,173 acres. Alexander Macomb, pioneer New York land plunger, a friend of Governor George Clinton and one of the appointed land commissioners, bid for an immense tract of 3,635,200 acres at eightpence per acre, payable in six annual installments, and got it. His acquisition is still designated in deeds as Macomb's Great Purchase. It now comprises most of St. Lawrence, Jefferson, and Franklin counties and constitutes the heart of New York's wonderful Adirondack Reserve, which the state of New York has bought and is buying back from private owners at heavy cost.

In bidding for the tract, Macomb was acting in conjunction with other capitalists. His silent partners appear to have been William Constable and Daniel McCormick, wealthy New York merchants. In fact, there are letters of Constable which show the purchase was planned by him, and his name appears in connection with the earliest resales of the acreage. Shortly after the purchase, when Macomb became bankrupt and was forced into a debtor's prison, he conveyed his interests to Constable and McCormick. Another land-jobber who was also interested in the deal was Jonathan Dayton, who was a partner of John Cleves Symmes in the purchase of Ohio land. Dayton has a township named for him in the Macomb Purchase.[5]

The sales of this and other big chunks of New York State at prices per acre of less than a loaf of bread did not pass without protest even in those early days. Cries of treason and fraud arose. One Dr. Josiah Pomeroy made oath that it was a scheme to annex New York to Canada. Handbills protesting the land-grabs were publicly distributed. Governor George Clinton, who was chairman of the State Land Commission, was bitterly attacked and threatened with impeachment. Aaron Burr, the state's attorney general, also one of the land commissioners,

[5]See Alfred Lee Donaldson, *History of the Adirondacks,* Vol. I, p. 66.

likewise had to endure much political criticism. But at the urging of Malancthon Smith, one of the land-jobbers of the period, who was a member of the New York legislature, this body did "highly approve the conduct of the Commissioners of the land office in the judicious sales by them."

In addition to the Ogden and the Macomb purchases, the state of New York, during the decade between 1790 and 1800, disposed of other sections of its public domain. Following this period, however, the political outcry against land-jobbers put an end to the whole disposal of large tracts. Subsequent sales were on a much smaller scale. The list of bidders and purchasers could have made up a social register of the time. There were the Cuttings, the Lows, the Roosevelts, the Ludlows, the Fenimore Coopers, the Watkinses, and the Livingstons—names which survive not only in their descendants but in the names of the townships, villages, and cities comprised in the areas of their purchases. The abundance of wild land both within and without New York State made it difficult for these speculators to profit immediately from their acquisitions, and a number forfeited their acreages for non-payment of taxes. When the land speculation fever died down at the turn of the nineteenth century, New York capitalists turned to trading, banking, and shipping as more steady sources of wealth and income.

Speculation in Pennsylvania and Virginia Land Warrants

Like New York, after the Revolution, Pennsylvania, Virginia, Massachusetts, and some of the other states possessed vast areas of unappropriated land. As was the common practice then, much of this was set aside for the Revolutionary soldiers. These soldiers in most cases were not granted deeds to specific plots but were given negotiable warrants entitling them to a definite acreage of land to be selected by them. These warrants were eagerly bought up by speculators, the detested land-jobbers of the period, and in some cases, particularly in Pennsylvania, the possession of transferred land warrants formed the basis for large concentrations of landownership.

Philadelphia appears to have been the center of the land-warrant business. The large land acquisitions of Robert Morris, John Nicholson,

James Wilson, William Bingham, and Timothy Pickering arose through wholesale and retail purchases of warrants. They did not limit themselves to Pennsylvania acreage but also acquired soldier warrants for tracts in Virginia and elsewhere. These land-hungry individuals, living far from the regions which they endeavored to acquire and exploit, employed local agents, called "discoverers," to select and survey lands purchased by means of the military warrants. Naturally this "absentee" system fostered fraud, villainy, and deceit. As stated by Timothy Dwight, in speaking of the gamble in Virginia military warrants, "several patents were often placed, successively, on the same tracts. These patents were sold again in other States. . . . When the purchaser went to look for his land, he found it already occupied . . . and himself the purchaser of a mere bit of paper."[6]

The Georgia "Yazoo" Lands

The young colony of Georgia, at the southern end of the colonial union, had performed its share in bringing about political independence, and following the Revolution, like its sister states, laid claim to the immense territory extending as far west as the Mississippi River. South Carolina, however, contended that part of this area was within its original charter limits, while the new federal authority maintained it was part of the national domain obtained directly from the British Crown. It was also claimed by Spain as part of Louisiana, ceded to that nation by the French.

While these competing and conflicting claims were being debated, the Chickasaws, Choctaws, Cherokees, and Creeks roved over the region at will. It was in their possession, and few whites dared to invade their ancient hunting grounds. Over these tribes the new United States Government established a protectorate and forbade any state or individual to deal with them directly or take action to dispossess them. In view of these difficulties, the impoverished state of Georgia was quite ready to accept any financial consideration for her doubtful claim and sought to dispose of the land at the earliest opportunity.

Nor were eager purchasers lacking! Despite its primeval condition

[6] See Timothy Dwight, *Travels*, Vol. I, p. 220.

and the fierce savage tribes, the territory had distinct commercial advantages. It bordered on the Mississippi River, which afforded a means of intercourse between the interior settlements and the Gulf of Mexico. It contained a number of navigable streams emptying into the Mississippi, and therefore gave accessibility to trade and barter, a prime factor in creating land values. One of these streams was the Yazoo River. For some reason or other, the name "Yazoo" was applied to the entire area now comprising Alabama and Mississippi.

An unprincipled character styling himself Thomas Washington, but whose real name was Walsh (he was later hanged at Charleston for counterfeiting South Carolina debt certificates), formed a "land association" called the South Carolina Yazoo Company. He and his associates, on November 20, 1789, presented an elaborate petition to the Georgia legislature urging confirmation of a grant of land. Another "land association," the Virginia Yazoo Company, in which Patrick Henry is reputed to have been the moving spirit, also made a bid for a slice of the region. A Tennessee Yazoo Company and a Georgia Yazoo Company were also formed for the purpose. The outcome was separate grants without much debate to three of these companies, by an act of the Georgia legislature, sanctioned by the governor on December 21, 1789. The act disposed of more than 25,000,000 acres, and the total compensation to Georgia was to be slightly more than $200,000.

However, not long after the act was passed, a hue and cry of fraud arose in Georgia, and a new legislature that convened repudiated the grants in an elaborate ceremony. In the meantime, President Washington was much disturbed by the transaction, and Jefferson, as Secretary of State, issued a proclamation denouncing it on August 25, 1790. The companies finally lost the grants through failure to meet the payments. The Georgia legislature then proceeded on January 7, 1795, to resell the Yazoo lands, this time some 30,000,000 acres of American soil, comprising the bulk of the states of Alabama and Mississippi, for the munificent price of about one and a half cents per acre.

When the Georgia folk began to realize the rotten deal put over by their legislators, a new howl of protest arose. There was indignation from the mountains to the sea. A new legislature, which met in January 1796, after three weeks' debate denounced the sale of the Yazoo territory as unconstitutional and void. Their next move was to cede the whole region to the United States, receiving for it $1,250,000. Five million acres of the cession were set aside to satisfy claims arising under the Georgia sales.

Although subsequent to the repudiation Georgia officials offered to refund the payments made by the land companies, few took advantage of the offer. Instead, they continued to subdivide their areas and sell their share certificates. One company established a sales office in Boston that did a "land-office" business. For years after the cession of the territory to the federal government, the "scrip" holders of the Yazoo companies petitioned Congress for reimbursement. Their claims were finally brought for adjudication to the United States Supreme Court, which on March 16, 1810, in the case of *Fletcher vs. Peck,* by a judgment read by Chief Justice John Marshall, held the sales by the Georgia legislature to be a contract which could not be invalidated by subsequent legislation. Four years after the decision, Congress finally agreed to a settlement of the Yazoo claims. In 1815 the Secretary of the Treasury reported payments for the purchase aggregated $4,282,151.12, represented by a new but reliable kind of Federal "Mississippi scrip." Thus the curtain was rung down on one of the most infamous scrambles by reputable citizens for land and its value increment in the history of the nation.[7]

Massachusetts and the Maine Lands

Massachusetts, after the Revolution, had ownership and jurisdiction of the vast area of what is now the state of Maine. Aside from a few grants already mentioned (see p. 70), the territory was unappropriated. There were, however, a number of squatters in the region, who were left undisturbed, and a few townships had been taken up by town proprietors and other purchasers. The Massachusetts Court was anxious to have settlers in the "Maine District" as a means of raising the value of the land they were trying to market. The Maine lands were

[7] For a detailed and authentic account of the Yazoo land frauds, see Charles Homer Haskins, *The Yazoo Land Companies,* American Historical Association, *Papers,* Vol. V, 1891, pp. 61–103.

therefore offered for sale by the state, in large and small tracts. Space does not permit giving details of these transactions.

However, there is one large grant which deserves being mentioned. This was a purchase by General Henry Knox, Washington's first Secretary of War. Knox, a Massachusetts citizen, had as a partner William Duer of New York, who, as we shall see later, was involved in Ohio land schemes. After the purchase both Knox and Duer became pressed for funds, and in their distress, for a mere pittance, they transferred to William Bingham of Philadelphia about two million acres located in what is now Knox and Waldo counties, Maine. The region became known as Bingham's Million Acres. The British banking house of Baring became a partner in the deal. Bingham's interest was willed to his five daughters, among whom was the wife of Alexander Baring, the English banker, afterward Lord Ashburton. The territory was held intact until around 1830, when it was offered for sale, and initiated a wild speculation in Maine timber lands, in which fraud and corruption played a prominent part.[8]

Summary

The foregoing brief account of land disposal by the separate states following the Revolution indicates the persistence of the confusion in land transactions, inherited from the colonial period. The colonial land systems, as we have seen, both fostered and hindered actual land settlement and use. The disposal of large tracts to individual absentee owners, whose only interests were pecuniary gain and a desire to get the advantages of the unearned increment, may have induced a more rapid settlement in some areas than a system of small allotments, but it created a series of economic maladjustments which caused political disturbances at a future period and led to inequitable social conditions.

Though many of the celebrated land jobbers of the period, chief among them Robert Morris and his associates, failed to realize gains from their vast land acquisitions, there was a widespread realization that land values were bound to rise with the growth of the country. The

[8]For an authentic statement of the interest of Baring in Maine lands, see Ralph W. Hiddy, *The House of Baring in American Trade and Finance*.

chief mistake made by the speculators was that they anticipated a more rapid rise than actually could occur, in view of the tremendous regions of vacant lands awaiting settlement. Another mistake was that they borrowed to make their purchases, and thus soon became "land-poor." Their lands lying unused were subject to taxation and, when not sold or rented, became a drain on the income of the possessors. If they could have held out, they would ultimately have been, in most cases, the gainers through the unearned increment. But liquid wealth at the time was limited. Actual cash money was scarce. The exaggerated "credit economy" could not continue unabated through the ages. Thus, in most cases, land transactions based on credit failed to yield benefits to the purchasers, owners, or the public. Land speculation, however, continued to be a fascinating lure, as it had been in colonial times and in the post-Revolutionary period. Whether it is an element in the nation's progress is a debatable question.

Chapter 8

The Early History of the Public Domain

During and following the period of the signing of the treaty of peace with Britain which ended the Revolutionary War, the vast territory beyond the Allegheny Mountains became the property of the federal government as then constituted under the Articles of Confederation. This development was the outcome of the disputes among the separate colonies as to ownership and jurisdiction over segments of the region extending from the Great Lakes to the neighborhood of the Gulf of Mexico. As already shown in the previous chapters, much of this region was unexplored and populated only by Indian tribes. But the "right" to it was bought dearly in blood and suffering by the colonists in their struggle against the French claim to occupation.

As some of the colonies had boundaries that did not abut any part of this region, they were unwilling to enter a union which thus cut them off from claims to a portion of this new territory. Appeasement came about only through the successive cessions of the claims of the various states in the Confederation to the national government. In this way, the public domain was created. It has proved to be a source of irritation, dispute, corruption, and even despair to the Republic for more than a century and a half. *Yet its distribution and development in this period form one of the most remarkable historical episodes in the story of civilized man.*

The Northwest Ordinance

The first project to dispose of a part of the public domain was an ordinance passed by the Continental Congress in 1785. Besides instituting a territorial government, it provided for the public sale of lands in the northwestern area (i.e., the region northwest of the Ohio River to the Great Lakes, ceded by Great Britain in the treaty of peace) in tracts not less than 640-acre lots at a minimum price of $1.00 per acre, or in larger tracts at wholesale, if approved by the Congress. It was provided that no areas were to be patented until after they had been surveyed, and all surveys were to make provision for parallel ranges, townships, and sections. As soon as sufficient ranges were surveyed and the maps prepared, the land could be sold or otherwise disposed of by Congress. Despite the fact that the Congress desired to obtain sorely needed funds by disposal of the lands—its "embarrassment of riches"—comparatively little land was disposed of under the Ordinance of 1785. This was ascribed to the high minimum acreage set for individual sales. However, Congress in 1787 made two sales at wholesale in Ohio, one to the Ohio Company of one million acres, and another of approximately the same acreage to John Cleves Symmes and associates. The details of these transactions will be described later.

The Northwest Ordinance, as we know it, was amended by the Congress of the Confederation on July 13, 1787. In addition to providing for the government of the Northwest Territory under federal jurisdiction, it re-enacted the provisions for land disposal but discontinued the policy of sales in large tracts at wholesale. In 1796, however, the act was again amended by fixing the price of the land at $2.00 per acre but left the provision of the minimum sale of a tract to 640 acres. As an offset to the increase in price, liberal credit terms were extended to purchasers.

This was an inducement to land speculators. However, sales to individuals were comparatively few, as 640 acres was too large to attract pioneer settlers, so in 1800 the minimum tract was reduced to 320 acres. As indicated in the accompanying table, the price of $2.00 per acre was continued until 1820, when it was reduced to $1.25 per acre. During the interval, however, Congress changed the credit terms (under which only one twentieth of the purchase price had to be paid immediately). Under a new payment plan, government bonds or specie only was acceptable and a partial-payment system adopted.

THE LAND ACTS COMPARED

	Ordinance of 1785	Land Acts of 1796	Land Act of 1800	Land Act of 1820	Pre-emption Act of 1841	Homestead Act of 1862
Minimum allotments	640 acres to an individual	640-acre lots in alternate sections	320 acres	80-acre lots	160 acres to an individual	160 acres
Minimum price	$1.00 an acre	$2.00 an acre	$2.00 an acre	$1.25 an acre	$1.25 an acre	Free, to actual settlers. $10.00 registration fee
Terms of payment	Cash or in debt certificates reduced to specie value	One twentieth of purchase price to be paid immediately	Payment in specie or government bonds. Partial payments	Cash; i.e., specie or bank notes	Cash	Title to land given after five years' cultivation of land

By this time Congress had despaired of gaining a substantial amount of revenue from the sale of the public lands. Many speculators who bought on credit failed to complete their purchases, and settlers were slow in making payments. In many cases they pleaded for extensions or abatements. Land offices were lax in making collections, and the whole scheme of land disposal became a political "hot potato" to the Congress. Corruption and fraud swept into the system, and waste characterized the whole land policy. As stated by W. A. Phillips in his book, *Land, Labor and Law,* it is unfortunate that a broad foundation was not set up in the Northwest Ordinance to secure the soil for the tillers thereof and to prevent an aristocracy from being founded on land monopoly.

Under the system of land disposal as originally set up in the Northwest Ordinance, the land was divided into parallel ranges, in which townships, each six miles square, were comprised. The township (a plan borrowed from New England practice) was thus adopted as a unit of land survey. The very name "township" was expressive of the intention that these surveyed squares would become the basis for a self-governing communal life. Each township contained thirty-six sections of equal size—i.e., a square mile—and a quarter section (160 acres), in due time, came to be regarded as the standard or average for the extent of a single farm or homestead. The charge of $1.25 an acre was sufficient to meet the costs of extinguishing the Indian title and of surveying the land, and to net the government substantial returns.

Despite the liberality of the terms of disposal, the sale of the public domain in the early period was relatively small. According to Dr. Adam Seybert,[1] no more than 121,540 acres had thus been sold prior to the act of May 10, 1800. These sales were made in the large cities; viz., 72,974 acres at public sale in New York City in 1787 for $87,325 in debt certificates, 43,446 acres at public sale in Pittsburgh in 1796 for $100,427, and 5,120 acres in Philadelphia in the same year at $2.00 per acre.

One reason for the paucity of land sales was the slowness in making land surveys. Another reason was that Indian titles were not ex-

[1] Adam Seybert, *Statistical Annals of the United States,* p. 362.

tinguished over a large part of the public domain. Then again, there were few generally accessible land offices, and these were not established until after 1800.

In the meantime, as surveys proceeded, land offices were set up at various localities within the regions where the public land was offered for sale. Settlers as well as speculators could make their selections and purchases at these land offices.

At the beginning of the nineteenth century, however, there was a considerable increase in public land sales. Seybert's figures show that the quantity of land sold under the system of land offices from July 1, 1800, to July 1, 1810, amounted to 3,386,000 acres, which produced $7,062,000. Of this amount, $4,888,000 was paid in specie or debt certificates, and the remainder was still due from purchasers.

Small as the proceeds from land sales were, they were sufficient to create political conflict. According to the early enactments, the sums received from public land sales were to be applied to the extinguishment of the national debt; but, as the older colonies, which became the original states, possessed their own public lands, the new states also desired to own and control the unsold public land within their respective boundaries. Thomas Jefferson, in his second inaugural address, in 1805, proposed a distribution of the public domain among the states and recommended that the proceeds of their sales be applied "to rivers, canals, roads, arts, manufacture, education and other great objects within each state." But Congress never got around to this idea. For decades thereafter, the disposal of the public lands was a subject of political controversy, second only to that of the slavery and tariff questions.

The plan of land disposal as adopted in this early period was undoubtedly fair and equitable. It was liberal, since its aim was to give easy access to landownership, and in conjunction with the early liberal immigration policy, it afforded opportunities to millions of European immigrants as well as native inhabitants to establish homesteads. It was undoubtedly responsible for the rapid settlement of newly acquired regions. But despite all this, there was "squatting" by settlers unable to pay for the land on the public domain, as well as unscrupulous speculation, particularly as regards the favorable sites. "Squatter sovereignty" thus became the slogan of the western pioneers who were actual settlers, and "town-jobbing" by local and absentee purchasers became a national nuisance. But more about this later.

Sale of Land to the Ohio Company

As early as 1784, when the federal union of the colonies was still in the balance and its continued existence was doubtful, the Congress took up the question of disposing of western lands. Bids for large tracts were not wanting. In 1785, Nathaniel Sackett, in behalf of himself and associates, petitioned for a grant of land, the boundaries of which would now cover most of the present state of Ohio. Sackett offered no consideration "except an ear of Indian corn annually as rental, if demanded." He did, however make it a condition of the proposed grant that the land be settled and cultivated by those who obtained title to it. To prevent land-jobbing effectually, none of the settlers would be permitted to sell his land for a space of years.

But the Continental Congress was too heavily in debt to give away the land. No consideration, therefore, was given to Sackett's petition. In the meantime, a reverend gentleman from Massachusetts, Dr. Manasseh Cutler, had been pondering over a colonization scheme in the Ohio country.[2] He was desirous of providing the hard-pressed New England yeoman with better and cheaper lands and, incidentally, he may have had ideas of pecuniary gain. At any rate, in 1786, Cutler, together with Rufus Putnam and a few others, formed a colonization scheme which he called the Ohio Company of Associates. The capital of the company was fixed at $1,000,000 in Continental debt certificates, and the shares in the project were publicly offered "for a consideration." It required a full year before one fourth of the proposed capital was subscribed, but Cutler thought the remainder could be readily obtained if Congress

[2]Manasseh Cutler was born at Killingly, Connecticut, on May 28, 1742, and graduated from Yale College in 1765. He then studied law and began to practice his profession at Martha's Vineyard, but soon gave this up for theology. Becoming a Congregational minister, he served as chaplain in the American Army during the Revolutionary War. In this capacity he became acquainted with Rufus Putnam, the hardy Revolutionary soldier, who, after making a trip beyond the Alleghenies, became an enthusiast of the Ohio country.

would give "the associates an option on a compact body of land on reasonable terms." This would require a modification of the land ordinance of 1785, which restricted sales to small tracts. To accomplish this, Cutler journeyed to New York to treat with Congress, and it is said he was instrumental in shaping the Ordinance of 1787, which established the government of the Northwest Territory and permitted the sale of unlimited areas at the discretion of Congress.

At this time, Colonel William Duer, an enterprising, wealth-seeking former British subject, was Secretary of the Board of the Treasury, an agency set up by Congress to replace Robert Morris, the Superintendent of Finance. The Board, then composed of three members, managed the depleted finances of the new federal Republic. Duer, therefore, would have a hand in arranging terms with Cutler, whom he wined and dined on his arrival in New York City. He not only promised him assistance but proposed himself as a partner in the deal.

The negotiations with Congress, however, were discouraging. Cash was demanded for the land, and this Cutler's associates did not have. Duer then advised Cutler that as a bait to the impoverished government his petition be increased from 1,000,000 to 4,000,000 acres, of which 3,000,000 should be assigned to another company composed of New Yorkers, of whom Duer would be the head. With so large a sum in prospect, Duer thought Congress would be willing to grant liberal credit terms.

The excess acreage comprised territory east of the Scioto River and west of the actual grant desired by the Ohio Associates. It thus became known as the Scioto Project.

The ruse succeeded. Congress approved the purchase by Cutler and associates of a tract in Ohio, covering 5,000,000 to 6,000,000 acres, at $1.00 per acre payable in specie, or in "loan certificates" reduced to specie value, or in certificates of liquidated debts of the United States. A payment of $500,000 was required on the execution of the contract. A similar sum was demanded when the tract was surveyed, and the balance was to be paid in six annual installments. It was provided, however, that as soon as the aggregate sum of $1,000,000 was paid, a patent for 1,000,000 acres was to be given. The title to the remainder was to be passed upon such conditions as the Board of the Treasury might agree upon with the purchasers.[3]

Thus the Ohio Company and William Duer's Scioto Project were launched as a joint proposition. The former may have been primarily a colonizing scheme without the stigma of speculation, but the Scioto Project was an out-and-out land gamble. In order to put the proposition through, Duer promised to advance $100,000 to Cutler to aid in making a first payment, and he promised that payment for the remaining 3,000,000 or 4,000,000 acres would be made by the Scioto Associates. This part of the deal was kept secret, and shareholders of the Ohio Company were kept in blissful ignorance of the connection of the Scioto speculation with their own enterprise.

Cutler had a difficult time obtaining the necessary funds to make the first payment. He conducted a vast selling campaign, appealing both to colonists and speculators to purchase shares in the undertaking. With some aid from Duer, who became a larger shareholder, he finally succeeded on October 27, 1787, in making the first payment of $500,000 in debt certificates worth somewhere between $60,000 and $130,000.

The history of the Ohio Company of Associates has been recorded in glowing eulogies as the earliest phase of the westward movement. A commemoration tablet in bronze to this effect has been placed on the Sub-Treasury Building in New York City. It notes that under an ordinance "passed here," Manasseh Cutler, acting for "the Ohio Company of Associates, an organization of soldiers of the Revolutionary Army, purchased from the Board of the Treasury for settlement, a portion of the waste and vacant lands of the [Northwest] Territory: and Rufus Putnam heading a party of fifty-eight on April 7, 1788, began the first settlement at Marietta, and on July 15, Gen. Arthur St. Clair, as first Governor, established civil government in the territory. From these beginnings sprang the states of Ohio, Indiana, Illinois and Wisconsin."

So runs the story; the project was free from the stigma of land speculation. "No land company in America," writes Archer B. Hulbert, the historian, "was ever formed with an eye more single to the welfare of

[3] See Joseph Stancliffe Davis, *Essays in the Earlier History of American Corporations*, Vol. I, pp. 132–36.

the poorest investor; no land company in our history surpassed the Ohio Company in its manifold efforts to better the case of the 'common people.' "⁴

All this is only partially true. The original prospectus of the company made an appeal to human cupidity, and many of the "shareholders" had not the least intention of emigrating to Ohio and had not the slightest interest in fostering land settlement for the downtrodden or impoverished Revolutionary soldiers. They were not interested in acquiring western lands. They wanted merely to profit from the rising market value of their "shares."

Measured by the financial outcome, the Ohio Company was not a success. It had to petition Congress for relief, as it was unable to make the required installment payments. Congress acceded by reducing the average price of the land by 50 per cent. The Ohio Company, therefore, received a grant of about 1,000,000 acres, for which it paid $500,000 in government debt certificates worth at the time from $12\frac{1}{2}$ to 50 cents on the dollar. For about 215,000 acres of the purchase, the Ohio Associates presented soldiers' warrants.

William Duer's Scioto Project fared much worse than Cutler's Ohio Company. It ended in a complete fiasco. Though the concern was never chartered and had not received a patent for an acre of land, the promoters of this notorious land gamble proceeded to sell in Europe, particularly in France, the portion of the region assigned to them by Cutler. To effect this purpose, they sent to France the American poet, Joel Barlow. After repeated failures to sell large tracts to individuals, particularly the hard-pressed noblemen, Barlow formed in France a subsidiary company, called the Compagnie du Scioto, of which he acted as agent and manager. Because he gave "shareholders" and land purchasers the right of immediate settlement, he "expected to raise the reputation of the lands to such a degree that they will sell them off at a great profit in the course of a year." Through glowing published accounts of the territory, he aroused the enthusiasm of intelligent Frenchmen and arranged for the shipment of a group of French gentlemen

⁴See Archer B. Hulbert, *The Records and Proceedings of the Ohio Company*, Vol. I, p. xcviii.

who were to make a settlement on the company's pretended property. These settlers were sold land with Barlow's warranty against every kind of eviction and attack.

The first shipload of French *émigrés* arrived in March 1790 and, with some difficulties, were carted off to Ohio. Among them were several prominent French noblemen who had purchased large tracts and brought along with them retainers—indentured servants of the worst class—some even taken from prisons. When they arrived at the place of settlement, euphoniously called "Gallipolis," they were painfully disappointed. Moreover, they were unfitted to endure the hardships of pioneer life. Many soon deserted. Duer attempted to appease them by seeking relief from Congress, but during this period, because of the collapse of his speculative schemes, he and some of his associates had to take up residence in a debtor's prison. As the land was not paid for and thus remained unpatented, Congress, merely as a charitable act, passed a law making small allotments to the settlers who remained at Gallipolis. John Bach McMaster, the eminent American historian, aptly describes the whole affair as "one of the ... most shameful pieces of land-jobbery that has ever disgraced our country."[5]

The Symmes Purchase

Aside from Cutler's purchase on behalf of the Ohio Company of Associates, in which the Scioto Project was involved, Congress made only one other sale of a large tract of public land for colonization purposes. This is known as Symmes' Miami Purchase. In its outward aspects it is very similar to that of the Ohio Company's purchase, but had more of the birthmarks of pecuniary gain.

John Cleves Symmes, who had been a member of the Continental Congress from New Jersey, picturing himself, in 1785, as a friend of the Revolutionary soldier and a promoter of western settlement, in association with Jonathan Dayton and Elias Boudinot, two prominent New Jersey politicians, succeeded in having Congress approve a petition for a tract of land, comprising about a million acres, lying on the Ohio River between the Great Miami and Little Miami rivers, a section in

[5]*History of the United States,* Vol. II, p. 146.

which Cincinnati is now located. The contract was signed on October 15, 1788, and the first payment of $82,198 in debt certificates and soldiers' warrants was made. Like Cutler, Symmes advertised widely for settlers and purchasers and extolled the advantages of the region. He professed no object of gain for himself, except "the exclusive right of electing or locating that entire and exclusive township which will be the lowest in the point of land formed by the Ohio and Miami River" (the site of Cincinnati).

Symmes began to push his land sales even before the land was surveyed. He sold on the expectancy of receiving a million acres, but when the survey was completed, it revealed the grant contained only slightly more than one half the acreage anticipated. This did not disturb Symmes and his associates, however, who continued to demand from Congress the full million acres, and he continued to sell tracts outside the designated area.

Symmes contracted to pay 66⅔ cents per acre for his grant in depreciated debt certificates. As Congress, after the approval of the Symmes grant, fixed the minimum price of public land to the public at $2.00 per acre, Symmes and his associates saw opportunity for an additional pecuniary profit in obtaining additional acreage, but Congress was obdurate and Symmes never received the amount of land he claimed. The total acreage patented to him was 311,862 acres, and the actual cost in specie was probably less than $50,000.[6]

The Connecticut Company

Symmes' Miami Purchase was the last sale by the government of land for colonization purposes at wholesale. But it was not the last of the Ohio land gambles. The state of Connecticut had persistently claimed, under its charter grant, title to territory beyond its western boundary. After much haggling and bickering with the federal government, a compromise was adopted in 1786 whereby Connecticut, by surrendering its claims, was given a strip of territory comprising 3,500,000 acres bordering on Lake Erie. This became known as the

[6] Symmes undoubtedly served the country well in settling the Miami tract on the Ohio. He took up his residence on the grant and was active in the administration of its welfare. He died, however, in almost hopeless poverty.

Connecticut Western Reserve. A part, covering about one half million acres, was set aside and allotted by the state to residents of New London, who had suffered from British depredations. This section became known as the Fire Lands.

The remainder of the area was sold to an association known as the Connecticut Company. However, because of dispute with the federal authorities regarding the political jurisdiction of the territory, the proprietors of the Connecticut Company for several years made little headway in disposing of the land. Finally, in 1800, in return for a surrender by Connecticut of all claim to land and its jurisdiction west of her western boundary, Congress acknowledged her right to ownership of the Western Reserve. This gave an impetus to settlement of the region. There began a Connecticut trek to the West that threatened to depopulate the state. The Connecticut Company lands were thus disposed of at favorable prices to the proprietors. In 1809 they divided the little that remained unsold and wound up the company.

Summary

After the unhappy experiences with the "colonizing companies," and when the national finances were re-established under Alexander Hamilton's funding schemes, Congress was wary of selling the public domain at substantial discounts to land promoters. There was, even at this early time, a cry against land monopoly, and the epithet of "landjobber" was not a pleasant one. Instead of selling the land in large tracts, Congress, as already stated, set up local land offices in surveyed areas to facilitate sales at retail. But the problems, both political and economic, of equitable land distribution persisted. Despite the evident intent of the nation's legislators during the early period to distribute ownership of the land to homesteaders, fraud, waste, and corruption prevailed in the parceling out of the public domain. This matter will be recounted in the next chapter.

Chapter 9

The Early Public Land Administration—
Town-Jobbing and Land Engrossment

When the year 1800 ushered in a new century, the land mania in America was at its ebb. Those who participated in it, if not already bankrupt through their wild speculations, were compelled to hold their acquisitions or proceed slowly to dispose of tracts at retail. The tendency, for a short time, was toward land acquisitions on a smaller scale.

This move was fostered by a change in the national land policy. As already noted, Congress, after the disappointments of the Ohio grants and the meagerness of revenue from public land sales, provided for sales in small allotments instead of large tracts. Through the suggestion of General William Henry Harrison, son-in-law of John Cleves Symmes, who had resided as the military commander in Ohio, Congress in 1800 passed a law reducing the minimum acreage allotted to single purchasers from 640 acres to 320 acres. Four years later this was further reduced to 160 acres; i.e., a quarter section. The minimum price of public land was set at $2.00 per acre regardless of the quantity purchased, and payments could be made in installments covering four years. To facilitate sales to all comers, land offices were established at accessible places in districts where surveys had been made and the lands were opened up for settlement. The principal offices at this early period were in Cincinnati, Chillicothe, Marietta, and Steubenville, Ohio. These served the Ohio country. Whenever a new tract was opened up for settlement, a public auction of sections and half sections was held for a period of three weeks. In this way the choicest tracts were expected to be picked up under competitive bidding. Thereafter the un-

Early Public Land Administration

sold portions could be obtained at the minimum government price.

The lure of fertile sections in the new "ranges" drew actual settlers to the West. Of course the private land companies and individual speculators continued to offer their lands, but they had to meet the competition of the government land offices. The prospect of fancy profits in private land deals was thus considerably reduced. It was only through "townsite" jobbing and the construction of internal improvements that a lively interest in land speculation could be maintained.

Town-Jobbing on Public Land Sites

Thus speculation in public lands, though declining somewhat in the early nineteenth century, did not cease, but took a different course. What was commonly called "town-jobbing" in those early days became the new form of land-grabbing. Choice sites for communities became the land speculator's dream. Whenever a government land office opened up a new district for settlement, businessmen, surveyors, lawyers, politicians, territorial officers, and others scrutinized the maps in the hope of discovering the possibilities of a favorable townsite. When some one of these decided that a certain section or half section was a desirable location for a town, they sought to pre-empt it. If they learned that others were after the same site and would offer competitive bids, they would endeavor to buy them off or swap bargains with them. Thus bribery and corruption became rife in public land disposals. Town-jobbing became a common practice.

The important beginnings of town-jobbing west of the Alleghenies can be traced to the large Ohio grants described in the previous chapter. All three of the principal "companies"—i.e., the Ohio Associates, the Symmes Purchase, and the Connecticut Land Company—laid out towns. The Ohio Associates founded Marietta; Symmes selected the site of Cincinnati; the Connecticut proprietors laid out the "village" of Cleveland. All these towns were divided into squares and lots. The central part of the town plot was composed of "in-lots" and the surrounding sections were designated as "out-lots." Both classes of lots were generally offered for sale simultaneously.

When Symmes thought he had done a good job with Cincinnati, he encouraged Jonathan Dayton, Governor Arthur St. Clair, and General James Wilkinson to select a site (which he believed was within his grant) for the town of Dayton, Ohio. In-lots in this town Symmes sold in Cincinnati at $10 per lot. Out-lots generally sold proportionately for less, but as the town boomers usually owned the surrounding land, the success of the town project meant also an enhancement of the price of the surrounding agricultural lands which were held by the same proprietors.

The institution of fee ownership of land in the public domain—the property of all the people—was established by law, and because of the prevailing *mores,* no questions seem to have arisen then regarding its postulates. Land increased in value as settlers made homes and farms in particular locations. But this increased value did not accrue to the people in common. It was largely appropriated by the speculators, who sold their holdings piece by piece as they were able to do so at higher prices.

From such beginnings originated the townsite mania. It has continued with very little interruption in the country ever since. It is now the leading form of land speculation. However, some towns in the Ohio country were established by colonizing groups, notably from New England. The Licking Land Company, formed in 1804 by residents of Granville, Massachusetts, was but one of several ventures of this kind. The participants in the company bought part of a tract in Ohio reserved for holders of military warrants, which warrants they acquired from the original owners. They then moved as a caravan across Pennsylvania into the Ohio Valley and took possession of their purchase in 1805. Two years later they formed Granville township and in its middle laid out a town "with 100-acre farms around it."[1]

With few exceptions, however, the aim of town building in the Old Northwest was to promote a profitable real estate transaction and not to serve as a land-settlement project. "Gain! Gain! Gain!" exclaimed Morris Birkbeck, an Illinois pioneer from Britain, who journeyed through this region in 1817. "Gain! is the beginning, the middle, and

---

[1] See Hubert Howe Bancroft, *Retrospection,* p. 77. Also *The Old Northwest Genealogical Quarterly,* Vol. 8, p. 241.

the end, the *alpha* and *omega* of the founders of American towns; who after all are bad calculators, when they omit the important element of salubrity in their choice of situations." He noted that, wherever there was a small cluster of houses, a town was laid out by someone who named it after himself and who sold lots at auction.[2]

The founding of Toledo, Ohio, on Lake Erie may be taken as a typical example of early land-jobbing. Located at the mouth of a sluggish stream, the Maumee River, the site was originally purchased from the government in February 1817 by two groups of speculators from Cincinnati, each of which began laying off lots on opposite sides of the river. One group, because of some unknown association, named its side Toledo; the other "town" was called Port Lawrence. The two rival land promoters began selling lots at about the same time. In order to avoid competition they soon combined as the Port Lawrence Company. But they attracted very few purchasers and as they failed to make the final payment to the government, the land was forfeited. In 1821, however, the surviving promoters succeeded in making an arrangement with the land office whereby they received back a part of the original purchase (the Toledo side). They again advertised their "town lots." This time the venture was more successful. It did not begin to thrive, however, until the boom days prior to the Panic of 1837. The townsite on the opposite side of the river was then also revived, and the lots, which had been neglected for almost twenty years, were again put up for sale.[3]

An English traveler, Joseph Briggs, whose diary was discovered about three decades ago, thus describes land-jobbing in the Northwest at this period:

> A speculator makes out a plan of a city with its streets, squares and avenues, quays and wharves, public buildings and monuments. The streets are lotted, the houses numbered, and the squares called after Franklin or Washington. The city itself has some fine name, perhaps Troy or Antioch. This is engraved and forthwith advertised and hung up in as many steamboats and hotels as the speculator's interest may command. All this time the

[2]*Notes of a Journey in America* (London ed.), p. 69.
[3]See Clark Waggoner, *History of Toledo, Ohio*, pp. 370–72.

city is a mere vision. Its very site is the fork of some river in the far West, 500 miles beyond civilization, probably under water or surrounded by dense forests and impassable swamps. Emigrants have been repeatedly defrauded out of their money by transactions so extremely gross as hardly to be credited.

Thus we can see that from the very beginning of our public land policy real estate speculation in the form of "town-jobbing," an evidence of the desire to gain the advantage of the unearned increment in land values, was an active and important occupation. Though it may have hastened settlements in unoccupied regions and induced population growth and concentration, it was accompanied by a regime of dishonesty, moral laxity, and political corruption. It interfered with the natural course of the westward movement of population and led to developments which produced poverty as well as riches. Had Congress and the Executive Branch of the federal government taken proper measures to forestall speculation and retain for the people the increased land values arising from the march of civilization within the public domain, the cost to the public would have been less and the benefits to all the people would have been much greater. Economic progress may not have been as rapid or as feverish, but the periods of "boom and bust" would have been less. On the whole, the nation would have had a more orderly and stable development. There would have been less economic distress and a more equitable distribution of wealth.[4]

Early Public Land Engrossment

Because of the wide prevalence of town-jobbing in the early period of public land disposal, it must not be thought that there was little or no engrossment of large areas by private interests. There was plenty of it. It did not, however, have the "wholesale" or political character of the colonial or early post-Revolutionary land deals, nor did it involve as many persons of social and political prominence. However, there were opportunities for engrossment of large tracts, with a view to resale at enhanced values.

[4]For further data on this topic, see Beverley Bond, Jr., *Civilization in the Old Northwest*.

The principal method of engrossing large tracts was through the purchase of soldiers' land warrants. Both the federal government and the states set aside tracts of western land as soldiers' bounties. To the claimants of these bounties they issued negotiable warrants. By buying up these military land warrants generally at a discount, individual speculators could acquire large areas, and some capitalists took advantage of these land-grabbing opportunities. Some were absentee owners—notably New Englanders—others were local promoters who took advantage of the adversity of the pioneers.[5]

An outstanding personality in the speculation in Ohio lands was General Duncan McArthur, one of the early governors of the state. A surveyor and Indian fighter, he assisted General Nathaniel Massie in 1796 in laying out the town of Chillicothe, one of the most successful town-jobbing ventures in early Ohio. While still occupying a log cabin in Chillicothe, he began surveying and locating lands in the Virginia Military Reserve. He soon acquired a reputation for land-jobbing superior to any others in the area. Through accumulation of Virginia military warrants, he was able to reap the advantage of his personal knowledge of the most fertile and accessible sections. Fortune favored his land speculations, though he was subjected to numerous lawsuits regarding his land titles. He became, by far, the largest landholder of the Scioto Valley. Entering politics, he joined General Hull in the defense of Detroit in the War of 1812. Paroled after the surrender of the post to the British, he later became a major general of militia and was a successor of General William Henry Harrison as commander of the forces in the Northwest Territory.

Following the War of 1812, McArthur continued his land-grabbing, and in these transactions he is said to have taken as much pride as a general who outmaneuvers his adversary on the battlefield. Though held in contempt locally as a "land-jobber," he was elected a congressman in 1824 and governor of Ohio in 1830. McArthur's biographer, his brother-in-law, referring to his land deals, states that "his conduct is not worthy of imitation, and though he acquired great wealth, it

---

[5]For a short statement of the interest of New England cotton manufacturers in western lands, see Caroline F. Ware, *The Early New England Cotton Manufacture*, p. 159.

brought to him more vexations and enemies than all the other acts of his life."⁶

Chillicothe, General McArthur's home town, and Cincinnati, Ohio, and Lexington, Kentucky, were the chief centers of land speculation in the Old Northwest during the first three decades after 1800. In this section the unoccupied public lands were rapidly being taken up. The New Englanders were settling along the borders of Lake Erie, Virginians and Pennsylvanians were taking up the southern areas, and foreign immigrants were pre-empting half sections or buying from speculators throughout the whole region.

As in former years, both settlers and speculators conducted their operations on a credit basis. Farms and town lots were sold "on liberal terms," and "wildcat" banks were organized in villages and hamlets to afford loans. The Second Bank of the United States, which was chartered in 1816, did a large business in granting loans secured by mortgages on land. At one time, it is said, it had under pledge almost all the area in and around Cincinnati. In 1823, defaulted real estate loans in that city alone exceeded two million and a half dollars. When interest was regularly paid, the debtors were not disturbed. But when arrears accumulated, the mortgages were foreclosed and the property sold, only to be repurchased by the bank.

All this brought on bitter political opposition in the Ohio region to "Nicholas Biddle's Money Monopoly" and aided in finally defeating the bank's request for a renewal of its charter. Voicing the western sentiment against the bank, Thomas Hart Benton exclaimed in the United States Senate: "I know towns, yea, cities . . . where this bank already appears as an engrossing proprietor. . . . All the flourishing cities of the West are mortgaged to this money power. They may be devoured by it at any moment. They are in the jaws of the monster! A lump of butter in the mouth of a dog! one gulp, one swallow, and all is gone!"⁷

Individual capitalists, as well as banks, engrossed large areas obtained from distressed real estate debtors and public land purchasers. Foremost

⁶John McDonald, *Biographical Sketches of General Nathaniel Massie, General Duncan McArthur, etc.* . . . This book was published in 1838, one year before McArthur's death.

⁷See Ralph C. H. Catterall, *The Second Bank of the United States,* p. 67.

among these who became rich buying up the holdings of distressed speculators was Nicholas Longworth, whose grandson was to become well known as Speaker of the House of Representatives. Coming from Newark, New Jersey, to Cincinnati in the wake of Symmes' settlers, Longworth took up the practice of law. From the beginning of his career he displayed confidence in the future of his adopted city. He bought up every piece of land and every town lot that his cash permitted. On one occasion (so the story runs) he defended a man accused of horse stealing. His client had no cash but offered in payment of legal services two secondhand copper stills in the possession of a friend. Longworth learned that the friend had a lot of several acres near the city and proposed that this be transferred to him in lieu of the copper kettles. The substitution was gladly made. On this transaction alone Longworth made a fortune, for in 1856 the "kettle land" was estimated to be worth two million dollars. His other property, extending from Hamilton to Sandusky, Ohio, was worth still more. When he died in 1863 he was reputed to be the richest real estate owner in the United States, with the possible exception of John Jacob Astor in New York City.

The Prairie Regions Opened Up!

In the course of a few decades following the first settlements in Ohio and Kentucky, unappropriated public lands were rapidly taken up and a considerable portion converted into farms. As the Indians were pushed back through warfare and treaties and the areas were surveyed and opened to public disposal, land-jobbing moved westward into Indiana and the Illinois country. Here was a different type of soil and topography—the prairie. Strange to relate in these times, "grass lands" were not looked upon favorably by the early American cultivators. Any ground that could not grow trees was regarded as of little value and was passed over even by those who selected homesites east of the Alleghenies.

This prejudice had to be overcome. It was a handicap to the spread of western land-jobbing. When it was proven, however, that bountiful corn and wheat crops could be raised on the Illinois lands without the difficult preliminary work of clearing and grubbing, and when sleek cattle thrived by feeding on the native grasses, the ancient prejudice departed. Settlers and land speculators began to move into the fertile plains beyond the Mississippi and Illinois rivers. This area, just prior to the Revolution, had been pre-empted by a group of politicians and Indian traders who formed an association known as the United Illinois and Wabash Land Companies. They claimed title through purchase from the Indians. Though they never received British or congressional approval of their claims, they offered for sale shares in the venture both at home and abroad. Despite their repeated petitions to Congress, which began even before the Revolutionary War ended, they failed to have their claims validated and never gained title to the territory.[8]

It was largely to offset claim to the region by the British and to obtain more territory for Virginia that this state equipped the George Rogers Clark Expedition, which drove out both the Indians and the British. In 1780 the Virginia authorities established a court at Vincennes (then a well-established French settlement) which assumed the right of granting lands to every applicant whom they approved. These claims to "granted lands" became a troublesome problem after Virginia surrendered the region to the federal government.

The members of the court set up by Virginia were naturally kind to themselves. "An arrangement was made," notes William Henry Harrison in 1802, "by which the whole country, to which the Indian title was supposed to be extinguished, was divided between the members of the Court." Most of these, however, abandoned their supposed acquisitions in a few years because of lack of purchasers. However, when the actual settlement of the region began after 1800, the claims of these "grantees" were bought up by speculators who infested the western country. These resold to others in different parts of the United States. "The price at which the land is sold," wrote Governor Harrison to James Madison, "enables anybody to become a purchaser; one thou-

---

[8]Several prominent men of the Revolutionary period were partners in the Wabash-Illinois land scheme. Among these should be mentioned Robert Morris and James Wilson of Pennsylvania and Silas Deane of Connecticut. Deane, while an agent for the Continental Congress in France, endeavored to sell shares in the project both in France and England.

sand acres being frequently given for an indifferent horse or a rifle gun." But whatever price purchasers paid, they actually received nothing, for their claims were never recognized by Congress.[9]

However, the title to lands along the Kaskaskia River, which were held by French settlers before the Revolution, was upheld by Congress. Most of these settlers had abandoned the territory after the United States acquired it. As might be expected, they sold their land titles for almost nothing. These titles were bought up both by resident and non-resident land-grabbers. Among the purchasers were such prominent men as William Henry Harrison, General Arthur St. Clair, first governor of the Northwest Territory; John Edgar, merchant of Illinois; William Morrison, and Nicholas Jarrot. The claims of these and others gave Congress a mess of trouble over a period of years. Out of a total of 2,294 claims presented, 1,171, or about one half, were confirmed.[10]

Early British Speculations in Western Lands

The rapid economic development of the Old Northwest and the consequent rise in land values there, as in the East, did not fail to attract European capitalists. The British were the principal participants. Of course during the Napoleonic Wars the British could spare little capital to be sent abroad. But conditions were different after 1815. The London banking house of Barings kept up close business relations with American firms, though they avoided large commitments in American lands. But they acted as agents and advisers of Englishmen, who desired profit and riches from rising American land values. How much capital was invested by British speculators in American soil in this period may never be known, but there is much evidence that British speculative interest in American growth and prosperity was greatly aroused in this period, and, along with the Americans in the East, British capitalists in this period employed agents to acquire both agricultural and urban real estate in the newly settled sections of the public domain.

The interest of the British in western lands was stimulated by a number of publications that circulated in that country. Some of these were

[9] See *American State Papers*, "Public Lands," Vol. I, p. 123.
[10] *Ibid.*, Vol. II, *passim*.

favorable, some unfavorable. Among those who influenced British interest in western land settlements were Morris Birkbeck and his partner, George Flower, a well-known English writer on rural economics. Both Birkbeck and Flower attempted to establish permanent colonies in the Illinois country. But both were disturbed and handicapped by land-jobbers. "Land-jobbers traverse this fine country," Birkbeck wrote, "like a pestilent blight. Where they see the promise of a thriving settlement, from a cluster of entries being made in any neighbourhood, they purchase large tracts of the best land, and lock it up in real *mortmain,* for it is death to all improvement."

> One of the greatest calamities to which a young colony is liable is this investment of the property of non-residents, who speculate on their prosperity, whilst they are doing all they can to impede it.... This holding back from civilization millions of acres, tends to scatter the population of these new countries; increasing the difficulties of the settlers manifold.... The western states are suffering greatly from this evil.[11]

Summary

The first four decades of the disposal of public lands were, as already indicated, a period of good intent, accompanied by a lax administration of the laws, a wild scramble for land engrossment, the beginnings of unscrupulous town-jobbing schemes and an open field for political waste and corruption. In these decades the European immigration and the westward movement of population which the colonial speculators had prematurely expected began to take place. The filling-in process was mainly fostered by a pioneer spirit rather than a leadership of wealthy and politically prominent promoters. But the factor of speculation, the desire of pecuniary gain from the unearned increment in rising land values, created by the advance of civilization, was prominent throughout this era, as in earlier and later eras of the Republic. This factor impeded the original intention of Congress to foster actual land settlement. Large tracts of the public land were acquired and held by

[11] See Morris Birkbeck, *Letters from Illinois,* also George Flower, *History of the English Settlement in Edwards County, Ill.,* and William Faux, *Memorial Days in America.* For data on interests of British capitalists in American land projects, see also Leland Jenks, *The Migration of British Capital.*

Early Public Land Administration

non-residents who, for the most part, neither tilled it nor otherwise improved it. Goaded by repeated outcries against this situation, Congress, despite the political opposition of southern political leaders, finally, in 1841, passed the Pre-emption Land Act. In the meantime, however, there had been added to the U.S. territory the vast area of the Louisiana Purchase and the peninsula of Florida. Most of these territories comprised unoccupied lands. The story of Louisiana land disposal, therefore, will next be taken up.[12]

---

[12]Speculation in public land in the southern states was quite as extensive as in Ohio or Illinois. The principal source for a study of this speculation is *The American State Papers. Public Lands.* Two suggestive articles are James W. Silver, "Land Speculation Profits in the Chickasaw Cession," *Journal of Southern History*, Vol. X, pp. 84–92, and Mary E. Young, "The Creek Frauds: A Study in Conscience and Corruption," *Mississippi Valley Historical Review*, Vol. XLII, pp. 411–37.

Chapter 10

The Louisiana Territory

The Louisiana Territory was ceded to the United States by France under a purchase agreement in 1803. Under the terms of the treaty of cession, the United States agreed to incorporate the ceded territory into the Union as soon as possible and to accord to the inhabitants "all the rights, advantages and immunities of citizens—and in the meantime, they shall be maintained and protected in the free enjoyment of their liberty, property, and the Religion which they profess...." This meant that all land titles, land grants, and other rights given by the Spanish and French administrators who formerly governed the territory must receive recognition in so far as they did not conflict with the principles of the federal Constitution.

All this gave an opportunity for hosts of schemers and "get-rich-quick" adventurers to present their claims to a large part, if not practically all, of the vast unappropriated region—which scarcely a half century before had engendered dreams of fabulous wealth creation on the part of John Law and other promoters of the Mississippi Bubble.

The Antedating of Spanish Grants

As soon as the Louisiana Purchase became known, land speculators in the region sought out and bought up all sorts of questionable land titles, grants, and conveyances, and when they could not find enough of them, they manufactured them. "No sooner was it known that the province of Louisiana was sold to the United States," wrote Moses Austin, then a resident of Upper Louisiana, to Secretary of the Treasury Albert Gallatin, "than a general and fraudulent sale of lands took place. . . . Concessions for any quantity of land were daily granted, bearing date in 1799, or further back if the claimants demanded. The number of acres granted was governed by the sum paid. It is not necessary to say to what extent this speculation has been carried on."[1] Rufus Easton, another Connecticut Yankee, then living in St. Louis, wrote President Thomas Jefferson in a similar vein: "About the latter end of June, 1803, when information arrived of the cession to the United States, instructions were given to the various agents of the Governor that grants and concessions be dated back to the year 1799, which was the general antedate . . . and that surveys thereof would be made of any tract from fifty to fifty thousand acres to any person upon payment of one hundred dollars for five hundred acres; and so great was the thirst for speculation, when money could not be obtained, horses and other property were received in payment."[2]

Because the Spanish governors had sought to attract settlers to the Upper Louisiana region, the local officials had granted free land under "headrights" and "colonization contracts." This policy was discontinued under the brief regime of the French, with the result that the dates of the fraudulent grants had to be set back to the Spanish period; i.e., before 1800. So freely were Spanish grants given that some Spanish officials were in the habit of attaching their signatures to the certificates before the location or the amount of the land grant was noted thereon. These sheets got abroad and commanded a price among the so-called "antedaters." These "antedaters" were mostly Americans who emigrated into Missouri and "squatted" on land without grant or conveyance by Spanish officials.

The frequency of these land grants bearing date of the closing year of the Spanish regime in Louisiana clearly indicated fraud and corruption. As early as February 29, 1804, President Jefferson informed Congress "of fraudulent practices for monopolizing lands in Louisiana, which may perhaps require legislative provisions." It was estimated that two hundred thousand acres of land, "including all the best [lead] mines,

[1] See *The Austin Papers*, Part I, p. 117.
[2] Louis Houck, *History of Missouri*, Vol. III, p. 36.

have been surveyed to various individuals in the course of a few weeks past." The most notorious antedater, it was charged, was Zenon Trudeau, former lieutenant governor of Louisiana and commandant of the Spanish garrison near New Orleans. Through bribes of speculators, he signed blank sheets of paper granting land and ordering surveys. In this way, the best lead and iron mines in Missouri are reputed to have been "granted" at the time the Louisiana Territory was transferred to the United States.[2a]

In 1805, Congress, having learned of these frauds, appointed commissioners to determine the validity of Louisiana land titles. Never was there a more difficult job given to a commission. Their work extended over a period of three decades. Corruption and fraud, threats and violence, suits and countersuits characterized their proceedings throughout. At times members of the commission suffered bodily attacks, and the lawless spirit and greed for land made it necessary for them to carry arms for their personal protection.

The land-grant controversies entered prominently into early politics of Missouri. The fiery Thomas H. Benton was elected to the United States Senate from Missouri in 1820 largely because he favored a liberal policy for the claimants. He defeated John B. C. Lucas, who was appointed a land commissioner by Jefferson and who favored a drastic policy in the validating of claims. Lucas himself in time became a large landowner in St. Louis through the purchase of a tract for $700. It is now worth many millions of dollars.

While the government commissioners were hearing and deciding land claims in the ceded territory, the Spanish grants were being hawked about among speculators. Eastern capitalists, as well as "land-grabbers" on the spot, eagerly bought them up. Familiar names appear among the lists of those whose claims were granted or denied. Daniel Boone, who moved from Kentucky into the Louisiana Territory in 1798 and became a commandant of the district under the Spanish regime, claimed and was granted 1,000 arpents (about 850 acres) by Congress in 1813, though he had not cultivated or improved the land as required by the original concession. Moses Austin, father of Stephen

[2a] *American State Papers, Public Lands,* Vol. I, pp. 188–89, 193–94.

Austin, founder of Texas, who settled in Upper Louisiana in 1797 and began mining lead at Mine-a-Burton near St. Genevieve, Missouri, was finally refused title to his "square league" of land on the ground that the grant was not completed prior to October 1, 1800. Rufus Easton, a local judge and politician, who early informed Jefferson of the "antedaters," also had a number of claims which were denied confirmation. So great was the ire of this land-grabber that he made a personal attack "with a bludgeon" on one of the claims commissioners, because of which he was sentenced to two weeks in jail. William Russel, a large jobber in the Spanish grants, submitted as many as 309 claims in the space of a few years, but of these only 23 were approved. John T. Smith, a notorious land thief, also presented a number of claims to both small and large plots, most of which were rejected. And so the cases ran, the decisions of the claims commissioners creating both political and financial animosities in the Upper Louisiana country.

The Squatter Claims

One of the problems of opening up the Louisiana Territory to settlement was the task of the national government in ousting squatters. Prior to the Louisiana cession many Americans had emigrated into the Spanish domain and had taken up lands merely on the verbal permission or acquiescence of the local Spanish officials. These settlers, because of willingness to live under Spanish laws, were called *hidalgos* (i.e., sons) by the Ohio people. Because they could furnish no legal evidence of title, they were ordered by the land offices to move from their holdings. The opposition to these orders caused disturbances that had considerable political reaction. The cry of "squatter sovereignty" arose throughout the region. Politicians sought offices by favoring this principle. Thus John Scott, who in 1816 presented himself as a candidate for the office of congressional delegate from Missouri—and was elected—boldly stated in his platform: "neither justice or policy required that the people of this territory should be removed from lands which they had ameliorated by their labour, and defended by their bravery."[3]

[3]See *The Austin Papers*, Part I, p. 258.

Despite this agitation for recognition of "squatter rights," Congress was obdurate, but this principle was one of the forces which eventually led to the enaction of the Pre-emption Act in 1841 and the subsequent Homestead Act in 1862.

Some Prominent Spanish Land Claims

Some of the Spanish grant cases were fought through the courts for many years. The litigation of Antoine Soulard for land granted him in Missouri covered a period of almost half a century. Soulard was a former officer in the French Navy who settled in Upper Louisiana and became a surveyor. He was recommended by the last French governor, Carlos Delassus, to the American authorities as one who could furnish the most reliable information regarding titles to Spanish grants, including those in New Madrid, the last post in Louisiana where free grants were made. Soulard and his two sons were granted more than 5,000 arpents (4,200 acres) in various parts of Upper Louisiana by Delassus. In addition, he received a grant of 59 arpents in and near the city of St. Louis. This latter grant became extremely valuable after the American occupation. It was assigned to E. H. McCabe, who prosecuted the claim. Though in the opinion of the land commissioners the claim was valid, the United States Supreme Court finally rejected it in 1830. In the meantime the land had been sold by the United States, but in 1856 the heirs of McCabe petitioned Congress for other lands to offset their claim—and Congress finally reported favorably upon the petition.

Another and more extended claim was that known as the Clamorgan Grant. Jacques Clamorgan, a native of Guadalupe, was a merchant, fur trader, explorer, and land speculator in the Upper Louisiana territory during the Spanish regime. As a reward for "exploration services as far as the Pacific Ocean," he petitioned on March 1, 1797, for a tract of land "on the west side of the Mississippi River, at a distance of a few leagues above the mouth of the Missouri River and bounded by Charmette (Dardenne) Creek and the Copper River, with suitable water frontage, and extending toward the west until the 'inland hills' are reached." The total acreage was estimated at 500,000 arpents (425,000 acres) and today would comprise a large part of Arkansas, just below New Madrid. The petition, it was claimed, was granted on July 3, 1797, by Baron de Carondelet, governor general of Louisiana. In addition, Clamorgan acquired other immense tracts in the same region along the Missouri and Mississippi rivers. The total acreage of his lands was estimated at about one million arpents. Land speculation, however, was not his only business. He was the promoter of the Missouri Fur Company in St. Louis, which traded extensively with the Indians. After the American occupation, he became a judge in the Louisiana Territory. But his fur company proving unsuccessful, he left St. Louis after a few years and settled in Mexico. His land claims were then assigned to others "as his legal representatives."

For many years, these "legal representatives," "trustees," and "assigns," as they variously called themselves, sought confirmation of Clamorgan's grants, stressing particularly the claim for the 500,000 arpents near the mouth of the Missouri River. Congress appears to have paid little heed to the repeated petitions for recognition of the claim, though the settlement of the region was retarded for a time because of its existence. The land was finally surveyed and opened to public entry and, because of its desirability, was soon taken up by settlers.

The federal commissioners again and again considered the question of the validity of the Clamorgan grants. In their final report, made on August 25, 1835, they stated that "the great importance of this claim has induced the commissioners to make a consideration of every fact connected with it." And they concluded that this grant to Clarmorgan had never been validated by the officers of the Spanish Government and had been abandoned by the claimant himself soon after it was obtained. Moreover, when the surveyor general of the United States made his surveys in the territory, he was not notified of the claim. "These circumstances induced the board to believe that the claimant abandoned his claim with the knowledge of the officers, to seek remuneration otherwise; or has been guilty of the neglect of his privileges under the grant. . . . The board, therefore, could not recommend this claim for confirmation."

Despite this rejection, speculation in the claim continued.

A peculiar interest is attached to the proceedings of the Clamorgan claim because of the participation of Daniel Webster. In spite of the repeated refusals of Congress to confirm the grant and the final adverse decision of the Board of Land Commissioners, the Clamorgan Land Association was formed in 1837 to take over the title. Like other land-grabbing concerns, the association was not incorporated, but it had a president and board of directors composed of prominent individuals. William A. Bradley was president; the Hon. D. Webster, senator, and the Hon. S. L. Southard, formerly governor of New Jersey, were directors. The association took over title to the claim from John Glenn and Charles M. Thurston, Baltimore capitalists, who purchased it from Pierre Chouteau. It issued 536 "shares," each share representing 1,000 arpents (850 acres).

The Hon. D. Webster gave the association a favorable legal opinion of the validity of the Clamorgan grant. Moreover, the deed of trust under which the title was held by the association was acknowledged before Chief Justice Taney of the United States Supreme Court. All this was published in two pamphlets entitled *Papers Relating to the Clamorgan Grant* and *The Clamorgan Grant*.

The shares of the association were not conspicuously offered for sale at a fixed price. In small type on the bottom of the title page of each pamphlet there is the bare statement: "The interest in this tract is divided into 536 parts, each part, therefore, will represent the interest of 1,000 arpents and a fraction." In this modest way shares in land companies were then advertised. To have solicited purchasers boldly would have condemned the proposition as a speculative land-jobbing scheme.

Success seems not to have attended the efforts of the Clamorgan Land Association. Congress, however, continued to receive petitions to compensate the "heirs" and "assigns." Thus in 1848 Henry Clamorgan, "one of the legal representatives of James E. Clamorgan," petitioned Congress. As late as 1851 another petition was received, and a Senate committee upheld the right to compensation and "reported a bill."[4] But there is no record that a bill was passed for a settlement of the claim, nor was the matter ever carried into the courts.

[4]Senate Report #354, 32nd Congress, 1st Session.

Another Spanish grant which was destined for many years to fill the annals of Congress was known as the De Bastrop Claim. It is of considerable historical interest not only because of the persistency of its prosecution through several decades but because it furnished the pretext of Aaron Burr's "western expedition," and also because it finally came into the possession of Stephen Girard, who philanthropically willed the land jointly to the cities of New Orleans and Philadelphia.

Philip Henry Neri, Baron de Bastrop, was one of the most picturesque and commanding figures associated with the early history of the Louisiana Territory and of Texas as well. He was a man of kindly, winning, and magnetic personality, an adventurer who sought to undertake great things but who met with misfortunes throughout his career. Although a native of Holland, he entered the service of Frederick the Great, becoming a member of his famous bodyguard of giants. Frederick ennobled him with the title "Baron de Bastrop," but Napoleon confiscated his property in 1795 and compelled him to flee to America. For a time he resided in Virginia, where he carried on trading with Europe and where he claimed to have acquired a large landed estate at Harrison, West Virginia. For some reason, possibly because of failure to pay his debts or because of passing out worthless bills of exchange, he took refuge in Louisiana. There he became friendly with the Spanish governor, Carondelet, with whom he made a contract in June 1797 for a grant of about 850,000 acres on the Ouachita River.

Bastrop agreed to settle five hundred families on his grant. Before the families were settled, however, or before Bastrop had time to carry out his plans, the execution of the contract was suspended by the Spanish Government. He therefore never received a patent, though he had succeeded in mortgaging a part of the property to Abraham Morhouse of Kentucky, whose financial assistance he had solicited in the deal.

Bastrop moved to Texas soon after the United States took possession of Louisiana. In consideration of a debt of $350,000, he deeded to Morhouse on January 25, 1804, two thirds of his pretended grant. The remaining third is reported to have been foreclosed in 1801, under a mortgage given in New Orleans. Or perhaps it was all mortgaged in

New Orleans and then sold by Bastrop to Morhouse. The baron's reputation for honesty in business dealings was not of the best. Haden Edwards of Nashville, Tennessee, whose Texas deals in 1827 were opposed by Bastrop, accused the baron of having borrowed $400,000 from American merchants by giving fraudulent bills of exchange on Dutch banks and then fleeing to New Orleans. He may have been such a scoundrel, but he has two American towns still bearing his name—one located in Louisiana and one in Texas.

Just how Aaron Burr at one time obtained a part—reported as 400,000 acres—of Bastrop's grant is not entirely clear. It is fairly certain, however, that it came either directly or indirectly from Abraham Morhouse, since the latter, through his assignees or representatives, remained in "full and complete possession until 1846, and had even paid taxes thereon." Colonel Charles Lynch of Lexington, who sold the property to Burr, either obtained it from Morhouse or was acting as Morhouse's agent.

"I have bought of Col. Lynch 400 M. acres of the tract called Bastrop's, lying on the Ouachita," Burr wrote a Mr. Latrobe on October 26, 1806. "The excellence of the soil and climate are established to my satisfaction by the report of impartial persons. I shall send on forty or fifty men this autumn to clear and build cabins. These men are to be paid in land and to be found for one year in provisions. It is my intention to go there with several of my friends next winter. If you should incline to partake, and to join us, I will give you 10,000 acres. I want your society; I want your advice in the establishment about to be made. In short, you have become necessary to my settlement. As the winter is your leisure I reason, if you should incline to go and view the country, you may do it at my expense."[5]

It is quite evident from this letter that Burr had at least intended making a settlement on the land, even though it may have been a mere pretext, or using it as a base for military operations against Mexico, or in order to separate Louisiana from the Union. Burr was certainly well acquainted with land-jobbing and land-development schemes. We have already seen that he was concerned in one way or another in several of

[5]Wandell and Minnigerode, *Aaron Burr,* Vol. II, pp. 87, 88.

the great New York land purchases. He was a close friend and political associate of Jonathan Dayton, through whose instrumentality it is quite likely that he obtained knowledge of the Bastrop tract. Dayton and General Wilkinson, we have already noted, were partners in western land deals.

Though some fifty or sixty of Burr's men started to the Ouachita River from Kentucky, nothing ever came of his purchase. It is quite probable that he made only the first payment of $5,000 and that, because of defaults in subsequent payments, the land reverted to the seller. Burr was interested enough, however, to draw a map of his "tract," which is now one of the prized possessions of the New York Public Library.

The connection of Bastrop's grant with Burr's conspiracy became generally known. As illustrative of the humor of the time, a political handbill issued during Burr's treason trial stated that "his quid Majesty [meaning Burr] was charged with the trifling crime of wishing to divide the Union and farm Baron Bastrop's grant." But the public was to hear more and more of the Bastrop grant long after the excitement of Burr's treasonable designs subsided. The Louisiana land commissioners refused to confirm the claim, and the petitions to Congress were equally unavailing. Finally the case came to the United States Supreme Court for decision and there received a "knockout" blow.

It came before the highest tribunal in this way: Stephen Girard was requested by the French bankers, Laffitte & Co., to collect a debt owed to them by one Carrère of New Orleans. Carrère offered 12,500 arpents of land on the Ouachita in settlement. This Girard accepted and credited Laffitte & Co. with the amount of the debt. He was glad to do this as he, in partnership with Robert E. Griffith and James Lyle, had already secretly bought, in 1822, other tracts in the Bastrop grant from the trustees of the heirs of Abraham Morhouse. They bought four tenths of the whole tract for $21,000. The purchasers divided it into 21 shares of $1,000 each, Girard taking 10 shares. Girard, however, later increased his participation, paying 15 to 21 cents per acre, until he had in all 200,370 acres. The estate he placed under the care of Judge Henry Buy of Monroe, Louisiana, under whose direction Girard spent $42,690 improving 30,000 acres.

Girard thought he was making a safe investment. He wrote Laffitte & Co. on June 7, 1829, "Congress has not done anything in it [i.e., the grant] nor do I expect they will do it for some time to come in consequence of the large tracts which they own themselves in that neighborhood, and are anxious to sell. I own myself upwards of 180,000 arpents of the aforesaid tract, and have commenced a settlement thereon where I have upwards of 30 slaves besides overseers, and feel perfectly tranquil as it respects the nature of the title."[6]

But all Girard ever received from his investment of upward of $100,000 was a few hundred dollars from cotton and produce grown on the land. At his death he willed one third of the tract to New Orleans and two thirds to Philadelphia. The city of Philadelphia brought suit for a confirmation of the grant. The Supreme Court held that Bastrop had not perfected his title, and denied the validity of the grant. The city appealed to Congress in 1859 to override the decision of the Court, but no action of this kind was ever taken.

Thus ended the famous Bastrop Grant. The Maison Rouge Claim, which was of a similar character and was also comprised in the "Ouachita" lands, likewise never received recognition.

Another interesting and long-drawn-out claim for lands obtained originally under Spanish grants also attracted public attention for a long period of years. This was known as the Myra Clark Gaines case. It involved, among other property, valuable real estate within and adjacent to New Orleans.

Daniel Clark was an Irishman who settled in New Orleans in 1784 when a youth of seventeen. Here he became a Spanish subject and waxed wealthy in trade and commerce. He was politically and socially prominent and of course was rewarded with liberal grants of land. He also bought up the grants of others, including the worthless Maison Rouge Claim. Among his acquisitions was a tract now in the parish and

---

[6]John B. McMaster, *The Life and Times of Stephen Girard,* Vol. II, pp. 409–10. For a detailed account of the Bastrop and Maison Rouge claims see Jennie O'K. Mitchell and Robert D. Calhoun, "The Marquis De Maison Rouge, the Baron De Bastrop, and Colonel Abraham Morhouse. Three Ouachita Valley Soldiers of Fortune. The Maison Rouse and Bastrop Spanish Land Grants," *Louisiana Historical Quarterly,* Vol. XX, pp. 352ff.

city of New Orleans which had been originally granted to Elisha Winter in 1791. The right to this land was approved by the Board of Land Commissioners in 1812. The patent was engrossed and made ready for the President's signature, but because of some objection the Secretary of the Interior arrested the patent. Clark died soon after the grant was confirmed but before its ratification by Congress. Before his death he conveyed this New Orleans property together with all his other real estate to Joseph Bellechasse, with the confidential understanding that they were to remain under his control for the use and benefit of Myra Davis.

Myra Davis was Clark's own daughter—the fruit of a secret marriage with Madame Zulime des Grange. At least the United States Supreme Court so decided in several suits brought before it. Her paternity was not discovered until Myra was a woman. Over the course of years thirty attorneys presented to the courts convincing arguments of their client's rights to the vast estate of the crafty New Orleans politician, congressman, and personal friend of Aaron Burr. In 1867, when Myra Clark Gaines was already an elderly woman, the Supreme Court confirmed her legal title to the immense acreage of real estate that had belonged to her father. Some of this was recovered through suits of ejectment, but much of the wealth thus obtained by the persistent litigant was swallowed up in court costs and legal fees.

As already noted, a valuable part of the estate consisted of 700 acres adjacent to New Orleans. This had been considered as national domain and was comprised in the grant of 200,000 acres awarded to General Lafayette by Congress in 1824. Lafayette needed money and sold the land. Thus innocent purchasers came into possession, and when the legal ownership was decided by the Court, the property was worth many millions. It was thus up to Congress and the city of New Orleans to compensate Myra. This was finally done after Myra Clark Gaines ended her litigious career in 1885.

The Myra Clark Gaines case is remarkable for the extended period of the litigation. It began in 1834 and was not settled until almost a half century thereafter. In delivering an opinion on the case in 1860, United States Supreme Court Justice Wayne remarked, "When, hereafter, some distinguished American lawyer shall retire from his practice, to write the history of his country's jurisprudence, this case will be registered by him as the most remarkable in the records of its courts."[6a]

Still another case involving valuable New Orleans property attracted nationwide interest. This was the claim to the New Orleans beach-front area by Edward Livingston, Andrew Jackson's friend and Secretary of State. Livingston was a member of the Scottish colonial clan of that name which for several generations held, under manorial rights, most of the present Columbia County in New York. The family had a reputation for land-grabbing, though Edward Livingston had become an attorney and was mayor of New York from 1801 to 1803. Thomas Jefferson then appointed him United States attorney for the New York District. While acting in this capacity he confessed to a shortage of public funds entrusted to him, owing, as he claimed, to the dishonesty of subordinates during his illness. This led him to take refuge in New Orleans in February 1804. The place then had a reputation as a resort for all those whose integrity had been questioned. In New Orleans, Livingston became a lawyer, politician, and land-jobber. Like Daniel Clark, he was friendly to Burr and became innocently involved in the latter's conspiracy. In this way he won the animosity of General James Wilkinson, then military commander of Louisiana Territory—and naturally Jefferson also became prejudiced against him.

Livingston had accepted some waterfront land in New Orleans as a fee for legal services. Much of it was the result of tidal action piling up the river silt. In 1808 the United States Government laid claim to this alluviation and ousted Livingston. To get the case before the country, Livingston sued Jefferson as a citizen for trespass. Jefferson then personally took part in the controversy. In 1812 he published his pamphlet of 103 pages entitled *The Proceedings of the Government of the United States in maintaining the Public Right to the Beach of the Mississippi, etc.* In this tract Jefferson took the opportunity to deny the charge that he was induced to seize the land because of malice toward Livingston.

[6a] Nolan B. Harmon, Jr., *The Famous Case of Myra Clark Gaines.*

The next year Livingston answered Jefferson in an equally vigorous manner. Livingston's reply was a pamphlet of 300 printed pages. Both documents attracted nationwide interest among the legal fraternity and were reprinted in the current law journals. Livingston accused Jefferson of endeavoring to deprive him of his property, from the sale of which he expected to discharge his shortage to the government. The controversy went from Congress to the courts and then back to Congress. It was not settled until after Livingston's death in 1836, when his widow received a large indemnity for the appropriated lands. In the meantime Jefferson and Livingston became reconciled. On April 4, 1824, just about one year before his death, Jefferson wrote Livingston a friendly letter congratulating him because the good people of New Orleans had restored him again to the "councils of our country," and expressing the sentiment that his election to Congress would bring aid "to the remains of our old school in Congress, in which your early labors had been so useful."[7]

Not all land speculations in the old Orleans country were founded on disputed Spanish and French grants. In this region, after the American occupation, town-jobbing and land engrossment were as rampant as in the Northwest Territory. Towns were laid out along the rivers or at crossroads, and lot auctions were advertised widely by handbills, newspaper announcements, and other means. Speculators also gambled on the probable or possible locations of state or territorial capitals or on county seats.

Thus Stephen F. Austin, destined in after years to become the founder of Texas, took up some land at Little Rock, Arkansas, in the expectation that the capital of the new territory would be located there. Others interested in lands elsewhere in the territory used their political influence to oppose Austin's selection. "Were it not for this man, Russell," Austin wrote his brother-in-law in speaking of one of his opponents, "our unfortunate family might yet be enabled to secure small, but decent competence for if his opposition was removed there would be no

[7] Jefferson's *Works*, ed. by H. A. Washington, Vol. VII, p. 342.

difficulty in getting the seat of the government moved to L. Rock. . . ."[8] Austin's speculation in Arkansas failed, but he was soon to take up another and more elaborate venture in Texas.

Stephen F. Austin and his family, through whom three generations of land speculators can be traced from Connecticut to Texas, also took part in the short but exciting "run-up" of what were commonly known as the New Madrid Claims. In December 1811 the populous settlement of New Madrid, Missouri, was visited by a severe earthquake. It tore up the land and demolished buildings. The inhabitants fled from the region and took refuge in the outlying sections. Though not required to do so by the Constitution or the statutes, Congress in 1815 passed a measure affording relief to the sufferers. The landowners were permitted to give up their holdings in the affected region and, in return, were granted certificates entitling them to locate an equal area on government land of their own choosing.

Thus the door for wild speculation was opened. Before the earthquake sufferers actually knew that a law for their relief was passed, a host of speculators came down from St. Louis and started to buy up their "certificates." As the certificates gave a choice of location to the holders, they were eagerly sought after by town-jobbers. The result of the rush was that, of a total of 516 certificates finally issued, only 20 remained in the hands of the earthquake sufferers.[9]

Imagine the disappointment of the speculators when William Wirt, United States Attorney General, gave an opinion in 1820 that the persons to whom the New Madrid warrants were issued had no right to transfer them, and that patents to the land claimed "must issue to the person who was the owner at the date of the [Relief] act, or . . . his heirs. . . . The Act," he stated, "attaches no assignable quality to the charity which it bestows; . . . It was not the intention of Congress to make these charities a subject of speculation. The law was passed to help the poor who had been rendered indigent by a visitation of God, not to enrich the speculator."[10]

[8]*The Austin Papers,* Part I, p. 359.
[9]*Ibid,* Part I, p. 317 ff.
[10]*American State Papers,* "Public Lands," Vol. III, p. 494.

This thunderbolt created consternation among the land-jobbers of Missouri. They made political fodder of it. As late as 1825 the General Assembly of Missouri, on behalf of the New Madrid speculators, petitioned the "Honorable Senate and House of Representatives of Congress to take the case of the claimants [meaning, of course, the speculators] under consideration and grant unto them such relief as justice, expediency and good policy may dictate." Concerning the speculation in the certificates, the legislative petition frankly stated:

> Those certificates [for public land] have been sold and transferred for a valuable consideration from one person to another, until they have passed through the hands of many individuals of the most worthy and respectable class of our citizens, from the time of their first being issued. They were purchased with great eagerness (and when lands were high) by the new settlers coming to this state . . . who have located [on] them. . . . Should the patents for the land be withheld, it . . . will be the means of breaking up many families, and cause the ruin of many of our most worthy and respectable citizens.[11]

Congress, in its public land policy, has frequently shown sympathy for actual settlers, but that august body has never had a high regard for or given much consideration to petitions of land speculators. In the case of the New Madrid Claims, there was little reason to be sympathetic. An agent of the General Land Office, writing to his chief from St. Louis on November 22, 1823, expressed the view that the law for the relief of the earthquake sufferers "has given rise to more fraud and more downright villany than any law ever passed by the Congress of the United States, and, if the claims are not immediately decided upon, will involve the citizens of Missouri in endless litigation and trouble. . . ."[12]

It does not appear that many great fortunes were founded on land speculation in the Middle West during the first decades of the acquisition of the Louisiana Territory. The amount of unoccupied land was too vast. Congressman Adam Seybert, in his statistical survey of the

[11]*Ibid.*, Vol. IV, p. 155.
[12]*Ibid.*, p. 47.

United States published in 1816, estimated that the government's acreage was then in excess of 400,000,000 acres. Surveys were continuously being made by the General Land Office and settlement was being opened to lands farther and farther west of the Mississippi River.

In New Orleans and St. Louis and other parts of Louisiana and Missouri, it is true, there were a number of large landowners, some of whom began their acquisitions during the old French and Spanish regimes. Others acquired their estates after the American occupation. Notable among these was John McDonogh, who at the time of his death in 1850 was the largest landowner in Louisiana. McDonogh was of Scotch-Irish stock. He was born in Baltimore on December 29, 1779, and upon coming of age he took up his residence in New Orleans. Here he became a merchant and shipper, but soon his chief occupation was buying up land. He bought a number of Spanish grants in West Florida, some of which were rejected on the ground of invalidity, while others were allowed. His real estate in New Orleans alone was valued in 1850 at over $2,000,000, and in addition he owned a large part of both the cultivated and the unimproved area of the state of Louisiana.

McDonogh never really speculated in land. Like John Jacob Astor, he bought to hold, and it is said of him that he rarely offered property for sale. Yet he did little to improve his real estate holdings. He seems to have invested his money upon the principle that time and the increase of population in Louisiana would vastly augment the value of his property. Accordingly, at his death the buildings on his New Orleans property were exceedingly dilapidated. There was, moreover, in the neighborhood of New Orleans at that time a quantity of land belonging to his estate that was still covered by the original forest, though it could have been cut up into building sites and farms and sold at a handsome profit to him. Vincent Nolte, a German trader, who was conspicuous in New Orleans business affairs, thus describes McDonogh in his reminiscences:

> McDonogh talked very little, and seldom mixed in general conversation, especially with ladies, whose society he avoided as much as possible. When he did open his lips, all that fell from them was praise of certain lands he had just purchased, and this

theme was inexhaustible. It was not in Louisiana alone that he carried on this system, but also in the neighboring States, and he continued it for more than forty years.[13]

Summary

Congress gave Napoleon $15,000,000 for the Louisiana Territory. It was a lot of money in those days. And there were many who doubted that the region was worth the price. Aside from the districts of New Orleans and St. Louis and a few other scattered settlements along the Mississippi River, the whole domain was then a boundless wilderness infested by savage Indian tribes.

All this was changed within a few years after the American flag was raised in New Orleans. The onslaught of speculators, lawyers, politicians, pioneers, and adventurers converted much of the barren empire into thriving and progressive farms and communities. Hardly a decade after the United States came into its possession, the combined wealth of a few individual newcomers exceeded the whole purchase price paid by the national government. Much of this was acquired through prudent urban real estate speculation and town-jobbing. Emigrants from the East, such as John McDonogh, Edward Livingston, and John B. C. Lucas, waxed wealthy in their real estate deals. Lucas alone, notwithstanding his hatred of the "antedaters" and land thieves, acquired a large portion of the present city of St. Louis. A tract of land here which he originally purchased for about $700 was in a few decades worth several millions. Like Astor, Longworth, and McDonogh, he did not sell but left his estate intact for his heirs. These founded the private banking house of Lucas & Co., for many years one of the leading concerns of its kind in the Middle West.

[13]*Fifty Years in Both Hemispheres*, p. 86.

Chapter 11

The Public Domain under the Pre-emption Acts

The greatest excitement in land speculation in the first two decades of the nineteenth century came at the conclusion of the War of 1812. Then with the Indian menace under control and new lands being opened for sale veterans of the war and other farm makers and speculators swarmed westward to seek out good locations. As new ranges were surveyed and opened for settlement speculators found gainful purchases of favorable sites. But the law required that newly opened sections must first be offered at public auction, so that competitive bidding sometimes drove up the price of choice sites to a high level. Of course, there was opportunity for collusion and fraud under this system, which was aided by lax and inefficient administration of the General Land Office.

In practice, the auction system did not result in the disposal of much of the public domain, and most sales were made at the minimum price. The extension of credit to purchasers was a handicap in obtaining revenue from the sales. A large percentage of the purchasers would fail to make the required payments. Up to 1819 the receipts from the public land sales amounted to $46,341,000, but the actual payment received was less than half this amount.[1] Congress, from time to time, had to pass relief acts in favor of the land purchasers. All this created dissatisfaction with the system of disposing of the lands. One main political objection was that a "squatter" who settled on government land was unable to have a pre-emption right when it was offered for sale and thus lost the capital and labor he had applied to his holding.

[1] Benjamin H. Hibbard, *History of the Public Land Policies*, p. 100.

Though in this period actual sale of public lands was relatively small, the amount of the proceeds was sufficient to create political controversy. As the new states with considerable areas of the public domain were admitted to the Union, they sought to obtain the benefit of unsold lands within their boundaries—a privilege given the original and older states. From the unsold public lands the new states had neither revenue nor taxable resources. As noted on a previous page, Thomas Jefferson, in his second inaugural address, proposed a "repartition" of the public income among the states and recommended an amendment to the Constitution, that from the proceeds of sales internal improvements and educational facilities should be encouraged. But Congress never took any action on this matter.

In the meantime, however, efforts were made to improve the administration of the public domain. In 1812 the General Land Office was established as a unit of the Treasury Department. It exercised supervision over local land offices as well as other land-disposal activities. To the General Land Office were transferred the functions of land survey and administration of land sales which had previously been performed by the War and the Treasury Departments. However, until 1833 land patents were still signed by the President, in whose name the patents were issued. About this time a tremendous land boom throughout the nation was in progress and sales of public lands skyrocketed.

In the meantime the national land business became a national burden and was a strong factor in promoting political sectionalism of the nation. As Andrew Jackson pointed out to Congress in December 1833: "From the origin of the land system down to the 30th September, 1832, the amount expended [on the public domain] has . . . been about $49,701,280 and the amount received from the sales deducting payments on account of roads, etc., about $38,386,624. The revenue arising from the public lands, therefore, has not been sufficient to meet the general charges on the Treasury, which have grown out of them by about $11,314,656."[2]

[2]James D. Richardson, *A Compilation of the Messages and Papers of the Presidents*, Vol. III, p. 63.

But the tide changed soon after Jackson delivered this message. In the early 1830s a speculation fever raged throughout the country. At that time, government lands, as well as other property, could be purchased with "rag money" created by "wildcat" banks. Then the "land-office business"—a term still in use though its application is long out of date—began in earnest. The public land auctions were attended by veritable mobs. They were scenes of great excitement. Premiums were paid by bidders for seats near the auctioneers, and bribery and other forms of corruption were used in the process of receiving and registering the bids.

The irregularities in bidding at the public auctions were too numerous to be recounted. A common form of fraud was secret agreements among the bidders to withhold offers for a selected section. Another was to bid up choice sites to abnormally high figures to scare away competitors. The effect of this, wrote an official investigator in 1834, "would be to enable any one man . . . to monopolize the entire sales, bid off the lands at whatever price he might put down competition; of course the people attending the public sales will have dispersed in a few days after the sales have been closed. They have no idea but all things in regard to the transaction are not fair. A short time after the sales, the person thus purchasing by agreement, forfeits the land; the whole affair is cancelled; the receipts destroyed, and the land becomes subject to entry in the usual manner, and this being known only to a few privileged individuals, of course, they can then enter the land at the minimum price."[3]

Another kind of public land fraud was related to pre-emption claims, such as certificates entitling soldiers, settlers, and Indians to the pre-emption or selection of lands in a designated location. These were commonly called "floats," because anyone entitled to land under a pre-emption right was said to have a "floating" claim to it. Such claimants were required under the act of 1834 to be bona fide cultivators and occupiers of the land. Many individuals taking up land with "floats," however, were merely "fake" settlers and soon sold out to speculators.[4]

[3]*American State Papers,* "Public Lands," Vol. VII, p. 524.
[4]In 1835, Benjamin F. Linton, the United States district attorney of western

As already noted, because of the great excitement attending the national land-office sales during the speculation fever just prior to the Panic of 1837, "doing a land-office business" became a common expression denoting great commercial activity and merchandising success. The tremendous increase in the sales of public lands indicates the extent of the virulent speculation fever. In 1825 the receipts from sales amounted to only $1,216,090. They rose to $2,329,356 in 1830, then continued as follows:

Years	Acres Sold	Receipts
1831	2,777,857	$ 3,577,024
1832	2,462,342	3,115,376
1833	3,856,227	4,972,285
1834	4,658,219	6,099,981
1835	12,564,479	15,999,804
1836	20,074,871	25,167,833
1837	5,601,103	7,007,523

The Impact of the "Specie Circular"

Thus the big bulge occurred in 1835 and 1836. It created a troublesome surplus in the national Treasury. Andrew Jackson was not pleased with the heavy receipts from land sales, for he and his cabinet realized that the land was bought with bank notes, much of which were depreciated and could not be redeemed in specie. Accordingly, on July 11, 1836, he took a bold step. He issued his famous "Specie Circular." It simply ordered that the land offices should accept only gold or silver or "land scrip" (i.e., soldiers' warrants) in payment for public lands.

The impact of this document was tremendous. Certainly land speculators could not then get specie! There was in fact little specie circulating in the country. The banks had very little specie in their tills to back up their outstanding circulating notes, and they could not meet an onslaught of holders demanding redemption of the notes in specie. Hence there was an abrupt abatement in speculation in public lands. The land offices were left deserted. When the financial crack came the fol-

---

Louisiana, reported that in his district there was a "notorious" speculation in floats by one individual, whom, however, he did not name.

lowing year, the Treasury found that, instead of surplus cash arising from lands already sold, the "old cat" was returned to its doorstep. Congress, by a large majority, passed a bill annulling the "Specie Circular," but Jackson was firm in his "hard-money" policy. He permitted Congress to adjourn without signing the bill.

The "Specie Circular" created as great an uproar in Congress as Jackson's war on the Bank of the United States. Prominent congressmen had been watching the wild speculations in government lands but avoided taking measures to abate it. The famous Foote Resolution, which brought forth Daniel Webster's most outstanding flight of oratory in his career—his "Reply to Hayne"—called for a cessation of land sales. This the southern statesmen opposed. Webster appears not to have been in favor of the resolution, but he, along with other New England and eastern members of Congress, was accused by the Southerners of seeking to hinder the westward movement for the sake of maintaining northern political influence. Webster resented the accusation. He took a keen interest in the public lands for political as well as personal reasons, for he had borrowed money to invest in public lands and is reputed to have had at one time as much as $60,000 thus invested. This, however, is doubtful.[5]

As a true statesman, Webster traced the cause of the land speculation of the period. The government itself, he said, was largely responsible for it, because it did not raise the price of its lands when everything else was going up in price. But, in his estimation, land speculation was not necessarily an evil. With characteristic oratory he told the Senate on May 31, 1836:

> "In everything else, prices have run up. But here [i.e., public land] the price is chained down by statute. Goods, products of all kinds, and indeed all other lands may rise, and many of them have risen, some twenty-five and some forty and fifty per cent; but government lands remain at $1.25 per acre. . . . The government land, therefore, at the present prices . . . is the cheapest safe object of investment. The sagacity of capital has found this out, and it grasps the opportunity. Purchase, it is true, has gone

[5] See Claude F. Fuess, *Caleb Cushing,* Vol. I, pp. 230–32, and Vol. II, pp. 85–88.

ahead of emigration; but emigration follows it, in near pursuit, and spreads its thousands and tens of thousands close on the heels of the surveyor and the land hunter. . . . Nor are we to overlook, in this survey of causes of the vast increase in the sale of lands, the effects, almost magical, of that great and beneficent agent of prosperity, wealth and power—*internal improvement.*"[6]

Henry Clay, like Webster, feared no evil from land grabbing. In defending the national land policy in the Senate in 1832, he pointed out that "to supply the constantly augmenting demand [for land], the policy has been highly liberal. . . . Large tracts, far surpassing the demand of purchasers, in every climate and situation, are brought into . . . market at moderate prices. . . . For $50 any poor man may purchase forty acres of first-rate lands."[7] Yet Clay admitted in another address that "a friend of mine . . . bought in Illinois last fall about two thousand acres of refuse land at the minimum price, for which he has lately refused $6.00 per acre. An officer of this body [the Senate], now in my eye, purchased a small tract of 160 acres at second or third hand, entered a few years ago, and which is now estimated at $1,900. It [land speculation] *is a business—a very profitable business,* at which fortunes are made in the new States—to purchase these refuse lands, and, without improving them, to sell at large advances."[8]

The Passage of the Pre-emption Acts

The outcry for "squatters' rights" won increasing support in Congress where earlier those opposed to squatting had been in control. In that earlier period unauthorized settlement on the public lands was prohibited and troops were despatched on more than one occasion to evict the settlers and burn their meager improvements. A number of special acts were passed giving squatters the right to purchase their claims of 160 acres at the minimum price. Then in 1830 Congress forgave all squatters who were illegally on the public lands and permitted them to purchase their tracts without competitive bidding. The pre-emption law

[6]Daniel Webster, *Works,* Vol. IV, p. 262.
[7]Colton, *et al., The Works of Henry Clay,* Vol. V, p. 429.
[8]*Ibid.,* Vol. V, pp. 429, 503.

of 1830 was re-enacted in 1832, 1834, 1838, and 1840, by which time it had become as regular as annual appropriation bills. All these measures were retrospective in that they forgave past intrusions.

On September 4, 1841, Congress passed a prospective pre-emption act that opened all surveyed public lands to squatting and in effect allowed a period of grace from settlement to purchase. By the fifties squatting was permitted on unsurveyed public land on which Indian rights had been surrendered. The essence of these acts was the right given an individual who complied with the requirements of actual settlement and cultivation to hold the land against others applying for it and at the end of a designated period to gain title by paying the customary price of $1.25 an acre.[8a] Regarding this legislation, Professor Paul Wallace Gates writes:

> After the passage of the general Pre-emption Act of 1841 the attitude of the federal government toward Western settlers had grown increasingly benevolent. It had become the practice, though not required by law, for the General Land Office to survey great tracts far out on the frontier and to delay advertising them at public auction for years. During that time squatters could settle upon them, erect a simple home and make such improvements as their means permitted. In effect they had the free use of the public land for a time, during which they could raise a number of crops and perhaps accumulate enough cash to buy their claims.[9]

The Swamp Land Acts

To appease the states in which there were large tracts of public land, Congress in 1849 and 1850 passed what is known as the Swamp Land Acts. This legislation permitted grants of land to states for drainage and reclamation purposes. It opened up, however, the opportunity for fraudulent practices as bold and as notorious as those under disposal of the land to private interests. The Swamp Land Act of 1850 provided that, to be classed as swamp land, each forty-acre tract must be overflowed, either at planting or harvest season, and that the proceeds from

---

[8a]Benjamin H. Hibbard, *History of the Public Land Policies,* pp. 144–69; Roy M. Robbins, *Our Landed Heritage,* pp. 30 ff.

[9]"The Struggle for Land and the 'Irrepressible Conflict,'" *Political Science Quarterly,* June 1951, Vol. LXVI, p. 251.

the sale of the lands by the states be applied exclusively to cost of reclaiming the lands. All that was generally necessary to obtain land under the acts was for some state or local official to swear that the lands were under water or in an undrained condition. The story is told that a state official once swore that he crossed certain lands in a boat, neglecting, however, to state that the boat was on a wagon which could readily cross over the dry land.[10]

Up until 1884 approximately 72,000,000 acres were selected by the states under the Swamp Land Act, of which about 58,000,000 acres were approved. Altogether, about 64,000,000 acres have been conveyed to states as swamp land, but about one third of this was granted to Florida. Much of this acreage was disposed of to private interests, without any action on the part of the states to drain or even improve it. George W. Julian, chairman of the House Committee on Public Lands in 1851, stated that under the Swamp Land Act some 30,000,000 acres of the most choice land had been granted to four Gulf states and Arkansas, which were sold to speculators or politicians at from ten to eighty cents per acre.[11] And in 1866 the land commissioner reported that more than 52,000,000 acres of agricultural lands in the same area, obtained by the states under the Swamp Land Act, were in the hands of speculators, both corporations and individuals, not engaged in agriculture.

Landlordism and Land Engrossment in the Pre-emption Period

Though the Pre-emption Act of 1841 was intended to forestall further engrossment of large public land acreage, this intention was, on the whole, never realized. Unlimited right of purchase was still permitted and capitalists in all parts of the country continued to buy in large quantities. Millowners and others purchased western lands, largely under the motive of obtaining a future rise in land values owing to the population growth of the region. They operated either with their own or borrowed capital and undertook the burden of meeting taxes, interest, fees, and other costs connected with landownership. If the anticipated

[10] Clawson, *op. cit.*, p. 72.
[11] Alfred N. Chandler, *op. cit.*, p. 498.

profits from sales did not materialize within the time they expected, "their taxes remained unpaid, tax titles of dubious value issued and patronage was thereby created for lawyers and the courts, and further financial aid given to the newspapers in . . . the much-fought-over 'tax delinquent list.' "[12]

The tremendous size of these tax-delinquent lists would give an impression that most holders of western lands, both resident and nonresident, were "land-poor" and made no money from their engrossments. However, as stated by Professor Gates, "In practically every town, large or small, the local squire, the bank president, the owner of numerous mortgages, the resident of the 'big house,' the man whose wife was the leader of 'society,' got his start—and a substantial start—as a result of the upward surge of land values in the nineteenth century."[13]

Because of inability to dispose of their holdings in a short time, a number of these absentee landlords resorted to the old colonial practice of seeking tenants for their lands. Thus Romulus Riggs of Philadelphia had acquired 256 quarter sections (40,000 acres) of land in the military tract of Illinois during the 1830s, which was partially covered with timber. He made agreement with squatters on the land whereby they undertook to prevent unauthorized cutting of timber in return for the right to use the land. He at first induced these squatters to pay the taxes, and later, when they had built a cabin and cultivated a few acres, he demanded a cash rent in excess of taxes. Thus was tenancy born on the frontier.[14]

According to Professor Gates, whose researches into western land-ownership have revealed a vast amount of unpublished factual material, frontier landlords and pioneer tenants were most numerous in central Illinois, where today the largest of the estates and the highest proportion of tenancy are still to be found. It was this region that in

[12]Paul Wallace Gates, *Frontier Landlords and Pioneer Tenants*, p. 2.
[13]*Ibid.*, p. 3.
[14]*Ibid.* Riggs, in partnership with William W. Corcoran, conducted a large banking business in Washington under the name of Corcoran and Riggs. This later developed into the largest banking institution in Washington, the Riggs National Bank.

the early 1830s began to attract speculators as well as settlers. The speculators, who were mostly absentee landlords, found that by making some improvements on their holdings they could attract tenants, and some of these resorted to tenancy on a crop-sharing as well as a cash basis. Among the large absentee landlords who resorted to this practice, in addition to Romulus Riggs, were Henry L. Ellsworth, John Grigg, Solomon Sturges, and William W. Corcoran. Despite difficulties and disappointments, they all reaped the advantage of the rising land values that followed the depression of 1837.

Commenting on the rise of absentee landlordism and tenancy in the West, Professor Gates states:

> The swift rise of tenancy is one of the most striking features of the history of the American prairies. Careful observers had no occasion to be shocked in 1880 at the publication of the first census statistics showing that this rise for tenancy dated almost from the very beginning of white settlement. A government land policy that permitted large-scale purchasing by speculators bears its responsibility for this early appearance and rapid growth of tenancy. The rise in land values that set in during and after the Civil War, and, of course, the increasing rents made it difficult for laborers and tenants to acquire ownership while the increasing capital demands of prairie agriculture and the unfavorable prices that produce brought in the seventies, and again in the early nineties, tended to depress many farm owners into the tenant class. . . . Nowhere in America at the end of the Century was tenancy more deeply rooted than in the prairies.[15]

Land Companies in Land Engrossment

During the period prior to the enactment of the Homestead Act in 1862, it became a common practice for speculators in public lands to organize themselves into companies. The process was, however, by no means new. It dates from the colonial period and was continued in the early post-Revolutionary period. Robert Morris, the most prominent land engrosser of this time, made use of this form of association, and it was followed by many others. At the height of the land boom, just pre-

[15]*Ibid.*, pp. 63–64.

ceding the Panic of 1837, a group of New York and New England capitalists, under the leadership of Charles Butler of New York, formed a company called the American Land Company. The authorized capital was $1,000,000—quite a large sum in those days. The specific object of the company was set down as "the purchase of land situated in the United States, particularly in the Western States and territories." It seems, however, that the object was to purchase cotton lands in the southwestern states, "at or near the government price." Anyway, about 70 per cent of the company's capital was applied to this purpose in the first year. To further purchases, the company went heavily into debt. It contracted to buy for $400,000 cotton lands in Mississippi "lately occupied by the Chickaw Indians," and title was to be obtained "directly from the Indians," to be approved by the President. But the most significant purchases of the American Land Company were made in town lots in Chicago, Toledo, and elsewhere. In Chicago the chief agent of the company was William B. Odgen, destined to become Chicago's first mayor and a leading real estate owner and railroad builder in that city.

In addition to the American Land Company, there were numerous other companies organized to operate on the same principles. They did not all originate on American soil. Several were owned and financed by British and Scottish capitalists. Thus George Smith, who later became a multimillionaire—not, however, through land speculation, but by issuing his "circulating notes"—came from Scotland to Chicago "as a prospector" in 1834. Impressed by the possibilities of gain in land speculation, he organized the Scottish Illinois Land Investment Company and acted as its agent. He also acted as agent for other British and Scottish companies and private bankers. Although he is reported to have returned to Scotland with enough dollars to purchase a kingdom, his Scottish Illinois Land Investment Company appears to have "gone by the boards."[16]

Despite the disappointments of some of these foreign speculators in American lands, the Scotch and the British continued to operate as individuals or in groups to buy, hold, and sell American soil. Several

---

[16] See Huston and Russell, *Banking in Illinois*, p. 107.

of the western states, fearing the effects of this absentee ownership, enacted laws to abate or discourage it.

Summary

Summing up the story of the disposal of the public domain in the period immediately preceding and following the passage of the Preemption Act, it can be said that this was an era in which there was the greatest political and economic confusion in the nation's land distribution. The whole question was tied up with the sectional disputes which then tormented the Republic, and because of the struggle between the southern interests, who wanted public lands sold as a source of national revenue, and the northern capitalists and western pioneers, who were experiencing difficulty in developing their holdings and gaining a livelihood, little or nothing was accomplished toward an orderly system of land distribution. The leading critic of public land policy in this period was Horace Greeley, who questioned the whole basis of the public-sale feature and the high price the government exacted for raw, unimproved land. He argued that for every dollar the government received from sales the actual settlers had to pay $2.50 or $3.00 in the form of usury, extra prices, sheriff's fees, and the cost of foreclosing. To penalize the settler by maintaining a system that entailed all these costs was a monstrous crime, in his estimation, and he used the pages of his prominent newspaper, the New York *Tribune,* to attack the land policies in both the East and the West. In this matter he was a potent factor in gaining support for the Republican party, which swept Lincoln into the presidency in 1860.[17]

[17] For an account of the political effects of the administration of the public land laws in this period, see Paul W. Gates, "The Struggle for Land and the 'Irrepressible Conflict,'" in *Political Science Quarterly,* June 1951, Vol. LXVI, pp. 248-54.

Chapter 12

The Public Domain Since the Homestead Act

Congress passed the Homestead Act on May 1, 1862. As in the case of the previous Pre-emption Act, this act was designed to aid the actual settler to obtain ownership of the land. The grant of "free land" to the settler was a question which had agitated Congress for twenty years, and it was closely linked to the slavery question. Successive bills were introduced in Congress to accomplish the purpose, but it was not until after the Republicans won the national election, and southern congressmen were absent, that the act was passed. It was hailed as a liberal land measure, but its implementation was impaired by other national land policies which removed large areas of valuable land from its application. Its benefits were also retarded by fraudulent entries and other unscrupulous practices, such as prevailed during the previous history of the public domain.

Under the Homestead Act, any citizen or any person who had declared his intention of becoming a citizen if twenty-one years of age, or the head of a family if not twenty-one years of age, could acquire a tract of land, already surveyed and not to exceed 160 acres, by maintaining a residence of five years upon the land and by making certain specified improvements thereon. There was one additional provision in the act, one which tended to defeat its very purpose. It was provided that after a six months' residence and improvement the applicant could acquire immediate title to the land by paying $1.25 per acre for it. This was contrary to the purpose of the act, which was to promote a large number of relatively small landowners who would retain title to the land and cultivate it. The right to acquire the land after a short residence, on which merely a log cabin could be built, gave land engrossers an opportunity to acquire favorable and adjoining tracts and thus, in a way, promoted rather than deterred concentration of landownership. It was, therefore, an incentive to fraudulent entries.

In amplification of the original Homestead Act, other public land measures were passed. The first was the Timber Culture Act of 1873. Under this measure a citizen could obtain a patent to 160 acres of land by cultivating trees on 40 acres of it. In 1878 the required acreage of planted trees was reduced to 10 acres. According to Marion Clawson, "probably no other statute was as generally evaded as the Timber Culture Act."[1] There was no limitation on the areas in which it could be applied, regardless of the unlikelihood of growing trees successfully on the land. Thus a patentee could plant and cultivate trees in an essentially prairie country if he planted and cultivated wheat at the same time. He could not be penalized if the wheat grew and the trees did not.

Another supplementary act, passed in 1877, was the Desert Land Act, designed to promote irrigation of arid lands. Like the Homestead Act, it required a period of residence and improvements, but it allowed an entry of 640 acres (later reduced to 320 acres), under the assumption that a larger acreage was required for irrigation. The applicant had to provide a water supply and he was charged a nominal price (usually $1.25 an acre) for the land. This act also is accountable for extensive frauds in acquiring public land. Other important acts relating to the disposition of public lands were: (1) an increase of the maximum area of homesteads to 320 acres in dry farming areas, passed in 1909; (2) the reduction of the residence period on homestead from five to three years, enacted in 1912; and (3) an act granting stockraising homesteaders 640 acres instead of 160, if they acquired land suitable only for stock-raising purposes. This act was passed in 1916.

Perhaps the most unique act relating to public land disposal in recent times was the so-called Carey Act, enacted in 1894. This act provided for large grants of land to states on condition that they be irrigated and, when thus reclaimed, the land be made available to actual settlers

[1] *Op. cit.*, p. 67.

only. Though generally applauded, on the whole the act did not work out well because the states were unable or unwilling to finance irrigation projects or they lacked the technical organization and skill to create them. To remedy the situation, the Reclamation Act of 1902 was passed, which provided for using the revenues from public land sales to finance irrigation construction. In applying the act, however, it was found that much of the land which could be included in an irrigation project was already in private ownership and therefore not available to homesteaders.

Summing up his discussion of the Homestead Act and the various other land acts modeled after it, Marion Clawson, a director of the Bureau of Land Management (the former General Land Office), in his book, *Uncle Sam's Acres*, has this to say:

> [These Acts] were the means whereby large acreages of land passed ... to private ownership. There was a lag between the date at which entries were made and the date at which the land was patented; the minimum lag was specified by law, and this might be extended in various ways. Many homesteads were never "proved up," but were relinquished by the applicant, who was then under certain circumstances free to take up another homestead elsewhere. Many entrymen made additional entries to bring their holdings to the legal limits. Thus, the number of entries is larger than the number of persons who ultimately got homesteads, and also larger than the number receiving patents. ... All told, more than 3 million homestead entries were made. Possibly, two thirds of these were successfully completed, resulting in the disposal of almost 300 million acres. ...[2]

The "Opening Up" of New Lands

As the public domain, subsequent to the Civil War, was rapidly taken up and transferred to private ownership under the various acts of Congress, the choicest lands for entry gradually were exhausted. Accordingly, when the General Land Office opened up new areas for settlement, there was a "rush" of applicants for entry. These "land rushes" were dramatic, but they were tragic episodes in American his-

[2] *Ibid.*, p. 69.

tory. Never was a more insane method of land disposal ever experienced. Wearying of the method previously followed, when long lines of supposed settlers (who in the main were likely to be "stooges" of speculators) confronted the land office having the task of opening up a new public land "strip," the General Land Office in 1889 hit upon another procedure.

The occasion was the opening up of the "Cherokee Strip," a large area of what is now Oklahoma. In this case applicants for land entries were lined up at a starting line and at the sound of a gun were allowed to rush forward to find and settle upon the tract of their choosing. The grand rush, dramatically portrayed in novels and moving pictures, gives the affair an alluring setting—but it resulted in violence, deaths, and frauds. Similar but smaller "openings" occurred in other areas, but the system has now been abandoned. As a substitute, the problem of allotting new openings of disposable public land has been solved by considering simultaneously all applications that are filed, and then, through a lottery, selecting the successful applicants. But it is not likely that there will be many such drawings in the future. Except in Alaska, public lands still available for homestead applications have dwindled almost to the vanishing point.

Frauds and Abuses in the Homestead Era

It was expected that the Homestead Act would not only encourage actual settlement of small holders on the public domain but would, in addition, tend to eliminate the fraud and corruption which had characterized previous periods of land disposal. But this did not generally happen. There were plenty of frauds and abuses, too numerous to mention. The law and its subsequent amendments and additions did not prevent land engrossment. Homesteaders, in many instances, did not really inhabit or improve the land and, after obtaining title to it, readily disposed of it to others, usually to land grabbers.[3] As stated by

---

[3] For the story of Homestead Law abuses, see *Government Handout, A Study in the Administration of the Public Lands,* by H. H. Dunham, New York, 1941. Despite the catch-penny title of this book—a Ph.D. thesis—it is a scholarly and authentic work.

W. A. Phillips, who was a member of the Public Lands Committee of the 43rd Congress:

> The preemption and homestead laws professed to do what they did not. The theory was that the land should be reserved for the cultivators. . . . Neither law secured that end. I have been very much at a loss in different stages of my land experience to determine exactly the sentiment in the public mind that has prevented a wise and far-reaching adjustment of the public land question. It could hardly be an accident. The first idea would be that the speculative and real estate interest was too strong to permit of wholesome, permanent legislation. Such a view . . . is not without foundation. But there may have been something else. Perhaps it was thought by men, not destitute of capacity, that it was desirable as early as possible to have the public domain in private hands, and by making it a chattel, providing for its easy transfer without let or hindrance, they believed all could be thus accommodated. If the hat-maker became dissatisfied with silk, felt and beaver skins, he could sell his blocks and smoothing irons, and buy eighty acres. If the pioneer, who imagined an Arcadia with the genial farmer sitting under his vine and fig tree, got tired of mauling rails, breaking prairie with oxen, and the ague with quinine, he could sell his "place," together with what a young squatter once proposed to sell, "his embediments," and try to get a position as a clerk in a store. . . . Young America might cry "scatter and divide all this national real estate; tangle it with no bars; make it easy to get and easy to sell, and thus it can best serve all interests." I have endeavored to define and exhibit what I have reason to suppose is a strong underlying sentiment. In regard to it I would only say that such a system might do in the squatting era. There is a future coming to the American land system with changed conditions.[4]

Commenting on the same topic, Marion Clawson, who has already been quoted in these pages, lays the blame for failure to prevent land frauds on inadequate administrative personnel. He states:

> More serious than trespass were the extensive frauds that occurred in disposition of federal land. Many laws imposed certain restrictions, such as settlement or improvement, as a condition for obtaining public land; others applied only to . . . swamp or over-

---

[4] W. A. Phillips, *Labor, Land and Law*, pp. 341–42.

flow, or non-mineral lands. The only way the Nation could have known that these conditions were being met would have been to have had an adequate force of competent honest men, freed as far as humanly possible from political pressures, and, of course, themselves divorced from any personal participation in land dealings. Perhaps, even so, it would have been impossible to control settlement and insure that it conformed fully to applicable law. The spirit that made for rapid settlement and conquest of the American continent was one uniquely impatient against restraint of any kind. Laws were invariably a compromise between the goals and objectives of the people in the older areas of the Nation and those of the people on the frontier. The compromises were tolerable to the frontier only because they were not more strictly enforced.[5]

Speaking further on the topic, Mr. Clawson points out serious defects in the land laws. They did not classify lands sufficiently or distinguish between the varying needs of settlers. "The land laws simply were not well designed to meet their ostensible objectives. The Congress did not have adequate personal contact with natural conditions in the public land areas to make wise decisions . . . based on their own knowledge, and they were unwilling to appropriate adequate funds to make the necessary investigations." They failed time and again to correct deficiencies in the laws called to their attention by the administrator of the laws.[6]

Concerning the effects of land engrossment by private capitalists, who garnered large tracts under the lax administration of the public domain, Professor Gates of Cornell University, who, as already stated, more than any other scholar has studied the land history of the Middle West, has this to say:

> Cattle kings and bonanza farmers retarded the growth of the community first by using their land extensively and later by encouraging and even requiring abusive and careless farm practices. Hired hands and shiftless tenants worked the land which small farm owners might otherwise have acquired. The hired hands were migratory workers who were undependable, drank heavily, sometimes shirked their work, and were frequently in trouble

[5] *Op. cit.*, pp. 83–84.
[6] *Ibid.*

with the law. The tenants, having no hope of acquiring ownership of the land they farmed, had little initiative to make improvements or to farm properly. Their chief concern was to raise the largest possible corn crop—their principal source of cash. Some of the second and third generation heirs of the cattle kings, especially if absentee landlords, showed a tendency to extract as much from the land as possible. Even where the modern farm manager was employed he also had a strong motive to make favorable cash rent returns to his employer. Some great estates developed into rural slums in the nineteenth century and even in the twentieth century exhibited backward social features that would shame poorer sections elsewhere.[7]

The evil has been done! The effects are not yet fully manifest! But the wasteful and inordinate manner of the distribution of the vast public domain is bound to have serious repercussions in the future. Despite the abundance of land, which Thomas Jefferson said would be enough for all for many generations to come, there still is in America, in large numbers, "the landless man." Landlordism and absentee ownership not only have persisted and prevailed but, as has been the experience of older nations, are increasing and more widely spread. The "land question" may be ignored economically and politically for some time to come, but it is bound to be a disturbance in the future unless proper action is taken to solve it.[8] We are land animals, and all of our material wealth, whether gadgets or airplanes, comes

---

[7] "Cattle Kings in the Prairies," in the *Mississippi Valley Historical Review*, December 1948, Vol. XXXV, p. 411.

[8] For a detailed account of the disposal policies of the public domain from 1900 to 1950, see E. Louise Peffer, *The Closing of the Public Domain*. In the concluding paragraphs of this historical study, p. 340, the author states:

"The attitude of the people of the United States toward their vast land holdings has been traditionally one of indifference. Even in the days of greatest public land activity, the interested public was small. It has been possible from time to time to arouse opinion sufficiently to obtain new public land legislation; it has never been able to sustain that interest for long. The public, until disaster stunned it into thought in the early 1930's, retained the old romantic view of the public domain—when it recalled that there was one.

"The old public domain of land open to entry and settlement has, like the American frontier, lost its significance in the contemporary scene. The closing phase has not been a heartening one, although it is difficult to see how it could have been otherwise."

from the application of labor to land and the products of land. Land is the ultimate source of whatever we produce and it is also the common inheritance of all living people, for them to use in common in their lifetime and to pass on under the rights of natural law to those who will come after them.

The California and New Mexico Land Grants

Before completing the history of the disposal of the public domain, there is yet to be considered: (1) the enormous grants to railroads and educational institutions, and (2) the grants, both valid and invalid, claimed by individuals and corporations that were made or claimed to have been made under the Spanish and Mexican regimes in California and New Mexico.

California occupies an exceptional situation as an episode in American land history. The discovery of gold there in 1848 soon after the American occupation drew a large movement of population to the region. They were not all "gold diggers." Among them were adventurers of all sorts seeking new riches. Many turned their attention to land acquisitions. "In all the new States of the Union," wrote Henry George in 1871, "land monopolisation has gone on at an alarming rate, but in none of them so fast as in California, and in none of them, perhaps, are the evil effects so manifest."[9] George evidently had in view the claims to vast territories which were put forward by individuals and corporations of almost all types, under grants purporting to come from both Spanish and Mexican sources—claims which, if valid, the United States, under treaty obligation, was bound to respect.

As had occurred previously in Texas, the Mexican Government, through its appointees, was exceedingly liberal in California in giving away parts of its public domain. It is estimated that prior to the American conquest there were approximately eight hundred "grants" to individuals. These comprised about eight million acres, or about one quarter of the cultivable area of the whole state. It was a wonderful opportunity for land-jobbers to acquire these "grants" from the reputed owners and to resell them, in whole or in part, at a profit.

[9] *Our Land and Land Policy*, p. 36.

Many of the Mexican grants were of a conditional nature, and legal titles in most instances were doubtful. Their validity had to be determined. As in the case of Louisiana a half century previous, Congress appointed a commission to investigate land titles in California and New Mexico. Owners of grants were called upon to prove their titles. In many instances this they could not do, since they had received no deeds or patents. Verbal gifts by governors and prefects had been quite common. All this made a wonderful harvest for lawyers, speculators, and politicians. "He was not much of a lawyer in those days," remarks Hubert Howe Bancroft, the California historian, "who had not a Mexican Grant in his pocket, the title to which his client paid for."[10]

The work of the California Lands Commission extended over many years, and there are probably cases still pending. It would be exceedingly tiring to cover even a substantial portion of the fraud, deceit, speculation, and villainy that prevailed in the settlement of titles to California lands. A group of Philadelphia speculators are reported to have established headquarters in San Francisco for the purpose of acquiring Mexican grant claims. Local politicians, financiers, and nonresident capitalists also sought to obtain windfalls by buying up the claims. The numerous reports submitted to Congress by the land-office officials and the special land commissioners appointed to investigate the claims contain frequent references to these fraudulent land-grabbing operations.

Among the prominent land grants declared fraudulent or invalid were the Limantour Claim (600,000 acres), the Santillan Grant, and the Mariposa Estate, the latter held by General John C. Frémont. Claims confirmed were 326,000 acres to the De La Guerra family, and 532,000 acres to the brothers Pio and Andre Pico. Both of these claimants failed to exploit their holdings and died poor.

Despite the culling of the Mexican land claims, California, according to Henry George and later investigators, has more large landed estates than any other state in the Union. From a report of the California Tax Commission, three hundred landed proprietors in 1916 owned over four million acres "capable of intensive cultivation and of

[10]*Retrospection*, p. 309.

supporting a dense population." The report states further: "The evil of such ownership in each year is becoming more apparent. We have at the end of the social scale a few rich men who as a rule do not live on their estates, and at the other end, a body of shifting laborers or farm tenantry. And so much for California, with more to come."

Mexican Land Grants in New Mexico

The story of jobbing in Mexican grants would not be complete without some reference to the land deals in California's sister state, New Mexico. The grants in New Mexico, like those in California, covered large areas of vacant lands and the boundaries were indifferently described. The grantees, also, claimed larger acreages than the patents called for. The reputed conveyances, moreover, were made much earlier than those west of the Sierras.

Following the cession of the Mexican territory to the United States, American speculators stepped in and acquired the most important claims. The titles to these New Mexican land claims were as troublesome to settle as those in California. Congress, however, did not take up the problem until a decade or more later, after the California mess was attended to. The courts, moreover, were slow in adjudicating New Mexico claims, and as late as 1890 there were still 107 claims pending. Most of these were not settled until 1904. Here, also, the lawyers found the land-claim business highly lucrative. One who became extremely wealthy was Stephen B. Elkins, in later life a United States Cabinet officer and a United States senator from West Virginia.

George W. Julian, who in 1885 was appointed United States Surveyor General of New Mexico, accused Elkins of buying up the Spanish grants at a small price and then, largely through his political influence, having the survey of the grants made to contain hundreds of thousands of acres that did not belong to them. By such methods, Julian stated, "more than 10 million acres of public domain in New Mexico became the spoil of land grabbers."[11]

Senator Elkins made himself conspicuous as a hero in successfully prosecuting the notorious Maxwell Grant. In 1864, Lucien Benjamin

[11] See *History of New Mexico, Its Resources and Its People,* Vol. I, p. 183.

Maxwell, one of the most striking early figures along the Rocky Mountain frontier, acquired from Carlos Beaubien and Guadalupe Miranda, original grantees, a tract of land in northern New Mexico that comprised almost the whole of present Colfax County, an area about three times the size of Rhode Island. Here Maxwell resided as a feudal baron, but his principal income was from sheep raising. The discovery of gold on his domain gave him plenty of excitement. He invested large sums in the development of placer mining. Like Sutter in California, he was met by an army of squatters and free-lance miners who refused to be ousted. In order to save the remnant of his fortune he sold his grant to an English syndicate for $1,250,000, which in turn organized it into the Maxwell Land Grant and Railroad Company. The Hon. Stephen B. Elkins was made its president.

All this was done before the validity of the grant was affirmed. This came in time, but meanwhile the company experienced financial difficulties. In 1875 it became bankrupt. Its lands were sold for unpaid taxes and its personal property disposed of at a sheriff's sale. Among the principal sufferers from the event were Dutch financiers who had purchased the bonds of the bankrupt concern.[11a]

Another notorious New Mexico land claim, which became a securities gamble and which, in 1893, was adjudged a criminal forgery, was the so-called Peralta-Reavis Grant. The promoter was James Addison Reavis, a St. Louis real estate dealer who, before he petitioned Congress to validate the supposed grant of 1,300,000 acres, sold releases to squatters on the land. The Southern Pacific paid him $50,000 for a right of way through the property. He obtained additional cash from other sources. But in 1889 the grant was declared to be an out-and-out forgery. He was subsequently convicted on this charge and spent two years in prison. The attorney who prosecuted the case remarked: "In all the annals of crime there is no parallel. This monstrous edifice of forgery, perjury and subornation was the work of one man. No plan

---

[11a]For further history of the Maxwell Grant see Herbert C. Brayer, *William Blackmore: The Spanish-Mexican Land Grants of New Mexico and Colorado 1863–1878*, passim.

was ever more ingeniously devised: None ever carried out with greater patience, skill and effrontery."[12]

Summation of Land-Disposal Policies

To enumerate adequately the shortcomings and errors of the public land-disposal policies is out of the question in this volume. The preceding pages, however, have indicated many of these shortcomings, and it is not necessary to repeat or enumerate them here. Perhaps it is best merely to quote from the most recent work relating to the land question, the excellent treatise, *Land Problems and Policies,* by V. Webster Johnson and Raleigh Barlow, and published by the McGraw-Hill Book Company in 1954. Commenting on the disposal policies in the distribution of the public domain, these two writers state:

> Perhaps the most fateful and potentially tragic development was the consistent adoption of alodial tenure in fee simple. This conferred on the individual owner a virtually unrestricted right of use and abuse, limited in practice only by the legal doctrine of nuisance, the tenuous application of the police power and the power of taxation subject to the constitutional principle of "due process."
> Much can be said of the granting of broad fee-simple rights of ownership. These grants fitted in with the virile pioneer spirit and in many ways influenced the rapid . . . development of frontier areas. . . . At the same time, however, the almost unrestricted right of use and abuse of land has resulted in devastation of a major portion of our forests, rapid dissipation of mineral resources, and serious deterioration of a large proportion of our range resources, and the social dislocations that flow from these devastations.[13]

[12]For a detailed account of the Reavis fraud see the magazine *Land of Sunshine,* Los Angeles, February and March 1898.
[13]Pp. 57–59.

Chapter 13

Texas Land Disposal

Texas alone among the states admitted to the Union after the adoption of the Constitution possessed and retained a public domain. This is because Texas, unlike the other states, was an independent republic at the time of its admission. But the interest of settlers and speculators in Texas lands began several decades before its annexation in 1845. And the story of Texas land disposal bears all the earmarks of the American system. It is a story of land engrossment, political corruption, and fraud. Concerning this, O. Henry, the noted author and a Texan, writing in 1894, stated:

> Volumes could be filled with accounts of the knavery, the double dealing, the cross purposes, the perjury, the lies, the bribery, the alterations and erasing, the suppressing and the destroying of papers, the various schemes and plots that for the sake of the almighty dollar have left their stain on the records of the [Texas] General Land Office. A class of land speculators, commonly called land sharks, unscrupulous and greedy, have left their trail in every department of this office, in the shape of titles destroyed, patents cancelled, homes demolished and torn away, forged transfers and lying affidavits.[1]

As early as 1827, Moses Austin, who then resided in Mine-a-Burton in Missouri and operated a lead mine under a presumed Spanish concession which was taken from him by the United States authorities, heard that the old Spanish system of granting land to colonizers or

[1] Quoted from Alfred N. Chandler, *Land Title Origins*, p. 453.

empresarios was still in vogue in Texas, and he undertook a journey to Bexar, then the capital of the province of Texas. Here he presented a petition to the Mexican Government for a land grant. Through the influence of an old Louisiana acquaintance, Baron de Bastrop (who had previously received a Spanish grant on the Ouachita River), the petition was finally granted and was sent to the Spanish governor for approval. Reaching home on March 23, 1821, after a journey of much suffering and privation, he immediately began advertising for settlers on his grant but died shortly thereafter.[2]

Moses Austin's oldest son, Stephen F. Austin, who at the time of his father's death was in New Orleans looking for a means of livelihood, decided to carry out the colonization scheme when he learned that the Spanish authorities in Mexico had approved the grant made to his father. The grant was for a tract of about 200,000 acres on the Colorado River, about 200 miles from Natchitoches, an American western border town. Three hundred families were to be settled on the grant, after which the unappropriated land was to go to the *empresario* as a premium. It was this premium land, together with the commissions charged settlers, that was the compensation Austin was after. He advertised widely for settlers and, despite disappointments and difficulties, carried out the project.

Before setting out to establish his colony, Austin issued a letter describing his plan. The colonists were to be given land in accordance with the size of their families and the number of their slaves. They were to settle on the land and make improvements thereon within a year. Each colonist was to pay $12.50 per hundred acres, payable in installments, in return for a survey and drawing up of papers.

Before Austin could settle his colony, Mexico threw off the Spanish yoke and he had to go to Mexico City to get a new confirmation of his

[2]Moses Austin, who had trekked from Connecticut to western Virginia and thence to Missouri, where he resided for several decades near St. Genevieve, became impoverished through speculation in the New Madrid Claims—certificates representing claims to land awarded by Congress to sufferers from the New Madrid earthquake in 1811. His troubles were further increased by the refusal of the Louisiana Land Claims Commission to validate his Spanish grant, on which he operated a lead mine. Becoming disgusted with the country "that ruined him," he resolved to immigrate again into Spanish territory.

grant. He remained there many months and made the acquaintance of General James Wilkinson and General Arthur G. Wavell, the latter an Englishman. Both of these ex-military men were interested in obtaining land grants. Wavell and Austin agreed to share in future Texas land grants they expected to receive.

In the meantime, other American speculators and adventurers were after Texas lands. From 1820 to 1840 this large area, occupied only by roving fierce Indian tribes, whom the Mexicans feared and wanted settlers to act as a barricade, was a lure to the land-hungry. From the swamps of Florida to the hills of Kentucky and Ohio, the sign G.T.T. ("Gone to Texas") could be found on many cabin doors. Some went to find new homes. But many were lured by the hope of land grants. Some of the wealthier ones organized Texas land companies. English translations of the Mexican colonization laws were distributed throughout the United States to awaken public interest, and glowing accounts were published regarding Austin's colony. Shares in Texas land associations and land companies were peddled to speculators in all parts of the country. Among the earliest of the Texas land companies was the Texas Association, organized in Nashville, Tennessee, about 1821. Sam Houston, destined to become the first President of Texas, was one of the original stockholders.

The independence of Texas wrested from Mexico after the Battle of San Jacinto increased the intensity of "the Texas fever." The task of distributing the unoccupied land was then transferred to the government of the new Republic of Texas, and the old Spanish policy of granting huge tracts to *empresarios,* individuals or companies who contracted to bring in settlers, was continued.

Oppressed by a heavy national debt, along with a severely depreciated currency, the new regime was in dire need of funds. And it was "land-poor." The result was that contracts were signed with numerous persons, mostly American adventurers, providing for the settlement of the Texas public domain. The contractors, who agreed to bring in a minimum number of families, each family to receive 320 acres, were to be rewarded with "premium land"—i.e., land not reserved for settlers. Some of the better known of these colonies were located in the north-central part of the state and extended from a point southeast of Dallas, north to the Red River, and far to the west. Among them may be mentioned the Peters, Mercers, Castro, and Fisher and Miller colonies. In extent, each covered an area as large as some of the smaller eastern states of the Union. The settlers who were brought in were largely Americans, but there were also Germans and Alsatians brought in by Henry Castro and the partners, Miller and Fisher.

In addition to these colonizing projects, the Republic of Texas and the state that succeeded it, anxious to increase population within its territory, offered land under a "headright" system and freely gave land as bounties to soldiers and others. After the liberation from Mexican rule, any immigrant who was the head of a family could receive a certificate for 1,280 acres, and a single man a certificate for 640 acres, provided they remained in the republic three years and performed the duties of citizenship. The amounts were reduced on October 1, 1837, to 640 acres and 320 acres, respectively. The total acreage granted under "headrights" and bounties is estimated at 36,876,492 acres.[3]

Another method of disposing of Texas lands was the sale of "land certificates." This was a means of obtaining needed cash by the debt-oppressed government. By an act of the Texas Legislature on December 10, 1836, the President of the republic was authorized to issue land scrip to be sold by agents in the United States for not less than fifty cents per acre. The most famous agent for this scrip was Thomas Tobey, who operated in New Orleans. This "Tobey scrip" floated throughout most of the United States and was almost as common as U.S. savings bonds are today. It was distributed during the wild era of land speculation which dominated the nation in the 1830s. As late as July 14, 1879, the state of Texas authorized further sale of land scrip at fifty cents an acre, most of the land being situated in western sections of the state. Altogether, the certificates sold represented almost three million acres.[4]

Galveston Bay and Texas Land Company

While *empresarios* and actual settlers were gradually filling eastern

[3]See Curtis Bishop, *Lots of Land*.
[4]*Ibid*.

Texas with immigrants during the decade between 1820 and 1830, a gigantic scheme of Texas land speculation was set on foot in the United States. This took the name of the Galveston Bay and Texas Land Company. It was organized in New York on October 16, 1830, to exploit the so-called "contracts of Lorenzo de Zavala, Joseph Vehlein and David G. Burnett to settle colonists on land in southern Texas." The region comprised the Galveston Bay district—a most desirable site—which Stephen F. Austin had endeavored to obtain from the Mexican Government as early as 1824.

The so-called "contractors" pooled their interests and, with the aid of several New York and Boston capitalists, formed an "association" to take over the rights. Three members of the association, Anthony Day and George Curtis of New York, and William H. Summer of Boston, were appointed trustees of the shareholders, to promote the fulfillment of the contracts and to obtain the approval of the Mexican Government. The Board of Directors of the company comprised several of the leading figures of the period in New York's financial circles. Chief of these was Lynde Catlin, president of the Merchants Bank—one of the prominent banking institutions in New York City at the time. Others were the Joseph brothers, who were then representatives in New York of the Rothschilds. The Joseph brothers were heavily involved in the financing of Texas land deals and were associated in this field with Samuel Swartout, a prominent New York politician, who, as Collector of the Port of New York, never accounted for over a million dollars of government funds.

Though Swartout's name does not appear among the directors of the Galveston Bay and Texas Land Company, he was undoubtedly interested. His family had started trading in Texas and carried on a shipping business between New York and Texas ports. Swartout's interest in Texas affairs continued until the financial crash of 1837, and he was one of the subscribers, along with J. L. and S. Joseph & Co., to the Texas Republic Loan floated in New York in 1836. The loan was not a success and so Swartout wrote Austin: "Nothing but lands will satisfy the lenders, and that at a low rate." He advised the republic to "let your lands pay the expenses of the war, if you sell them only at 5¢ per acre."[5]

The Galveston Bay and Texas Land Company sent General John W. Mason of Michigan to Mexico City to get the Mexican Government's approval of the contracts. The company had already invested $125,000 and was anxious to see some return from this investment. Mason offered to settle twelve hundred families before January 1, 1838, if the grants were approved and if the Mexican Government would permit the entry of the settlers and allow them to hold lands.

Despite these offers, the proposition fell flat. Beyond sending out fifty-seven "emigrants" as an advance guard, who were not even permitted to make a landing in Texas, nothing further was accomplished. However, in the meantime, the promoters of the company issued stock to themselves and sold "Texas scrip" broadcast. They also issued a pamphlet in which it was subtly hinted that there was some uncertainty whether the contractors' grants they had acquired could be legally assigned to others. Moreover, at the time, Mexico had passed a law forbidding further admittance of American settlers in Texas.[6]

The "Texas scrip" of the Galveston Bay and Texas Land Company, which was sold at from five to ten cents an acre, carried a claim to land but gave no title of ownership or even a pre-emption, except in the event that the number of applications from emigrants exceeded the number required. Under such condition the company would select land for scrip holders who desired to emigrate. But few of the scrip holders cared to emigrate. They speculated on a rising value of the scrip. As a writer in the *North American Review* remarked: "Such is the cupidity and blindness, that anything that looks fair on paper passes, without scrutiny, for a land title in Texas." Thus was a gigantic fraud fostered on the American people.[7]

The rapid colonization of Texas by American and foreign immigrants

[5] See *The Austin Papers*, Vol. III, p. 342. Also Dyer, *Early History of Galveston*, p. 4.
[6] See *Address to the Reader of Documents Relating to the Galveston Bay and Texas Land Company*, pp. 4–7.
[7] The Galveston Bay and Texas Land Company was not connected with the Galveston City Company, which bought land, sold shares, and developed the city of Galveston.

under the *empresario* or contract system, whereby, in return for bringing in settlers, the contractor was given a commission payable in land, was destined to bring about the loss of the vast province to Mexico. Like the Americans of the colonial period, the American-Texans became dissatisfied with "Mexican tyranny" when this tyranny attempted to restrict the system of land settlement. As already noted, the Mexican Government in 1831, wishing to curb the heavy influx of undesirable non-Catholic immigrants, issued an order forbidding settlers to come into Texas except when destined for colonies whose loyalty had been tested. This was treated by many Texans of American origin as "a scrap of paper," much like the British Proclamation of 1763 against colonial western settlement.

Through Austin's influence, however, the order was repealed, but thereafter, instead of using the *empresario* system, the Mexican Government substituted direct sales to speculators—preferably to its own citizens. Some of these so-called "Seven-League Grants" were bought up by speculators.

The object of the Texas provincial government at the time was to obtain funds for its distressed treasury. This reckless policy of disposing of the soil aroused indignation among the Anglo-Texans, and they revolted. However, as already indicated, when the Texans achieved their independence they, likewise in need of revenue for their government, used much the same methods and granted tracts, constituting principalities in size, to "contractors" and proceeded by other means to dispose recklessly of the domain for mere pittances. Land was given liberally for educational purposes—the largest grant was to the University of Texas. There were also grants for eleemosynary institutions, for internal improvements, for ironworks, and for the building of railroads.[8] Texas, like the federal government today, now has a relatively small acreage of

---

[8]Until the Texas public domain was exhausted, railroad promoters were granted sixteen, in some instances thirty-two, alternate sections of 640 acres each for each mile of railroad built and put into operation. These grants, which ran to thirty-two million acres, were often illegally and fraudulently acquired, and the promoters obtained more land than they were entitled to receive. Chandler, *op. cit.*, p. 459. S. G. Reed, *History of the Texas Railroads,* pp. 129–31.

public domain left, for of the 171,000,000,000 acres in the state, not more than 5 per cent is undisposed of or unoccupied.

When the fabulous wealth of the soil of Texas, with its fertile lands and underlying mineral and oil resources, is taken into consideration, one can look back with amazement at the recklessness and waste that characterized its disposal. Today in Texas individuals and corporations own vast domains. As cattle ranges or as goat farms, as cotton or onion fields, as oil pools or sulphur deposits, these lands have gained immensely in value, creating millionaires of some and paupers of others. All the incalculable wealth involved grew up as civilization advanced. The fruits of ownership belong to a relatively few. The growth and development were the work of many.

Chapter 14

The Early Railroad Land Grants

Almost from the beginning of the distribution of the public domain it was the policy of Congress to donate land for local improvements and public use. Thus, in 1796, Congress granted three tracts of land, each a mile square, to Ebenezer Zane, who constructed a road in Ohio—"Zane's Trace"—and who conducted a ferry in the neighborhood of Zanesville. Also, it should be borne in mind that under the early land acts there were reserved for public use or disposal in each township sections for educational and religious purposes. Land was also donated directly to the states for road building. It was not until 1833, however, when the canal and railroad mania was at its height, that a grant on a wholesale scale was made for a public improvement. In that year Congress gave Illinois the right to apply to railroad construction the national land that had previously been granted the state for construction of the Illinois and Michigan canal. Little was it realized then that this act was the beginning of land-jobbing promotion on a tremendous scale, and, though aimed to benefit material progress, it would carry in its wake rampant speculation, townsite jobbing, political corruption, and downright fraud.

During the fever of violent speculation which characterized the period of rapid western settlement from about 1820 to 1837, it was frequently suggested, and even importuned, that internal improvements be fostered by free gifts of public land. There was then a craze for canals and turnpikes, for bridges and railroads. Landholders wanted these in order to enhance the value of their properties. The promoters of the improvements wanted land so that they could reap the profits which would come from rents accruing to higher land values as well as from the income derived directly from the utilities. Thus land was the bait! Land was the quarry!

The use of the public land as a bait to promote economic development was advocated in all sections of the country. No political party was opposed to it and no geographical section complained about it. As early as 1828, Daniel Webster, staunch "Old State" New Englander, advocated in a speech at Faneuil Hall, Boston:

> In most of the new States of the West, the United States are yet proprietors of vast bodies of land. Through some of these States and sometimes through these same public lands, the local authorities have prepared to carry expensive canals, for the general benefit of the country. Some of these undertakings have been attended with great expense, and have subjected the States ... to large debts and heavy taxation. The lands of the United States, being exempted from all taxation, of course bear no part of this burden. Looking at the United States, therefore, as a great land proprietor, essentially benefited by these improvements, I have felt no difficulty in voting for the appropriation of parts of these lands, as a reasonable contribution by the United States to these general objects.[1]

With this reasoning, other statesmen of the time voted to distribute in both modest and in large quantities parts of the national heritage of free land. River improvements, wagon roads, canals, and railroads received cessions of the public domain.

Early Grants to Railroads

Railroads became the largest beneficiaries of the congressional largesse. After 1840, the railroad rage took precedence over the canal craze. Real estate developments and land booming went hand in hand with railroad construction. Rail highways were promoted in many cases, not with the idea of profiting from their operation, but with the prime motive of increasing town and rural land values. Large landowners of the period were therefore concerned in early railroad projects. Thus,

---

[1]Daniel Webster, *Works,* Vol. I, p. 169.

soon after the organization of the Baltimore & Ohio Railroad in 1823, a group of capitalists, some of whom were promoters of the project, formed the Canton Company in Baltimore. They acquired a large tract of land near the city that could be served by the railroad. They expected the value of this land to increase greatly because of both access to the railroad and the harbor. Although the Canton Company and the railroad company remained separate corporations for over a century, their interests coincided. It was not until 1930 that the Canton Company came under the control of the Pennsylvania Railroad, but not without protest of the rival carrier, the Baltimore & Ohio Railroad.

The right of railroads to hold and dispose of real estate was regarded as a special advantage by early railroad promoters. The original prospectus of the Mt. Carmel and New Albany Railroad of Indiana in 1838 took note of this: "Were the Company to purchase a million acres of land adjacent to the work, *the increase alone* in the price of the lands so purchased would, before the work is half completed, pay for the entire construction of the work. The bare location of the route would triple the price of every acre of land within two miles of it. All that is wanted is capital to invest in lands, and go on with the work for a short time without being compelled to make sale of them."[2]

In the same belief, individuals and corporations eagerly granted rights of way over their properties to railroads in order to enhance the value of the portions they retained. Donations of lands, both public and private, to transportation companies as a speculation thus became an established policy. Overbuilding of railroads and canal facilities was a logical result. Waste of capital and political logrolling were evils that accompanied the nation's material progress.

Illinois Central Railroad—The First Large Railroad Land Grant

Although Congress had previously granted lands to corporations and individuals for the purpose of creating and maintaining public utilities of various kinds, the first substantial grant for a railroad enterprise was not made until 1850. In that year the Illinois Central Railroad was or-

---

[2] See Cleveland and Powell, *Railroad Promotion*, p. 199.

ganized. As early as 1836, however, Congress was petitioned for a land grant for a similar enterprise.[3] A similar measure was advocated by Senator Sidney Breese in 1844. He desired to secure for the proposed Great Western Railroad of Illinois the right of pre-emption of public land along its lines. This meant that the railroad would pay the government price for the land, if it were acquired, but of course the lands would be paid for only as they were sold at an advance above the government price. Hence it is quite evident that early railroad building in the West was closely interlaced with land speculation.

Congress had already made a gift of public land to Illinois in 1827, in aid of the construction of a canal between Chicago and the Illinois River in order to create a "Great Lakes to Gulf Waterway." This project and the land donation engendered a fever of land speculation in the region around Chicago. Before the route of the canal was even marked out, lands supposedly adjacent to it increased rapidly in value. William B. Ogden, who, as already noted, previously went to Chicago in the interests of the American Land Company, wrote on May 3, 1836, that he purchased nearly two thousand acres along the canal at five dollars per acre. "It is considered a good investment at $10," he stated, "for it would not be only on the canal, but near the flourishing town of Joliet." In Chicago, "canal lots" brought ridiculously high prices, but most of the sales were canceled because of defaults in payment following the financial crash in May 1837.

As the canal was slow in building and costly, and as railroads were demonstrating their superiority over other means of transportation, Illinois sought to apply the canal land grant to construction of a railroad. Though Congress consented to this diversion in 1833, the grant was not used because of the curb on internal improvements caused by the 1837 Panic and the bankrupt condition of the Illinois State Treasury. However, in 1836 one Darius B. Holbrook, an Illinois town-jobber who was interested in promoting Cairo City, obtained a charter for the Illinois Central Railroad Company. He petitioned Congress for a land grant under a new Illinois charter. He was opposed in the Senate by Stephen

[3] See *American State Papers,* "Public Lands," Vol. VIII, p. 593.

Douglas, then senator from Illinois, on the ground that Holbrook's railroad was "a stupendous private speculation to enable the Cairo Company to sell their chartered privileges in England."

Douglas offered a substitute plan. He proposed a land grant directly to the state of Illinois, to be used in aid of private railroad construction. This bill was enacted by Congress on September 20, 1850. It did not convey a definite acreage. It granted alternate sections of land (each one mile square), extending six miles on both sides of a railroad to be built as part of a rail line between Mobile, Alabama, and the city of Chicago. Because only alternate sections were granted, speculators could not obtain directly from the railroad company large contiguous tracts. Moreover, if the railroad's lands rose in value, the government's sections would rise proportionately. Thus the government might participate equally with the railroad in the profits obtained from the land grants. This pattern, designed primarily to block monopolization of land along the railroad, was continued in all subsequent grants.

Capitalists were attracted by the possibility of enriching themselves through control of the land grant that promised such swift appreciation in value as virtually to provide the cost of building the Illinois Central Railroad. A group of wealthy New York and Boston bankers, brokers and railroad men, mostly Whigs, induced Robert Rantoul, Democratic senator from Massachusetts, to present their request for the grant and a charter to the predominately Democratic legislature of Illinois. Success came to Rantoul's efforts; the land grant and charter were secured.[4] To attract attention to the lands, Rantoul wrote a typical real estate advertisement of the time entitled *Letter on the Value of Public Lands in Illinois,* in which he spoke enthusiastically of the worth of the lands to the railroad project and predicted that the Illinois Central lands would in ten years rise to from $10 to $12 an acre.

He was not wrong. In scarcely ten years thereafter the Illinois Central Railroad announced that it had 1,100,000 acres, less than one half of the original grant, still for sale at $5.00 to $25 per acre. Meantime,

[4] Paul W. Gates, *The Illinois Central Railroad and Its Colonization Work,* pp. 44 ff.

the government-reserved sections had been quickly snatched up, mostly by speculators.

It can be readily assumed that the early speculative interest created in the Illinois Central Railroad was based upon its land grant. An English capitalist, reporting on the company in 1856, wrote: "This is not a railroad company, it is a land company." Anthony Trollope, the English novelist, who visited the United States during the Civil War, made a similar remark: "Railroad Companies," he wrote, "were in fact companies combined for the purchase of land. They purchased land, looking to increase the value of it five fold by the opening of the railroad . . . it is in this way that the thousands of miles of railroads in America have been opened."[5]

The main activity of the Illinois Central promoters in the early period was to sell lands. They advertised them extensively in alluring pamphlets both at home and abroad. Moreover, the company was enabled to obtain cash by mortgaging its lands (though of course it had legal title only to such sections along which its lines were already constructed). A large part of the land profit was expected to come from the sale of lots in towns of its own creation. A station was established every ten miles and the surrounding plots divided into lots which were offered at various prices according to the prospects of the location. Town-jobbing and railroad building thus went hand in hand.

Altogether, the Illinois Central Railroad Company received about 2,600,000 acres. In less than twenty years after obtaining the grant, only about 450,000 acres were unsold. A complaint was made to Congress in 1870 that the company was then "holding its land for advance in prices, instead of offering them to settlers."

The records of the General Land Office in Illinois show heavy sales along the line of the railroad to large and influential speculators at the minimum price of $2.50 per acre or slightly above it for the alternate sections. Stephen A. Douglas, John Wentworth, John S. Wright, and other prominent names appear among purchasers. Not only did politicians and land boosters buy land along the railroad, but they sought

[5] See William K. Ackerman, *Early Illinois Railroads*, p. 75, and Anthony Trollope, *North America*, Vol. I, p. 143.

to influence the location of the route. Jesse Fell of Bloomington, Illinois, a large western land-jobber, was instrumental in getting the Illinois Central to Clinton, Decatur, Bloomington, and other towns in which he held real estate. All this fostered political "wire pulling and corruption."

The land grant to the Illinois Central led to a host of similar projects. Congress was swamped with petitions. Every townsite promoter or landed nabob put in applications. The western congressmen, in whose states were vast stretches of public domain, were kept busy backing up the claims of their constituencies for federal aid in railroad promotion. In these activities, corruption, bribery, logrolling, and other questionable political practices flourished.

Horace Greeley, whose slogan "Go West, young man," placed him among the friends of the pioneer settlers, could see no need of "hiring or bribing capitalists to construct railroads." He advocated limited land "ownership" as an antidote to land speculation, and he even hinted his approbation of "squatter's rights." "The mischiefs already entailed on the Industry and Business of country by Land Speculation," he wrote in his paper, the New York *Tribune,* "are incalculable. . . . Only those who have seen much, reflected much, have any full idea of them. Wherever, upon a natural harbor, a bay, a head of navigation, or a waterfall, a village begins or promises to spring up, there, the speculator or his agent is early on hand, and pounces on the unoccupied land within a circuit of a mile or two. This he holds back for a price treble to sixty-fold that he paid for it."[6] By releasing capital tied up in vast tracts of unproductive land held by speculators, there would be money enough, Greeley thought, to construct railroads without the aid of land grants.

Greeley made a tour of the West in 1847 and while there discovered the heavy traffic in military land warrants. The warrants were bought up in great wads, in both the East and the West, and the owners converted them into large tracts of vacant land of their own selection. They needed settlers to make the lands valuable, but settlers now followed railroads and canals instead of going ahead of them. Hence the numer-

[6] July 17, 1847.

ous railroad projects. Maps in emigrant guides to the western states published in this period show veritable networks of "projected railroads," most of which were never even surveyed. All the "projectors," however, had in mind possible land grants as a means of putting their plans over. "By stimulating the building of roads, where they are not wanted, and where the leading cause for building them is the gift of public lands, we shall throw such discredit (when the breakdown comes) on our western roads, that the building of useful roads will be retarded or indefinitely postponed." Thus wrote John Murray Forbes to Charles Summer on February 14, 1853. Forbes was then engaged in the construction of the Burlington Railroad, which was seeking a land grant for its line in Iowa.[7]

Summary

Sober-minded statesmen realized that railroad operation in the sparsely settled areas of the Great West was not a profitable business proposition. It was different from the transportation situation in the East. Here population centers were already sufficiently large and prosperous to furnish traffic immediately. But in the new states, still in the process of pushing back the Indians and in preparing the soil for human sustenance, rail traffic had to be developed. This required a comparatively long period. Under the circumstances, the prospects of dividends on capital invested in western railroads were remote.

It was therefore not from choice but rather from necessity that the railroads were proffered lands amounting in extent, in some cases, to empires or principalities as a reward or a bait for their construction. On the whole, prospective profits of operating railroads in most sections of the country had little influence in inducing capital investment in these enterprises. The opportunities for making money in land speculation, in townsite projects, in construction contracts and numerous other schemes were more generally the lure than operating legitimate transportation facilities. In some cases, as, for instance, in the Illinois Cen-

---

[7] See Henry G. Pearson, *An American Railroad Builder*, p. 189. See also Richard C. Overton, *Burlington West. A Colonization History of the Burlington Railroad*, pp. 31 ff.

tral, the proprietors of the railroad could have donated the entire original cost of construction and still have realized a capital gain from their land sales. The Illinois Central is reported to have cleared about $25,000,000 from the disposal of its domain. Its success, however, is exceptional. The largest and most richly endowed land-grant railroads were less fortunate. The Union Pacific and Northern Pacific, for example, fell into receivership before they reaped the reward of their land grant. The land-grabbing activities connected with these gigantic ventures will be next considered.

Chapter 15

The Transcontinental Land Grants

Following the Illinois Central land grant in 1850, a number of similar grants were made to encourage the construction of railroads and canals in the Middle West. It was not until the Civil War, however, that Congress finally enacted the Pacific Railroad Act, which for almost two decades was planned and debated in its halls. As early as 1843, Asa Whitney, a New York merchant, published a pamphlet in which he urged the construction of a railroad to the Pacific, to be aided and supported by a grant of public land. The matter was considered seriously by Congress and the nation at large. But the bickering of sectional interests as to the most desirable route prevented Congress from taking action. In 1853, Jefferson Davis, as Secretary of War, sent out parties to make surveys of the most feasible routes, but no agreement could be reached as to which should be chosen.

In the meantime, land speculators and prospectors gambled on the anticipated route. It was not until the secession of the southern states in 1861 that the so-called central route was selected by Congress to connect with the Central Pacific Railroad of California, which began construction at San Francisco under a land grant, the Puget Sound terminus being abandoned. The eastern end of the railroad was to be "on the hundredth meridian of longitude, west from Greenwich, between the South margin of the Republican River, and the North margin of the valley of the Platte River at a point to be fixed by the President of the United States."

The railroad was to have free right of way over government domain and, in addition, *was to be given ten miles on each side in alternate sections.* All this made an aggregate acreage of about 12,000,000 acres —a vast inland empire, the like of which had never before been known to be held in single private ownership.

But this was not all. The government was to furnish a construction loan in 6-per-cent 30-year bonds at the rate of $16,000 per mile of road through the prairies, $48,000 per mile over the Rockies, and $32,000 per mile between the Rockies and the Sierras, not to exceed, however, a total of $50,000,000.

This apparently liberal donation brought out opposition and cries of land-grabbing. But these protests went unheeded and the landless Atlantic states joined with the "land-poor" West in favoring the project. "I give no grudging vote in giving away either money or land," exclaimed the Massachusetts senator, Henry Wilson. "I would sink $100,-000,000 to build the road and do it most cheerfully, and think I had done a great thing for my country. What are $75,000,000 or a $100,-000,000 in opening a railroad across regions of this continent that shall connect the people of the Atlantic and the Pacific, and bind us together? . . . Nothing! As to the lands, I don't begrudge them."

Possibly the senator was right. Twelve million acres was an ocean of territory that would require decades to fill with people. The land was offered by the railroad promoters at from $2.00 to $10 per acre and sold in 40-acre tracts upward, with liberal terms of credit. A vast influx of population would have been required to settle them during the period of construction. Moreover, the Homestead Act of 1862 made it possible to acquire land free of cost, and this competition was a serious handicap to the railroad company in disposing of its vast domain.

But it was not the vast tract of vacant land that attracted speculators. Mere acreage is not what the railroad promoters most desired. *It was the favored townsites, terminals, and way stations that were the objects of pecuniary exploitation.* This is borne out by the town-lot speculation of some of the original proprietors of the Union Pacific Company, the company organized to take over the Pacific railroad project. One of these was the notorious George Francis Train, who formed a company chartered in Nebraska which he called the Crédit Foncier of America.

This is not to be confused with the Crédit Mobilier of America, which also received its name from Train. The latter company undertook the construction of the railroad for the Union Pacific Company. Train endeavored to exploit real estate in Omaha—the eastern terminus of the railroad—and in Columbus, Nebraska, but with apparently little success.

There was hardly a location in any way suitable as a station or a junction point on the proposed rail line that did not develop into a "mushroom city" because of the activity of land speculators.[1] The same may be said of the route of the Central Pacific in California, which had received a similar grant of land in aid of construction. The Southern Pacific, another transcontinental rail project, also came in for a handsome land bounty, and its promoters also became deeply concerned in townsite and terminal land-jobbing.[2] And it was thus with the Northern Pacific project, the story of which we are about to tell.

The Northern Pacific Railroad

A final transcontinental railroad project to which Congress made liberal land grants and which became a football of land speculation was the Northern Pacific Railroad. This road was given twenty sections of land in the states and forty sections in the territories for each mile of main line, together with a four-hundred-foot-wide right of way through the government lands. It was to follow the northern route extending from Lake Superior to Puget Sound. The promoters had the statutory assurance that patents to the contiguous land would be issued as each twenty-five miles were constructed, and that the even-numbered sections retained by the government would not be sold for less than $2.50 per acre. Altogether, the total grant was to be for about 47,000,000 acres.

This free donation of a landed domain larger than all New England attracted at the time little attention, and the act of Congress creating

[1]For some details regarding this, see Sabine, *The Building of the Pacific Railroad, passim.*
[2]See Stuart Daggett, *Chapters on the History of the Southern Pacific.*

it passed without much opposition. "It was a faulty measure," wrote John Sherman in his memoirs, "making excessive grants of public lands. . . . It was an act of incorporation, with broad and general powers, carelessly defined, and with scarcely any safeguards to protect the government and its lavish grant of land. Some few amendments were made, but mostly in the interest of the corporation, and the bill finally passed the Senate without any vote by yeas and nays."[3]

Despite the lavish land grant and strenuous efforts at financing, the company found that it was quite unable to obtain the $100,000,000 required for the road's construction. There was a time limit placed on the period of construction, and they were forced repeatedly to petition Congress for an extension. British capitalists refused to become interested in the project. But rescue came from the then most prominent banker in America, Jay Cooke of Philadelphia. Cooke, "The Financier of the Civil War," had already become financially interested in the Lake Superior and Mississippi Railroad, which was to extend from St. Paul, Minnesota, in a northerly direction to Duluth. This railroad also had a congressional grant of about 1,500,000 acres, mostly timber land. Believing this timber to be a valuable asset of growing value, Cooke extended his landholdings in the region. He was impressed by the commercial advantages of the city of Duluth—"The Zenith City of the Unsalted Seas." This site, he said, must "become an important point as the terminus of the road," and though he admitted it "may not equal Chicago, there must be a large town there within a few years after the road shall be in operation."[4] On the basis of this belief, Cooke, in addition to financing the Lake Superior and Mississippi Railroad, promoted the Western Land Association of Minnesota, a concern similar to that proposed by George Francis Train along the line of the Union Pacific, the object of which was to exploit real estate values in towns along the route.

In extending his land speculations, the next logical step of Cooke was to acquire an interest in the projected Northern Pacific Railroad. He

[3] *Forty Years in the House, Senate and Cabinet*, Vol. I, p. 335.
[4] Ellis Paxson Oberholzer, *Jay Cooke, Financier of the Civil War*, Vol. II, p. 105.

admitted that it was a big proposition. But in May 1869 he reported he "had practically determined to take hold of it." However, on the advice of his partners, he first would have an expert survey the route and the engineering problems involved. The country through which the railroad was to traverse was described by General Sherman "as bad as God ever made or anybody can scare up this side of Africa." The engineers, however, gave favorable reports. The chief engineer, Milnor M. Roberts, stated that "the immense landed property of the company as a body in connection with valuable town sites and water powers will ultimately be worth more than the entire cost of the railroad." And Henry Cooke, Jay's brother and partner, insisted that, "if successful, the financing of the Northern Pacific would be the grandest achievement of our lives."

So in this way Jay Cooke and Company, the leading banking house in America, became identified with the Northern Pacific.

However, before entering the project, Jay Cooke and Company made the following stipulation: "A company shall be organized for the purpose of purchasing lands, improvement of town sites, and other purposes, and the same shall be divided in the same proportion; that is, the original interests shall have one-half and Jay Cooke and Company shall have one-half."

Jay Cooke formed a "pool," in which notables of the time were offered participation, to raise $5,600,000 for financing the project, of which $5,000,000 was represented by bonds and $600,000 by capital stock. With this modest beginning he proceeded to advertise the securities of the Northern Pacific Railroad at home and abroad through pamphlets, circulars, and other means. He gave prominence to the company's land grant, and in a map traced the route of the line encased in its accompanying land. This resembled the shape of a banana, and thus the Northern Pacific came to be known popularly as "Jay Cooke's Banana Belt."

Despite the stupendous efforts put forth to attract investors, which were similar to the methods used by Cooke when he was the selling agent for United States Government bonds, the project was doomed to an initial failure. His firm was forced into bankruptcy on September 18,

1873—and this brought on the financial panic of that year. Not long thereafter, the Northern Pacific Railroad also became bankrupt. However, the land company which Cooke organized in connection with the railroad remained intact, even during the period of the Northern Pacific receivership, which extended into 1875. Its capital stock was acquired by the successor corporation of the Northern Pacific, and its affairs were not wound up until 1891.

The Origin of the "Bonanza Farms"

The Northern Pacific Railroad, before its bankruptcy in 1873, had issued and sold through Cooke's efforts mortgage bonds, which gave the holders the right to convert their holdings at any time into the land of the company at the rate of $2.50 per acre at 110 per cent of face value of the bonds. Few took advantage of this privilege until after the financial collapse. It was then that Jay Cooke openly advised the bondholders to make the exchange as a way out of a bad situation. He had more faith in the future value of the lands than in the profitableness of the railroad.

Several large holders of the Northern Pacific bonds, feeling that it was better to own wastelands than to have a doubtful equity in a partially completed and visionary railroad, engrossed large tracts in the Red River Valley, North Dakota, by converting their bonds. Here the virgin soil was in a condition for cultivation without clearing, and homesteaders had demonstrated that wheat could be grown in this section. Several of these former Northern Pacific bondholders began to grow wheat on a large scale, under absentee ownership, and their properties became known as "bonanza farms." Some of these individual farms had acreages of ten miles square. William Dalrymple, a pioneer bonanza-farm manager, during the years 1876 to 1879 reported yields on his lands of more than twenty bushels of wheat to the acre. At this time, wheat prices were high and Dalrymple estimated net profits of from ten to twelve dollars per acre per annum. The land exchanged for bonds at the depreciated value of the bonds could be purchased during the railroad's receivership at around fifty cents per acre.

Among the owners of the bonanza farms who also were officers of or large investors in the Northern Pacific were General George W. Cass and B. P. Cheney. These, along with others, obtained additional sections by purchase from homesteaders. They employed managers to work the farms and are said to have recovered their losses in the railroad project in a short time. Corporations also engrossed the lands by buying up the Northern Pacific bonds. The American and Sharon Land Company, the Baldwin Corporation, and other concerns consolidated large tracts and worked them as a unit. Thirteen large farm holdings in Minnesota and Dakota at this time included 174,000 acres, or an average of more than 13,000 acres per farm. Gradually it became profitable for the owners to divide up and sell off their large acreages. In this way most of the bonanza farms during the period from 1875 to 1900 disappeared.

During the era the bonanza farms flourished they were not popular economically or politically, and there were public utterances of discontent regarding their operations. William Godwin Moody, a radical writer of the period, thus stated his objections to them in 1880.

> The owners of these large tracts have bonanzas, yielding great profits, not one dollar of which is expended in beautifying and permanently improving their vast estates, beyond that necessary for the care of the stock and tools, nor in sustaining a permanent population. Their homes, their pleasures, their family ties, are not upon their farms. Their wealth is flaunted in the gaieties and dissipations, or expended in building and developing some distant city or country. But the owner and cultivator of the small farm in its neighborhood, upon which he has planted his rooftree, and around which are gathered all his hopes and ambitions, finds it impossible to pay his taxes, clothe and educate, or find any comfort for his wife and little ones. The case of the small farmer is steadily going from bad to worse. The two can not exist together; the small farmer can not successfully compete with his gigantic neighbor under present conditions. He will inevitably be swallowed up. It is at best but a question of time.
>
> Thus are vast areas, in the very heart of our country, barred and closed to the occupation and ownership of our people in small tracts, and the making of homes for a strong and thrifty population, but are made centers of weakness that are sure, soon or late, under present tendencies, to spread over the whole land.[5]

[5]*Land and Labor in the United States*, pp. 58–59. Also see James B. Hedges, *Henry Villard and the Railways of the Northwest*.

When the Northern Pacific Railway was reorganized in 1875, it reacquired most of the magnificent grant which had been conditionally conveyed to its predecessor. The machinery of land colonization, which had been interrupted by the failure of Jay Cooke and Company and the subsequent Panic of 1873, was again put in motion. The energetic landselling campaigns which had been inaugurated by Cooke's agents at home and abroad were intensified. A rush of population into the region followed. Lands in Minnesota and North Dakota rose rapidly in value. The railroad sold land not only to settlers, but also to speculators. In numerous instances, accordingly, the condition requiring purchasers to cultivate a certain portion of the land was omitted from the sales contract or was disregarded. The Weyerhaeusers bought immense tracts to preserve for timbering. In this way they became the timber kings of America.[6]

Others bought tracts with a view to holding them for later development and rise in value or for town-jobbing purposes. The eagerness and necessity of the railroad company to realize cash from its patented lands in order to prosecute construction work as far as Puget Sound led to its making sales to these speculators, who retarded immigration and settlement and later became serious competitors of the railroad company when it undertook to dispose of its lands at advanced prices. However, the company continued with its colonizing and land-jobbing activities. In 1882 it had 831 active local land agents in the United States and Europe.[7]

The vigorous land-disposal policy of the Northern Pacific was fruitful in its results. The company reported to the Interstate Commerce Commission in 1917 that gross receipts from land sales amounted to $136,118,533, and it still retained a large acreage. The total cost of originally constructing the road was estimated at $100,000,000.[8] Accordingly, the prediction of Milnor Roberts, Jay Cooke's engineer, was

[6] See Chap. XVIII.
[7] For a history of the Northern Pacific land-selling activities see James B. Hedges, "Colonization Work of the Northern Pacific Railroad," *Mississippi Valley Historical Review*, Vol. XIII, pp. 311 ff.
[8] See *Hearings of the Joint Congressional Committee on the Investigation of the Northern Pacific Land Grants,* March 18, 1925, p. 2020. The gross proceeds received from the sale of donated lands of the Northern Pacific were $138,483,-626, in 1927. The expenses of administering, sale and taxes, were $37,555,498.

correct. The immense landed property of this company would be ultimately worth more than the entire cost of construction.

But this is stating it mildly! The receipts reported by the railroad company from its land sales constitute only a part—and probably a minor part—of its gains from its donated domain. The "land" and the "improvement companies" created as subsidiaries of the railroad and owned by it also made vast profits, which trickled into the coffers of the company or of its stockholders. These subsidiary companies, consisting of land, mining, and other concerns, have constituted the mysterious "hidden assets" of the Northern Pacific Railroad Company, by means of which its shares have been boosted from time to time by stock manipulators.

The Northwestern Improvement Company has been an important landholding subsidiary of the Northern Pacific. What business this company is engaged in, or what it owns, has been largely withheld from the public. Its operations, however, have been profitable. In 1908 it declared a dividend from accrued earnings, equal to 11.26 per cent on the capital stock of the railroad company. In some years the Northwestern Improvement Company paid as much as $5,000,000 into the railroad company's treasury.

Summary

Altogether, it is estimated by Marion Clawson, a director of the Bureau of Land Management (formerly the General Land Office), that about 91,000,000 acres, or 8.8 per cent of the public-domain disposal, constituted land granted to railroad corporations. Another 40,000,000 acres were granted directly to the states in aid of public improvements. The question arises: Was this a proper, necessary, and beneficial policy? There may be arguments for and against it. Certainly it should be admitted that a rapid extension of the railroad system, particularly in the sparsely settled West, could not have been undertaken profitably by private enterprise. Some public assistance was necessary to connect the

---

This left a net balance from the lands of $100,928,128, or sufficient to cover the original cost of building the railroad. In addition, there were still in the possession of the Northern Pacific 6,249,339 acres. Federal Coordinator of Transportation, *Public Aids to Transportation*, Vol. II, part 1, "Aids to Railroads," p. 111.

distant reaches of the Republic. But the question also arises, as it has in the past: Was the method employed—the give-away in fee simple (i.e., complete and absolute ownership) of vast stretches of the people's heritage—the proper and most equitable and socially desirable method to obtain the objective? Could not a more moderate and less spectacular plan of financial aid have been devised? It should be borne in mind, as pointed out by Mr. Clawson, that one consequence of the various land grants was to reduce materially the area of land open to homesteading, and hence to diminish considerably the importance of homesteading as a method of parceling out the national heritage of land among the nation's inhabitants. The residence requirements and the acreage limitation to individual purchasers did not apply to the land grants, so the homesteading principle adopted in 1862 was seriously weakened in this way. Moreover, the door was opened to land monopolization through these generous and unrestricted grants, and thus the policy early adopted by the nation's leaders in favor of wide distribution of landownership had been, to a great extent, nullified. As indicated in the foregoing pages, large grants of land to single interests is the easiest way to encourage land engrossment. Many of the large landowning interests today have had their origins in the railroad land grants.[9]

[9] Clawson, *op. cit.*, p. 75.
William Godwin Moody, already referred to in the text, writing in the early 1880s on the railroad land-grant policy, p. 117, stated:
"It would have been far better for the people and for the government, that the whole body of the lands within the railroad grants, had been donated on the homestead conditions. At the first suggestion such a proposition might be deemed extravagant. But a little reflection will quickly show that it is by no means as objectionable as the grants that have been made. In the first place, under the homestead provisions, the railroad companies could not have created and fostered vast monopolies of the lands, nor have peopled the public domain with aliens; neither could they have wholesaled the people's heritage to alien capitalists, for speculation and colonization. The lands would still have been held for homes for our own people and the naturalized citizen. The system of tenant farming, now so prevalent, would not have received the unnatural development that has marked its growth in the last twenty years, and the railroad companies would not have raked Europe for aliens to occupy the people's lands. But the railroad companies, under the grants as they now stand, do all these things that are not possible under the homestead provisions, and extort from the people a far greater amount, in their speculative operations, than they would receive from the whole body of the lands when disposed of under the homestead provision."

Chapter 16

Political Repercussions of Public Land Policy

It has frequently been stated that the history of the nation can be written in terms of the public domain. To be covered adequately in all its aspects, therefore, would mean a full recounting of the nation's history. This we do not propose to do. All that is intended herein is a brief outline of political developments that are hedged around a period extending over a century and a half, in which the treatment, disposal, and utilization of the public domain were debated in legislative halls, in public assemblies, in political parties, and in philosophic discussions.

When the nation was formed under the Articles of Confederation, the public domain was considered as a national resource in territorial expansion, in natural wealth, and as a means of providing revenue for the national treasury. The Congress passed the Ordinances of 1784, 1785, and 1787. It created the Northwest Territory. It prohibited slavery and guaranteed religious liberty in it and provided that the disposal of the soil should be left to the federal government without interference or hindrance by local, state, or territory authorities. The question soon arose, however, "What is to be done with the land?" "Give it to the soldiers," was a widespread demand of the time. "Use it to pay off the national debt," said others. "Guard it and keep it for future use," counseled others. And there were those who held that anyone who desired should have an unobstructed right to settle on it.[1]

---

[1]Speaking of this subject, Amelia Clewley Ford, in her study, *Colonial Precedents to Our National Land System as It Existed in 1800,* writes:
"From the first the nation regarded its new public domain primarily as the source of funds which were so urgently needed. In this respect it was in an identical position with some of the former colonies, particularly Pennsylvania, and

Thomas Jefferson, in 1782, estimated that five million acres could readily be sold at a dollar an acre in government "debt certificates" and the whole national debt soon could be paid with the proceeds of progressive sales. Alexander Hamilton, more astute in business affairs, however, had a better idea of land values. He opposed the issue of currency based on land as security, and held firmly to the belief that wild unoccupied distant lands in immense tracts could afford little relief from the national debt burden. He was satisfied to pledge the lands as security for national obligations, but advised strongly the withholding of their wholesale disposal until conditions created sound values and a genuine demand for them. Indeed, Hamilton was one of the few outstanding statesmen of the early national period who was not lured into the maelstrom of wild-land speculation. As Secretary of the Treasury, his work in re-establishing the national credit relieved the infant Republic from the necessity of sacrificing its domain to the land-jobbers, and his plan for an orderly distribution of land to settlers and others was adopted by Congress.

The Early Conflict of Opinions

It is not the intention here to discuss the numerous debates in Congress and elsewhere relating to the public domain. This has been done in a number of monographs and doctoral theses and has been well covered by prominent American historians. But outside of legislative halls,

---

with many of the new states; consequently it felt the same intolerant attitude toward the squatter whose presence was inconsistent with profits or legal procedure. It was natural that Congress should be uninfluenced by the indulgent legislation of Virginia and North Carolina, which states had always favored settlement rather than revenue, but it is to be wished that it might have profited by Pennsylvania's long experience, and established at once some method of adjustment or compromise, and thus escaped the long struggle and the mass of legislation that ensued before the final surrender to the squatter's persistency. But instead, the policy of summary removal by force, such as Pennsylvania had used in 1750 against the settlers on Indian lands only, was adopted by the new national landlord against all squatters indiscriminately. . . . Colonel Harmar, the federal military officer north of the Ohio, had, among other duties, that of preventing illegal encroachments on the public lands. The commissioners for Indian affairs had instructed him, January 24th, 1785, to 'employ such force as he may judge necessary in driving off persons attempting to settle on the lands of the United States.' The necessity of such action was soon abundantly proved." Pp. 140–41.

in newspapers, in periodicals, in political and workingmen's conventions, forceful opinions and proposals were expressed in opposition as well as in defense of the public land policy. Because of the almost constant prevalence of land speculation and the engrossment of large areas, there was bitter denunciation of land-jobbers in all sections of the country, and proposals were put forth from time to time to limit land-ownership held by single interests. These outcries, it is true, came largely from radical reformers, but similar views were also expressed, as we have already shown, by such revered statesmen as Thomas Jefferson and John Adams, as well as by philosophic writers such as Thomas Paine, Edwin Burgess, Gerrit Smith, Horace Greeley and George Henry Evans. The urge for land reforms, of course, was not isolated from the outcry for other social reforms, such as betterment of the workers' condition and improvement of health, sanitary and housing conditions.

Notable among the early agitators for land reform in America was George Henry Evans. On October 31, 1829, Evans began publication in New York City of the *Working Man's Advocate,* a publication that for a period gained wide popularity and became the official organ in New York of an independent political party called the Workingmen's Party. Evans was active in seeking a liberalization of the public land laws and in the advocacy of free public lands. In this he was antedated by another publication, the *Mechanics Free Press* of Philadelphia, which in 1821 advocated that the public land be reserved as a donation to citizens of the United States.

A more radical proposal was made by Thomas Skidmore, a printer active in the Workingmen's Party, who in 1829, in a pamphlet entitled *Rights of Man to Property,* declared that the real basis for social injustice was the unequal distribution of landed property. He advocated abolishing inheritance of land and a distribution among the people of an annual social dividend from the land.[2]

---

[2] H. S. Zahler, *op. cit.,* p. 21. A work published by Stephen Simpson in Philadelphia in 1831, entitled *The Workingman's Manual, A New Theory of Political Economy,* attacks the national land system and the upholding of the royal grants which led to the monoply of land, and regret is expressed that royal titles to land were not abolished forever when the federal Constitution was adopted.

It should be noted that these proposals had already been made in the late eighteenth century by more prominent philosophers. Thomas Paine, in his *Agrarian Justice,* and Thomas Spence, in *Real Rights of Man,* had put forth similar ideas. But the significance of these later proposals is that in the United States at the time they were made there existed a vast domain of unoccupied land, and the proposals could be readily put into practice. There was no question of compensation of vested interests! There was no need for a political or economic revolution! Evans and his associates, as well as his followers, in applying their theories to the public domain, were merely voicing their opposition to land monopolization and to land speculation. They had as chief supporters of their doctrines the active labor organizations of the time—organizations which, despite legal and political opposition, were fast gaining in social importance.[3]

Among the more concrete proposals relating to the distribution of the public domain made by Evans and his associates were that the maximum quantity of land any individual might own should be limited by law; the unrestricted right to dispose of land by sale or bequest should be ended; and the power of creditor to seize a homestead by writ of execution should be abolished. Only by these means, these reformers contended, could monopoly in land be averted. They strongly advocated that public land should be given free to a landless person who actually settled on it, but prohibited the sale or rental of it by such a settler. Thus there was a prologue to the Pre-emption and the Homestead Acts, neither of which, however, went as far as limiting the settler's right to dispose of the land he received after it was patented.[4]

Followers of Evans

Two prominent followers of Evans' line of thought on the land ques-

---

[3] According to Helene Sara Zahler, the theory of Evans was as follows: "Title to land comes from use, not purchase! The public land belongs to the people not the government." He held that free public land, by absorbing surplus labor, will prevent wage cuts and unemployment. "The public land, therefore, should not be sold, because acquisition by private owners would end its usefulness by siphoning workers from the city." *Op. cit.,* pp. 29–30.

[4] George Henry Evans died in February 1856, just about six years before the passage of the Homestead Act.

tion were Gerrit Smith and Horace Greeley. Gerrit Smith, son of a wealthy landowner who had been a partner of John Jacob Astor, was elected to Congress from Peterboro, New York, on an anti-slavery and land-reform program in 1852. A plank of this platform stated that "the right to the soil is as natural and equal as the right to light and air." On February 21, 1854, at the time the Homestead Bill was under discussion, Smith introduced in the House of Representatives the following set of resolutions:

Whereas, the members of the human family, notwithstanding all contrary enactments and arrangements, have, at all times, and in all circumstances, as equal a right to the soil as to the light and air, because as equal need of the one as of the other.

And whereas this invariably equal right to the soil leaves no room to buy or sell or give it away; Therefore

1. Resolved, That no bill or proposition should find any favor with Congress which implies the right of Congress to dispose of the public lands, or any part of them, either by sale or gift.
2. Resolved, That the duty of the civil government in regard to public lands, and indeed to all lands is but to regulate the occupation of them; and that this regulation should ever proceed on the principle that the right of all persons to the soil—to the great source of human subsistence—is as equal, as inherent, and as sacred, as the right to life itself.
3. Resolved, That government will have done but little toward securing the equal right to land, until it shall have made essential to the validity of every claim to land both the fact that it is actually possessed, and the fact that it does not actually exceed in quantity the maximum, which it is the duty of government to prescribe.
4. Resolved, That it is not because land monopoly is the most efficient cause of inordinate and tyrannical riches on the one hand, and . . . abject poverty on the other; and that it is not because it is, therefore, the most efficient cause of that inequality of condition, so well-nigh fatal to the spread of Democracy and Christianity, that government is called upon to abolish it; but because the Right, which this mighty agent of evil violates and tramples under foot, is among those clear, certain, essential, nat-

ural rights which it is the province of government to protect, at all hazards, and irrespective of all consequences.[5]

Gerrit Smith, who was a free trader as well as an anti-slavery advocate, followed out his principles in his career.[6] During his life he offered thousands of acres in northern New York lands, which he had inherited from his father, to landless persons. He spent much of his wealth in publishing and distributing radical essays and, despite the failure of his schemes to settle jobless workmen on his land, he continued his interest in land reform until his death in 1874.

Horace Greeley, a prominent molder of public opinion, through his newspaper, the New York *Tribune,* and through his prolific writings, was a strong advocate of reform of the national land system. He became a convert to the national reform platform of Evans, though remaining a leader of the national Whig Party. He favored the anti-rent movement in New York. As late as 1851 he advocated that the New York manors be broken up regardless of the validity of the holders' original title and proposed that any single ownership of arable land above 320 acres should be taxed in order to force their sale until "the genuine and thorough Free Soil principles of enabling every man to act under his own vine and fig tree (we prefer the apple) shall be approached."[7] Holding the distress of the factory workers as a social evil, he invented the slogan, "Go West, young man, go West." He agitated for the passage of the Homestead Bill by Congress and voiced satisfaction with its passage, expressing the view in the New York *Tribune* on May 20, 1862, that "the long struggle for land and the landless was at last consummated."

After the passage of the Homestead Act in 1862, agitation for further reforms of the national land system continued. The large grants of land to railroads, the continued engrossment of areas by land specu-

[5]*Congressional Globe,* 33rd Cong.; 1st Sess., 1853–54, Appendix, p. 207.
[6]For a short account of Gerrit Smith's life and work, see the pamphlet, *Gerrit Smith on Land Monopoly,* by William Lloyd Garrison, the Younger. Also see Octavius B. Frothingham, *Gerrit Smith, A Biography,* and Ralph Volney Harlow, *Gerrit Smith.*
[7]Zahler, *op. cit.,* p. 51n.

lators, the lax administration of the land laws, and the political corruption of the time, combined with alternating periods of economic distress in the industrial areas, furnished the incentives for further action to assure a more equitable distribution of the public domain. As in the earlier period, the agitation was tied up with the growing labor movement and the outcries against concentration of capital, particularly in land and urban real estate.

Among the leading advocates of further land reforms in the post-Homestead Law period were William Godwin Moody, whose book, *Land and Labor,* had a considerable circulation, and W. A. Phillips, a western congressman, who in 1886 published a book in London entitled *Labor, Land and Law.* Phillips was a member of the Committee on Public Lands of the House of Representatives in the 43rd Congress, and in his book severely attacked the national land policy, particularly the administration of the Homestead Act. He stressed the fact that there had been no adequate effort to keep the public land out of control of non-resident holders or to prevent the development of a landlord-tenant system. He was, in a way, though not outspokenly, a supporter of Henry George's theories.

Among the most active promoters of the Homestead Act, in and out of Congress, was George Washington Julian of Indiana. One of the organizers of the Republican Party, he was elected to Congress in 1860 and for eight years served as chairman of the Committee on Public Lands in the House of Representatives, in which capacity he was largely instrumental in guiding the working out of the land laws. He was an active writer with advanced radical views and in 1898 proposed a constitutional amendment that would permit woman suffrage. In 1885 he was appointed surveyor general of New Mexico and was both instrumental in exposing the land frauds in that region and in calling attention to land engrossment. Julian was an advocate of free use of land on the broad ground of natural rights, and he favored grants of land as a relief to landless laborers in the older states. In one of his addresses he stated: "It is for us . . . to check monopoly of the soil, and the exactions of capital in the old States, by withdrawing the landless laborers of the country from their crushing power, and at the same time giving them houses and independence on the public lands."[8]

In 1866, Julian succeeded in preventing the grant of military bounty warrants to war veterans, which, being negotiable, would have practically nullified the Homestead Act. Later, in 1868 and 1871, he tried to get Congress to make all agricultural lands in the public domain available only to homesteaders. Both in and out of Congress he vigorously attacked land monopolization and land speculation.

The "Safety-Valve" Theory

Throughout the nineteenth century, advocates of land reform stressed the importance of having public land available to the landless as a "safety valve" against political and economic discontent. The so-called "westward movement" has been regarded by several American historians, notably by F. J. Turner,[9] as a factor in discouraging radicalism and revolt in the political and economic arena, and therefore the public domain has had an important bearing on American institutions.

It is frequently stated that the discontented factory worker, the unsuccessful trader, the unemployed mechanic could, at any time if he wished, "go West" and become an independent farmer and landowner. The opposition to liberalizing the public land laws by New England and other industrial sections of the East is pointed out as recognition that when cheap land is not available wages can be kept down and the number of job applicants can be increased. Not all writers, however, agree with this assumption, and Henry George, in particular, took little note of it as a means of settling the land question. Opponents of the theory point out that in the actual process of land settlement the migrants are almost never identified as wage earners, though there are frequent references to the presence of farmers moving West from the East and of immigrants from across the seas settling on western lands. "If there was a substantial movement of wage-earners," according to

---

[8]Quoted in Zahler, *op. cit.*, p. 143n.
[9]See F. J. Turner, *The Rise of the New West, 1819–1829;* also his *The Frontier in American History*.

Professor C. Goodrich and S. Davison, "the story remains to be told, and if there was not, the theory stands in need of correction."[10]

Studies by Professor Arthur H. Cole of Harvard University and a special report prepared by the General Land Office show that cash sales of the public domain were greatest in boom times, declined precipitately with the coming of a business depression, and continued the downward trend for some time thereafter. Professor Cole attributes as the greatest influences in the fluctuation in land sales the impact of immigration, the provision of "internal improvements," such as roads, canals, and railroads, and the cyclical influence of business booms and speculation.[11]

It is clearly shown in a chart which has been prepared by Professor Cole that commodity prices and the receipts from land sales fluctuate in parallel lines and, in addition, as Dr. Cole contends, show a close, almost parallel relation to the immigration volume prior to the homestead period. Accordingly, Professor Cole concludes that it is "evident that the several public-land states were all more or less affected in the more prominent speculative episodes, but at the successive periods the areas most powerfully affected were the newer states."[11a]

There is thus considerable evidence that the public land policies, even under the more liberal Pre-emption and Homestead Acts, were not the means of affording a "safety valve" against the oppression of the worker or the relief from economic discontent, nor the abatement of business depressions. More likely, as Henry George has pointed out, economic depressions were the effect of speculative land booms, with their consequent inducement to depressions and the fluctuations in unemployment. Certainly the Panic of 1837 was generated largely by excessive land speculation, as was also the one that followed in the year 1857. Land speculation is an attempt to gain the benefits of the rising value of land and its accompanying unearned increment. The rush to garner

[10] See "The Wage-Earner and the Westward Movement" in the *Political Science Quarterly*, June 1935, p. 161.

[11] "Cyclical and Sectional Variations in the Sale of Public Lands," in the *Review of Economic Statistics*, January 1927, Vol. IX, p. 43.

[11a] *Ibid.*, p. 53.

this gain causes the movement to overreach itself. Thus it is usually followed by a temporary collapse. As stated by Henry George:

> Given a progressive community, in which population is increasing and one improvement succeeds another, and land must constantly increase in value. This steady increase naturally leads to speculation in which future increase is anticipated, and land values are carried beyond the point at which, under the existing conditions of production, their accustomed returns would be left to labor and capital. Production, therefore, begins to stop. Not that there is necessarily, or even probably, an absolute diminution in production; but that there is what in a progressive community would be equivalent to an absolute diminution of production in a stationary community—a failure in production to increase proportionately, owing to the failure of new increments of labor and capital to find employment at the accustomed rates.[12]

[12]*Progress and Poverty,* Fiftieth Anniversary Ed., the Robert Schalkenbach Foundation, New York, 1953, p. 264.

Chapter 17

Landownership and Land Disposal in Local Politics

While the Congress was engaged in passing legislation for the disposal of the public domain, there was taking place in the old as well as the new states a series of political reactions regarding not only the question of the means and methods of disposal but also the basic principles underlying landownership and land tenure inherited from the colonial period and handed down by subsequent legislation in the different states.

We have already stated in the previous chapter that there were two schools of political thought regarding national land policy. One, the liberal school, composed of pioneer farmers, large and small spokesmen for the laboring classes of eastern urban communities, and protagonists of the theory that actual ownership of land by the masses promotes true democracy, insisted that the public domain should be disposed of quickly and on easy terms. Opposed to this liberal school were the conservatives, who maintained that the public land should be a great national resource from which the government should derive funds to be spent for the well-being, happiness, and education of all the people. To this school also belonged owners of land in the eastern states, who feared the competition of the cheaper and more fertile lands of the West, as well as eastern manufacturers, who professed to see in these lands a magnet that drew away their labor supply.[1]

Thus one party regarded the disposal of the public domain as a means

[1] See Helene Sara Zahler, *Eastern Workingmen and National Land Policy, 1829–1862*, pp. vii–viii.

of preserving a "safety valve" against political and economic discontent, and the other regarded it as a means of preserving a national resource and a means of promoting economic welfare.

John Adams, along with Thomas Jefferson, was an adherent of rapid and widespread disposal of public land to the masses. In one of his philosophical writings he stated:

> Property in the soil is the natural foundation of power and authority. Three cases of soil ownership are supposable. First, if the prince own the land he will be absolute. All who cultivate the soil, holding at his pleasure, must be subject to his will. Second, where the landed property is held by a few men the real power of the government will be in the hands of an aristocracy or nobility, whatever they are named. Third, if the lands are held and owned by the people, and prevented from drifting into one or a few hands, the true power will rest with the people, and that government will, essentially, be a Democracy, whatever it may be called. Under such a constitution the people will constitute the State.[2]

Adams complained at one time that "an attempt was made to introduce the feudal system and the canon law into America." He published a letter from the French economist and statesman, Turgot, to Richard Price, dated Paris, March 22, 1778, in which Turgot said that in America due attention had not been paid to the great distinction, and the only one founded in nature, of the two classes of men—those who were landlords and those who were not. Thus the American method of treating the land question did not escape the observation of reflective minds in Europe. In the same letter, evidently in reference to the idea of territorial possessions by the colonists as discussed in the Continental Congress, Turgot said, "The pretended interest of possessing more or less territory vanishes also when the territory is justly considered as not belonging to nations but to the individual proprietors of the soil."[3]

The political repercussions of opposing views on the land question can be noted not only in the numerous debates in Congress but in the legislation of the states and the political agitation of land reformers of

[2] *Works*, Vol. III, p. 466.
[3] *Ibid.*, p. 281.

the period. It has already been noted that during or soon after the Revolution most of the states took legislative action to abolish primogeniture and entail as features of landownership. The new states followed along the same lines. During the period from the adoption of the Constitution to the enactment of the Homestead Law in 1862, there were not only constant agitations for "free land" and "squatter sovereignty" but also local and state movements for reform of land laws.

The debates in Congress that led to the enactment of the Pre-emption and the Homestead Acts give evidence both of national and local radical movements of the time that there was opposition to the tendency toward land monopolization, which, it was claimed, was forcing "the youth and vigor of the country to a state of dependency upon the manufacturing aristocracy." On the other hand, there was opposition in the East to a "giveaway" policy of the public land on any drastic revisions of land tenure. Thus in 1840 the New York legislature protested against the sale of lands "at a price below the present minimum as a virtual violation of the trust and pledge under which they were received, as wasting the common fund, and by inducing exhausting emigration from, as well as diminishing the value of land, in the older states."[4]

And so the controversy raged—a matter of profound national and local concern, almost equal to that of the slavery question.

Land Reforms in the East

New York State

While Congress was wrangling over the public domain, several individual states were concerned with their own land problems. Some of these problems were inherited from the colonial era. Others came about through economic and political developments, which called for land reform.

New York State was one of the important sections of the nation which became involved in a serious controversy relating to landownership. It has already been shown that the land system, inaugurated by the Dutch and fostered and extended by the English, was based to a

[4] See *New York Assembly Document, 1840*, Vol. VI, No. 234, p. 20.

considerable extent on land tenancy. The grants to "patroons" under manorial rights did not cover a large part of the state's area, but in time, when the number of settlers increased and land rents were raised, the system became obnoxious. Even in colonial times, an inequitable distribution of landed proprietorship retarded the growth and economic progress of the region. There were in this period a number of agrarian conflicts, some involving the patroonships and their masters.[5] As settlements along the Hudson and the Mohawk rivers increased, and land, because of engrossments by manorial lords, got scarcer and more valuable, discontent arose among the rural population, chiefly among those who were land tenants. They suffered disadvantages compared with the settlers on the lands farther to the west, who had obtained large areas from the wholesale disposal of the state's unoccupied lands following the Revolution.

However, these tenants had one economic advantage. This was the ease with which a farmer could transport his produce to market. But this advantage was largely offset by the increased value of the rented land and the consequent demand of landlords for higher rents. Moreover, many farm tenants in New York State came from New England and, on general principles, they were opposed to rents.

The patroonships and manors created grounds for dissatisfaction. The landlords of these large areas were fast becoming an aristocratic class, having its basis in landownership. Like the feudal lords of Europe, they were, through intermarriage, extending individual holdings. Whenever they were afforded the opportunity, they raised the rents of their tenants and otherwise made it more difficult for them to gain a decent livelihood. In addition to the patroonships, other large landowners were following a policy of leasing their lands. This policy was extended to the areas of new lands opened up in the western portion of the state.[6] As late as 1848, when many landlords had already abandoned the lease

[5] For an account of these conflicts, see Irving Mark, *Agrarian Conflicts in Colonial New York, 1711–1775.*

[6] David M. Ellis, *Landlords and Farmers in the Hudson-Mohawk Region, 1790–1850,* p. 54.

system, Governor John Young estimated that 1,800,000 acres in New York State were under lease.[7]

After rumbling complaints extending over several decades, the dissatisfaction broke out in what historians call "the Anti-Rent Movement in New York." It flared up in 1839 and reached its peak in the middle 1840s, though it continued intermittently until well after the Civil War. As stated by David Maldwin Ellis: "It became the channel whereby reformers of many stripes attempted to bring about constitutional changes within the state and land reforms within the nation."[8]

The uprising took the form of a strike against rent payments. The landlords experienced serious difficulties in trying to collect their rents and were frequently met with violence. The rent strikers took the name of "barnburners." They resisted landlords, sheriffs, and the militia. They became a powerful political factor, causing the state legislature to take notice and seek to appease them by enacting relief measures.

In 1840, Governor William Seward, in his message to the state legislature, urged passage of laws which would "assimilate the tenures in question to those which experience has proved to be more accordant with the principles of republican government and more conducive to the general property and the peace and harmony of society." He followed these remarks with a special message proposing remedial legislation. As a result of his appeals and in response to the flood of petitions from disgruntled tenants, the New York legislature, on May 13, 1840, set up a commission to investigate the problem.[9] This related particularly to the dispute between the powerful Rensselaer landlord and his tenants.

In the meantime, disturbances between landlord and tenants continued. Violence was of frequent occurrence. The "Anti-Renters" became a political organization. Finally, the New York Assembly appointed a committee, of which Samuel J. Tilden was chairman, to make recommendations to settle the problem. Tilden's keen legal mind dis-

[7]*Ibid.*, p. 227.
[8]*Ibid.*, p. 226.
[9]*Ibid.*, p. 240.

covered a way out. He pointed to legal phraseology in conveyances to tenants that made them "freeholds" and not "leases." He also recommended a change in the laws regulating devises and descents, which would enable a tenant to convert an annual rent into a principal sum.[10]

Tilden's recommendations, among which were the abolition of distress, taxation of ground rents, and, as mentioned, the right of the tenant to buy out the landlord's interest, were, of course, strongly opposed by the landlords. However, the recommendations were, after a time, adopted in so far as the constitutional prohibition of invalidating a contract permitted.

A New York State constitutional convention held in 1846 was called specifically to enact land reforms. Horace Greeley, though not a delegate to the convention, urged it, in addition to other reforms, to provide against anyone acquiring more than 320 acres of land after July 4, 1847. He was against land engrossment both in the state and in the public domain. The convention, in addition to forbidding future lease of agricultural land which contained a reservation of rent or service for a longer period than twelve years, reasserted the law of 1787 abolishing feudal tenures, except rents and services lawfully created and reserved. But it did not disturb the existing legal pattern of landownership or place any restriction on land engrossment.

After several decades of rioting, legal wrangling, and political and legislative action, the old form of the leasehold system in New York State was thus finally abolished, and the long fight of the Anti-Renters and the "Barnburners" ended in success. In reality, the movement was more than a local affair. "By dramatizing the evils of land monopoly and by identifying their cause with the demand for more democracy, the antirenters helped to arouse the nation to the importance of land reform. Within less than twenty years Congress was to enact the famous Homestead Act which, despite its many faults, was an important milestone in furthering Jefferson's dream of a nation of small independent farmers."[11]

---

[10]*Ibid.*, p. 274.

[11]Ellis, *op. cit.*, p. 312. See also E. P. Cheyney, *Anti-Rent Agitation in the State of New York, 1839–1846*, University of Pennsylvania Publications, No. 2.

New England Land Problems

At the time of the Revolution, most of the arable land in the settled portions of New England had come under private proprietorship. The pressure of population on the arable area had at this time already begun. Land values rose, and, as already noted, New England pioneers sought relief in westward migration.

There were, however, outlying sections within New England which were still largely vacant and the settlement and ownership of which gave rise to conflict. These sections now comprise Vermont and Maine. The territory of Vermont was known in pre-Revolutionary days as the "New Hampshire Grants." We have already seen that the territory was claimed by both New Hampshire and New York. In order to forestall New York's claim and jurisdiction, Governor Benning Wentworth of New Hampshire, acting on the principle that possession was nine points of the law, hastily and recklessly made free grants in the region to both New Hampshire and Massachusetts citizens. It is estimated that, between 1749 and 1764, 131 townships were granted to more than six thousand persons. Whole "towns," comprising 23,000 acres, more or less, were granted to selected groups of individuals who had no intention of ever settling on the lands. Samuel Adams, the patriot, was among the grantees. He was known as a speculator in both New Hampshire and Maine lands in this period. Governor Benning Wentworth granted himself about 65,000 acres and is reported to have accumulated considerable wealth from heavy fees exacted for grants.[12]

Despite the Wentworth grants to prominent New England individuals, the territory of Vermont was soon overrun by squatters who refused to be ousted. Among the prominent leaders of the squatters was Ethan Allen, the hero of Ticonderoga. While New York and New Hampshire were waging a legal battle over the Green Mountain area, he was organizing opposition to both. His bold move to protect his "squatter followers" led to the creation of the State of Vermont.[13]

---

[12] See *Publications of the Colonial Society of Massachusetts*, Vol. XXV, pp. 33-38. Also *Publications of the New York Historical Society*, "The New Hampshire Grants."

[13] When Governor Wentworth in 1749 began to make his bountiful New Hampshire grants to land-hungry New Englanders, the New York authorities

But the greatest conflicts with squatters in New England occurred in Maine. This vast northern New England region had been originally granted to Sir Ferdinando Gorges in 1639, who associated with himself in the deal John Mason, a London merchant. These two adventurers, however, never actually took possession, and their claims were strongly contested by the Massachusetts authorities. Finally, Massachusetts obtained title by a quitclaim purchase from the heirs of Gorges. Although as early as 1661 the colony of Massachusetts sold to a few individuals a large tract along the Kennebec River known as the Kennebec Purchase, and another to the Pejepscut Company, the bulk of territory remained unsettled and was largely in a wild condition. About a quarter century before the Revolution, however, settlers began to seep into the region and squatted on the land. This gave rise to political difficulties, disturbances, and violence comparable to that which was experienced in New York State during the tenant uprising. Unlike the southern colonies, New England did not favor squatters and regarded them as illegal possessors. Accordingly, after the Revolution, Massachusetts enacted measures and took steps to oust them in Maine. Moreover, after the Revolution, the Massachusetts state treasury was in a bankrupt condition, its circulating currency depreciated; and, like New York, it was desirous of obtaining revenue from the sale of its unoccupied domain.

Following a rapid increase in squatter settlement in Maine, the Massachusetts authorities became alarmed, since it interfered with the

---

brought protests against this high-handed business to the British Crown. A commission was appointed to settle the dispute. This commission decided in favor of New York and allotted to the future Empire State all territory west of the Connecticut River. The attorney for New York in the case was James Duane, destined to become the first mayor of New York City. He became the owner, through his father, of 6,000 acres of land lying west of Albany, which now comprises the town of Duanesburg, and in addition acquired large tracts in the Mohawk Valley, where he was active in attracting German settlers from Pennsylvania. He also bought heavily of Vermont "grants" after 1764, when the region was allotted to New York. His land speculations here, however, were not successful. When Vermont was granted its "independence" following the Revolution, Duane's title to lands therein was not upheld. All that his heirs received was the sum of $2,621 from the total amount of $30,000 which the Vermonters paid to New York for a quitclaim to all rights of the latter's citizens in the Green Mountain State.

sale of land in large blocks. Accordingly, in 1786 the governor was ordered to issue a proclamation prohibiting squatting on Maine lands and warning squatters they would be dealt with "according to law." This did not have the desired effect, so in 1788 another compromise was provided, whereby on payment of five Spanish dollars the squatter would be deeded 100 acres, to be laid out in the standard manner so as to include his improvements. This leniency, however, did not accomplish its object, and the strife with the squatters continued.

The Massachusetts state authorities incorporated Maine into a "district" and proceeded to make surveys of the territory and to advertise "the townships" for sale on a wholesale basis. In order to further these sales, the state appointed a committee to investigate "trespassers," as squatters were designated, and to demand payment from those who were in "illegal possession." But there was little success in this move. The squatters insisted on holding their lands and refused payment therefor. A compromise of the situation was then sought in the enactment of a statute whereby purchasers of "townships" on which there were settlers prior to January 30, 1785, were to allow each such settler 50 acres, so laid out as best to include his improvements, and to give the privilege of buying, in addition, 50 acres of unallotted land at not more than three shillings an acre.[14] The squatters were thus allowed settlement and pre-emption rights.

As the Maine lands were sold by Massachusetts at wholesale—i.e., in township units—the treatment of squatters became a problem for the private proprietors to settle. The state usually provided that each proprietor should allow a settler 100 acres, but left the proprietors and the settlers to come to terms between themselves. This was a source of conflict. The lack of uniformity in the treatment of squatters by the state and by the private proprietors caused the less favored to complain. The proprietors, being absentee landlords, employed agents to deal with the squatters, and these felt impelled to drive hard bargains in order to retain their positions. All this led to political disturbances and, at times,

[14]See Amelia Clewley Ford, *Colonial Precedents of Our National Land System, as It Existed in 1800,* bulletin of the University of Wisconsin, No. 352, p. 135.

to something like open warfare. Juries refused to convict for the killing of a sheriff who was enforcing an ouster order against a settler. Partly as a means out of the political difficulty, Massachusetts in 1820 consented to the creation of Maine into a separate state but received the right to one half of the proceeds from the sale of the public lands.

General Henry Knox of Revolutionary fame, who, in partnership with William Duer, became for a short time a large proprietor of Maine lands, counted over 500 squatters on his estate, which now comprises the present counties of Waldo and Knox in Maine. Knox fixed a price for land held by the squatters, but many resisted paying the charge, which was set at $2.50 per acre. Before a complete settlement of the dispute with the squatters was accomplished, however, Knox disposed of the bulk of his Maine lands to William Bingham of Philadelphia.

Knox and William Duer's vast Maine holdings were locally named "Bingham's Million Acres." It was in fact about two million acres. The Bingham heirs, absentee owners, desired cash rather than wild land burdened with annual tax assessments. They appointed agents, chief among whom was General Harrison Grey Otis, to dispose of the acreage, but these agents, after spending the heirs' money in building roads and other improvements, one after another, gave up their jobs.[15] Under the provisions of acquisition from Massachusetts, the lands were to be sold to actual settlers before patents could be granted. The Bingham heirs employed political influence to get the period of settlement extended from time to time, and by using methods bordering on bribery they finally obtained a patent from Massachusetts. They then proceeded to offer the land and the timber on the land for sale. In September 1828, whole "townships" were offered at auction, at a minimum price of seventy-five cents per acre. This brought about wild land speculation. Some "townships" were bought at the minimum price one day and resold at a 25-per-cent advance the next. Purchasers flocked from Boston and elsewhere to bid for "townships." There was fear of a shortage of timber at the time, and as Maine woodlands had a dense timber growth, they would thus become extremely valuable.[16]

[15] See *Maine Historical Society Collections*, Vol. VIII, p. 359.
[16] For an account of the Maine timber-land speculation, see Hugh McCulloch, *Men and Measures of a Half Century*, pp. 214–16.

Fraud and corruption accompanied the sale of these timber lands. Tracts were sold that did not exist. In the interest of large holders, maps were prepared on which lands were represented as lying upon watercourses which were scores of miles away from them. Notes were given for land and endorsed without the expectation of making payment. In one of the many lawsuits arising out of the speculation, the defendants denied the validity of the debt on the ground that "eastern land speculations . . . in general were so tainted with fraud, deception, cheating, lying, and swindling, that the very term had become proverbial for those vices." And on this ground the jury failed to return a verdict.[17] As Hugh McCulloch, Lincoln's Secretary of the Treasury, a native son of Maine, stated: "It happened strangely enough that the largest losers in this land speculation were prudent men, who kept aloof from it until it had reached the highest point, and the tide was ready to turn."

Land Politics in the Former Proprietary States

Pennsylvania and, to a considerable extent, the other states to the south that were formerly proprietary colonies escaped the political disturbances and dissatisfaction arising out of land tenure. The quitrents were only partially paid and in many cases were so insignificant as to become harmless and easily avoided. Yet, in spite of all this, quitrents were unpopular. They were, in a way, a substitute for taxes, and attempts were made with considerable success to tax the quitrents in the hands of the landlords. This was done in Pennsylvania and Maryland.[18]

The outbreak of the Revolutionary War practically put an end to the quitrent system in the colonies, but it persisted in certain areas. With the overthrow of British rule in Pennsylvania, Chief Justice McKean, in an opinion given to the General Assembly, declared that quitrents "would be utterly subversive of the rights, safety and happiness of the good people of this State, and dangerous to civil liberty in general, as evidently tending to revive and confirm an unwarrantable aristocratical power and influence . . . inconsistent with its true intent and therefore

---

[17]See *Hunts Merchants Magazine*, Vol. II, pp. 497-98.
[18]See Beverley W. Bond, Jr., *The Quit-Rent System in the American Colonies*, Chap. XV.

not to be admitted in a government founded upon equal liberty and authority of the people."[19]

In implementing this decision, Pennsylvania abolished the quitrents claimed by the proprietors and assumed ownership of all their unallotted lands but confirmed their reserved manors and the manorial rents as private property of the proprietors. With a sense of justice that was unique at this time, the Pennsylvania legislature voted to compensate the Penn family for loss of their quitrent rights by a payment of £130,000 "in remembrance of the enterprising spirit of the founder, and the expectations and dependence of his successor." This, as Professor Beverley Bond points out, was a good bargain for the proprietors, "for the actual returns from their quit-rents were unsatisfactory."[20]

Maryland followed much the same action as Pennsylvania in relieving the inhabitants of quitrents. By a legislative act of 1780, quitrents were abolished as incompatible with the sovereignty of an independent state. The payments of quitrents in Maryland had been a continual source of discontent, not so much because of the amount of the payments, which were unscrupulously enforced, but because it was regarded as tribute to an absentee landlord—who did nothing to aid the actual owners of the land. "No power on earth," declared the Maryland State Senate in 1783, "can place the free people of Maryland in the disregarded position of tenants to a superior lord, a foreigner or a British subject."[21]

Despite its obnoxious political aspects, the quitrent system in both Maryland and Pennsylvania had one beneficial result as regards land distribution. As stated by Bond:

---

[19] R. M. Cadwalader, *A Practical Treatise on the Law of Ground Rents in Pennsylvania*, pp. 46–47.

[20] The abolition of quitrents in Pennsylvania did not mean the end of a ground-rent system. This system persisted over a number of years. See Cadwalader, *op. cit.*

[21] The survival of ground rents in Baltimore—which persisted for several centuries and which only in the last few years is being discontinued—as in Pennsylvania, is not a survival of the quitrent system. The ground rent is merely an ordinary rent that is limited in time, though by a renewal clause it could become perpetual, like a feudal charge. See Lewis Mayer, *Ground Rents in Maryland*, p. 48.

The enforcement of quit-rents rendered unprofitable the holding for an indefinite period large unsettled tracts as were taken up in New York, and thus promoted the division of the land into small holdings. Hence, in pre-Revolutionary times there were no private holdings of large tracts in Pennsylvania or Maryland. Accordingly, there was no serious problem of squatter sovereignty or agrarian unrest, or tenant revolts such as occurred in New York State and in Maine.[22]

As noted previously, in no section of the American colonies was the quitrent system of land tenure more inefficient and ineffective than in the Carolinas. Though the "Fundamental Constitutions" of John Locke were designed to set up a feudal regime, of which his patron, the Earl of Shaftesbury, was to be the overlord, and high quitrents were demanded of the settlers, the inefficiency of administration, combined with the refusal or avoidance by tenants to pay the rents demanded of them, made the whole system much of a farce. The large arrears of the tenants and the general dissatisfaction with the feudal regime, therefore, constituted an incentive to overthrow the proprietary government. The proprietors' lands in 1728, at their own request, were taken over by the British authorities by purchase, and up to the time of the Revolution the governments of the "Crown Colonies of the Carolinas" were struggling with the mess of collecting arrears of quitrents and settling the land problems, which induced constant political dissatisfaction among the inhabitants. It is not surprising, therefore, that the Carolinas early joined in the revolt against the Crown and abolished the quitrent system. The same may be said of Georgia, where even the British Government, assuming the rights of the proprietaries, was unable to make the quitrent system work and where it was ignored to such an extent that the early constitutions of the state did not formally mention it.

Summary

It will be seen from this brief account of the repercussions of the colonial land systems that landownership and its distribution had in-

[22]For an account of the workings of the quitrent system in Maryland, see C. P. Gould, *The Land System in Maryland.*

fluenced local political sentiment in the various states following the Revolution. It was only natural that in the early days of land settlement on this continent the land-hungry immigrants sought and prized landownership. Their desires were largely the result of "landlessness" in the European nations in which they had their roots. They knew what landlessness meant; they knew the exactions of landlords, whose monopoly they could not tolerate or endure. They knew in a way the nature of the unearned increment they desired to acquire, and, above all, they knew that land was the best guarantee against starvation and poverty. Thus the vast availability of land in America was a "safety valve" against political unrest. Except in a few areas, such as noted above, there was a general indifference on the part of the public for almost a century after the Revolutionary War to matters pertaining to land tenure and land control. But when ownership of land became restricted or set at a high price, the public gave vent to political and agrarian unrest. In later times this was demonstrated in such radicalisms and reforms as the populist movement, the Granger movement, the single-tax movement, and other land-reform agitation.

Chapter 18

Forest and Mineral Lands Developments

Most of the treatises and discussions of land acquisition and landownership in the United States have neglected the importance of forests and minerals as products of the land. These natural resources, like agrarian and urban areas, have largely come into the hands of private owners, and their use and destruction have not generally inured to the benefit of the people as a whole. Moreover, the problem of monopolization is here also important. Timber and mineral resources are from their very nature exploited under different conditions than are arable lands, and this affects the character of their ownership. Small operations are limited and, in most cases, economically impractical. Large-scale operations, on the other hand, require large areas of unified ownership, and this intensifies the trends toward monopoly. These facts make the history, policies, and trends in the use and in the development of forest and mineral resources of the nation of especial significance.

The Forests and Their Exploitation

Forests have been a most important natural resource of the United States. They have served to furnish an ample timber supply, have built up by-product industries, and have been a contributing factor in the conservation of soil, water, and power resources. The United States had originally within its advancing territory a forest area larger than any other nation. But as settlements advanced and as population increased, primeval forests had to be cleared for agricultural use. This necessitated the elimination or alteration of much forest area. Forest lands, which at one time covered more than one half of the nation's territory, have now dwindled to less than one fourth, and only a limited portion of this is available for exploitation. Moreover, despite recent efforts of the federal government, the states, and private interests toward timber conservation and timber culture, forest destruction proceeds faster than population increases, and the consumption of native timber is estimated to be greater than the natural growth.

Before the disappearance of the frontier of settlement, American forests were destroyed mainly to provide agricultural lands. Yet even in early colonial days, lumbering was an important industry. The British relied on it largely for a supply of masts. It was the basis of the colonial shipbuilding industry. The forests of New England were prized also as a source of maple sugar and for pearl- and potashes.

Though timbering then was a local industry, limited to a few forested areas adjacent to rivers that could float the logs, it has in more recent times developed into an industry on a national scale. With improved transportation facilities, markets for timber products expanded and amplified, and large-scale output has replaced much of the output of local sawmills. All this has led to concentration of forest ownership by large corporations. In 1910, the United States Bureau of Corporations reported that at that time one half of the privately owned timber resources in the country were held by about 250 owners; and of these, several, notably the Weyerhaeuser corporation and a few others of whom we shall speak later, controlled the bulk of it.

Concentration of ownership has since continued. Notwithstanding large timber areas held in national forests, it is estimated that four fifths of the timber-growing land in the United States, exclusive of Alaska, is still privately owned, even though large areas have been acquired by the federal and state governments as forest reserves and recreation areas.

Under private exploitation, the timber resources of the nation have been recklessly wasted. Areas which in the early days of the Republic were the leading timber and pulp producers, such as New England, Pennsylvania, and New York, have been largely denuded, and the production of timber moved, first to the region of the upper Great

Lakes, and then to the Pacific Northwest, though some timbering areas in the South still persist. In this shifting process, the opportunity was afforded for the engrossment of forest lands by large corporations and wealthy individuals. It has already been shown that the opportunity arose in many instances through the acquisition and engrossment of timber areas lying within the limits of railroad land grants. Contiguous areas were readily added, and, in this way, the nation has been threatened with the private monopolization of its timber resources. This has led to efforts to obtain a greater knowledge of the pattern and extent of ownership of forest lands, along with demands for conservation and protection of the future national forest and timber resources.

But, in spite of these movements, it should be borne in mind that, regardless of public pressure for conservation, it is the private owners of timber land who have it in their hands to determine whether a desired program can be put into effect. The object of private ownership is pecuniary gain, and this in many cases may induce owners of forest lands to denude and market their timber resources as rapidly as possible. In this way they escape taxes, interest, and guardianship charges that would be borne by them if they extended their operations over a long period of time. By mass-production methods to lower operating costs, the land is denuded of its entire merchantable timber, and the nation is deprived of a necessary and important natural resource for its future welfare and even for its existence.[1]

Government Timber-Land Disposal

In the early years of disposal of the public domain, no distinction was made between timber lands and agricultural lands. In the Northwest Territory as well as in the region south of the Ohio River, the land was mostly in a natural primeval forest condition, so there was little need for this distinction. In the Great Plains states, however, there was little in the way of forests, and in order to encourage tree planting, Congress in 1873 passed what is called the Timber Culture Act. Under its

[1] See Report on Senate Resolution 311, 66th Congress, 2nd Session, 1920, known as the "Capper Report on Timber Depletion . . . and Concentration of Timber Ownership." See also *Report on Forest Land Resources,* National Resources Board, Washington, D.C., 1935.

provisions, land was given without charge if the donees agreed to plant trees. No greater opportunity was ever given to fraudulent entries of the public land. Repeated recommendations were made by the head of the General Land Office that the act be repealed, as frauds were beyond the reach of correction. The act was finally repealed in 1891.

Congress also passed in 1878 the Timber Land Act, but limited its provisions to the states of California, Oregon, Nevada, and Washington Territory. Under the act it was stipulated that public land valuable chiefly for timber but unfit for cultivation could be opened to private entry. Single entries by individuals and associations were limited to 160 acres, and the condition was set down that the entry should not be made for speculation, nor for the benefit of any other person than the party making the entry. The applicant was required to swear, among other things, that he had made no contract or agreement by which the title he might receive from the United States would inure in whole or in part to the benefit of any person but himself. These provisions were undoubtedly wise, but they were, as the land commissioner stated in 1883, "widely evaded," adding, "It is understood that large operators cause their employees and other persons to make the necessary affidavit, enter the lands, and then convey to their employers or principals. In this manner large tracts of timber lands in California, Nevada, Oregon and Washington Territory are controlled by single persons and firms, contrary to the intendment of the statute."[2]

The commissioner noted further that "the rapid decrease in the timber areas of the country invites attention to the methods of appropriation of public timber lands"[3] and suggested a modification of the law. He advised that timber lands be reserved by law from ordinary disposal and sold only after appraisement under sealed bids, and at not less than the appraised price.

Probably the worst frauds in the disposition of the public domain were committed under the Timber Land Act. An instance of this is

[2] Thomas Donaldson, *The Public Domain, Its History, with Statistics,* House Misc. Doc., 47th Cong., 2nd Sess., no. 45, part 1, p. 306.
[3] *Ibid.,* p. 1166.

cited by Marion Clawson. "Along the Pacific Coast," he says, "where much of the lumber was shipped by boat, it was the common practice to round up a group of alien sailors off a ship, have them fill out first papers toward citizenship, and then file on a tract of timber land which was available at a nominal price. This would be sold to a timber company and the timber cut, without citizenship going any further."[4] Other frauds were connected with the unauthorized cutting of timber on government land. In order to correct these abuses, Carl Schurz, when Secretary of the Interior, recommended that timber land not be sold but that timber operations be permitted on federal land under federal supervision and sold to operators instead of being given away. But no legislation dealing with forest-land administration was enacted until 1891, when the national forest system was established. The Timber and Stone Acts were then repealed.

However, under the timber acts, approximately 35,000,000 acres of land were lost to the people, most of which entered into the maws of large private concerns.

The Weyerhaeuser Timber-Land Holdings

The largest concentration of timber-land ownership today is that of the Weyerhaeuser Timber Company. This concern owes its origin largely to the activities of Frederick Weyerhaeuser, a German immigrant who, after several local ventures in lumbering around Rock Island, Illinois, moved to St. Paul, Minnesota, where he became acquainted with James J. Hill, the railroad magnate, whose company, the Northern Pacific Railway, held large tracts of timber land. Hill was anxious to dispose of the remaining landholdings of his railway empire. In 1899, the land commissioner of the Northern Pacific Railway took Frederick Weyerhaeuser to South Bend, Washington, on a timber-inspection trip. The result of this journey was a purchase on January 3, 1900, by Weyerhaeuser and his associates of 900,000 acres of Northern Pacific timber lands at a price of $6.00 per acre. Thus the Weyerhaeuser Timber Company was organized. By subsequent additional acquisitions of timber lands in the Pacific Northwest, this company has become

[4] *Op. cit.*, p. 85.

the largest private owner of timber resources in the United States, if not in the world. Its present holdings, mostly in the states of Washington and Oregon, are in excess of 3,000,000 acres.[5] The company gradually developed a broad policy of timber exploitation and preservation, with the object of conducting a permanent and expanding production. This is the reversal of the policy of many other timbering concerns, whose object has been to cut the merchantable timber as rapidly and completely as possible under the circumstances, in order to reap quick and large profits. The Weyerhaeuser Company has co-operated with state and federal authorities in measures to preserve the supply of timber in the territory in which it operates.

Another large aggregation of timber-land holdings, held under much the same policy as the Weyerhaeuser concern and also located in the Pacific Northwest, is that held by the Crown-Zellerbach Corporation.

Why the Public Should Own Forest Land

In no field of land economics is it more apparent that the interest of all the people is best served by public ownership than in the case of forest land. The history of private exploitation of the nation's forests makes this obvious. The grounds for this conclusion are nowhere better expressed than in the introductory paragraphs of a monograph prepared for Congress in 1933 by S. B. Show, then federal forester of the California region, entitled "The Probable Future Distribution of Forest Land Ownership."[6] These are his words:

> Stability of ownership of forest lands is a prerequisite to the stability of forestry. The bulk of the commercial forest lands are now in private ownership, but significant changes in ownership are taking place with great rapidity, and on a Nation-wide scale. Extensive tax delinquency in the cut-over regions; failure of any considerable number of owners to take advantage of the special forest tax laws enacted by many States specifically to help the

---

[5] For details on the concentration of timber holdings in 1912, particularly the Weyerhaeuser holdings, see the Bureau of Corporations, *The Lumber Industry*, 4 parts, 1913–14.

[6] *A National Plan for American Forestry*, prepared by the Forest Service, U. S. Department of Agriculture, in response to Sen. Res. 175, Senate Documents, 73rd Cong., 1st Sess., no. 12, vol 2, 1253.

private owner remain in the forest-land business; the rapid exploitation of forests with scanty provision by the owners for continuing in the forest-growing business; and the very large areas of forest land offered at distress sale to public agencies—all are indicative of existing changes in forest-land ownership. These trends are even more significant as symptoms of widespread and imminent changes in the distribution of ownership.

Formerly forested land, now or recently used for farming, is being abandoned as unsuitable physically or economically for farming, and is thereby becoming available again for forest production. Major changes in the character of ownership of such land are obviously inevitable if it is to be managed for its highest value of forestry.

Other sections of this report bring new information to bear on the forest situation and the forest problems of the nation. To a very high degree, these finally focus on the question of ownership—whether existing ownership is accomplishing the full conservation of forest values so clearly needed, whether it is likely to, and whether a realignment of ownership should be deliberately sought, regardless of the trend toward breakdown of private ownership and the consequent shift toward public ownership. Other sections of this report in fact suggest or recommend increase in public ownership as a means of accomplishing such purposes as watershed protection, balancing the timber budget, and conservation of recreation and wildlife values:

> Public acquisition programs by some of the States and by the Federal Government are already established, but with the exception of a few outstanding States such as New York, Pennsylvania, and Michigan, they are going ahead slowly. These public programs with few exceptions were based on what today appears to be an underestimate of the public values of forest lands, or on an overestimate of the stability of private ownership and management, and of the degree to which private ownership conserves them.
>
> Clearly, a fresh appraisal of the probable distribution of forest land ownership is needed, one that takes account both of what is likely to happen anyway as a result of the breakdown in private ownership, and of what should be done in the direction of public ownership to meet the known needs of the forest situation. Such

an analysis, which this section of the report attempts, is beset by many difficulties. Major trends, involving hundreds of millions of acres of land, varying economic conditions, deeply planted habits of political thought and tradition, and complex interrelation and conflict between public and private needs and values, are not to be resolved into formulae accurate to the last decimal point. Estimates and approximations have necessarily been used in analyzing the problem, and great accuracy in the conclusions cannot be claimed. But even rather wide approximations, and the differing results obtained from various approaches to the problem, emphasize rather than obscure the conclusion that very large shifts from private to public ownership are both inevitable and necessary.

The Disposition and Concentration of Mineral Lands

Mineral lands, as such, have been a prize acquisition in America, as in other countries. It is, of course, well known that the precious metals were eagerly sought after in the New World, and the English, French, and Dutch, along with the Spaniards, made it a strong if not a prime motive for conquest and exploration. But Spain appears to have been the only European nation which met with considerable success in this objective. Yet it should be noted that in the early English colonial charters the monarch reserved the right to a royalty on gold and silver that would be taken from the soil. This was the only claim to property by the King that was specifically mentioned in the original colonial charters.

Failure to find and exploit the precious metals was a blessing in disguise to the British colonists, since it forced them to devote their energies to agriculture, manufacture, and the utilization of other natural resources. The search for and the exploitation of the baser metals, however, were not neglected. Colonial mining for many years was confined largely to digging iron ore from bog deposits and the crude mining of iron, copper, and lead in isolated spots. Production was not large, however, and was applied mostly to domestic use. Since the colonists were prohibited by the British Navigation Laws from manufacturing metal products on a large scale, mining was largely a limited industry throughout the colonial period, and no special importance was attached to mineral lands. Such lands, as a rule, were not distinguished from agricultural lands.[7]

In the early days of the disposition of the public domain, the same policy was largely followed, though in the Northwest Ordinance of 1785 mineral lands were specifically reserved from sale. Mineral lands then, however, were not distinguished from agricultural lands when there was no outward evidence of the presence of minerals. The feesimple title gave the owner the right not only to the use of the soil but also to the growth on it and the minerals beneath it.

As early as April 16, 1800, Congress authorized the President to collect information relative to the copper mines on the south side of Lake Superior. This resolution contained a clause "to ascertain whether the Indian title to such lands as might be required for the use of the United States, in case they should deem it expedient to work the said mines, had been extinguished." Thus Congress at this period seems to have had in mind the direct working and control of mines in the United States.[8]

Likewise, Congress, on March 3, 1807, by Section 5 of an act for the sale of certain lands in Ohio and Indiana, "provided that lead mines in Indiana, with as many contiguous sections of land to each as the President might deem necessary, should be reserved" to the future use of the United States, and any grant of a tract of land thereafter "containing a lead mine" which had been discovered previous to the purchase of the tract should be fraudulent and void. The same act authorized the President, however, to lease the lead-bearing lands for a term not exceeding five years.

"This inaugurated the policy of the United States of leasing mineral lands," a policy not always put into practice and rarely adequately and

[7] There were, however, a few projects to carry on the mining and processing of minerals on a large scale during the colonial period. Notably among these were the Principio Company in Maryland, of which George Washington's father was a promoter, and the Durham Furnace in Bucks County, Pennsylvania, which was at one time owned by George Taylor, a signer of the Declaration of Independence. Another was the Hopewell ironworks, also in Pennsylvania, the location of which is now preserved as a national monument. These undertakings continued in operation over more than a century.

[8] Thomas Donaldson, *op. cit.*, p. 306.

honorably administered.[9] As President Polk stated in his first annual message, on December 2, 1845:

> The system of granting leases has proved to be not only unprofitable to the Government, but unsatisfactory to the citizens who have gone upon the lands, and if continued, must lay the foundation of much future difficulty between the Government and the lessees.

Following this advice, Congress, in 1846, provided for the sale of reserved lead mines in sections of the Northwest for cash. In the next year this was extended to include the iron-ore lands in the Lake Superior region.

Finally, in 1851, Congress authorized the classification of public land into "non-mineral" and "mineral." Pre-emptors and homesteaders were limited to the non-mineral lands, and mineral lands were withheld from railroads and other utilities that received land grants. The basis of the classification of land as "mineral" was evidence that the General Land Office had in its possession knowledge as to whether there were minerals in commercial quantities on the land. This basis, in view of inadequate staff and the limited extent of mineral exploration knowledge at the time, was defective. When lands that had been originally applied for were classified as non-mineral and later proved to be mineral in character, the patentee would still claim the mineral content. In this way, large areas of mineral land were obtained privately by prospectors and others, who in many cases had secret knowledge of the land's mineral content. This was but one of the defects in the "good-intentioned" land laws that afforded opportunities for fraud and corruption.

Impact of the California Gold Discoveries

The California gold rush in 1849 rendered inoperative the mineral-land laws in that region. It was impossible for the federal government to enforce them, as the federal jurisdiction was not then completely established. Local law was enforced largely by the use of the rope. "General" John Sutter, on whose land gold had been discovered, was overwhelmed by squatters who conducted mining operations almost at

[9] *Ibid.*, p. 307

will. In view of this, the "general" appealed to Congress for compensation, but despite years of efforts by himself and his heirs, the bold California enterpriser, whose empire was destroyed by the "curse of gold," never received what he claimed was a just reward. The years he spent on the doorsteps of Congress cost him a vast sum, and he died poor in Washington on June 17, 1880.

The "gold rush" was ruled by local California law and custom, and it was not until 1866 that Congress, in recognition of the situation, passed an act providing that the public lands in the region be opened to exploration and occupation by citizens or those who declared their intention to become citizens (and this meant practically everybody), subject to local law and customs that were not in conflict with the national laws.

Finally, in 1872, another act was passed which, with minor modifications, has continued in effect down to the present time. Under this act a claimant was required to make "a valid discovery" of mineral "sufficient to justify a prudent man investing further of his time and money in its extraction." A claim was valid without patenting as long as the claimant did $100 worth of "assessment work" on it annually. After $500 worth of improvements had been made on a valid claim that had been surveyed, a patent to the land could be obtained by payment of $5.00 per acre for lode claims and $2.50 per acre for placer claims. Lode claims were limited to 600 by 1,500 feet, with the long axis parallel to the course of the lode. Under these arrangements, more than 1,000 patents were issued annually from 1882 until 1913, reaching a peak of 3,000 claims in 1892. Despite the large number of individual claims and patents, in a brief time the mineral lands in California and the neighboring states came under ownership of wealthy individuals and large corporations.

The liberality of Congress to get-rich-quick gold seekers was due both to political influences and to the desire to encourage the production of precious metals to aid the Civil War effort and thereafter to aid in restoring the national currency to a specie basis. Because of the rapid decline in mineral prospecting in the West at the turn of the century, there has been no occasion to change the law.

In the meantime, oil—"black gold"—on the public lands became a problem. In 1898, Congress extended the placer-mining law to petroleum deposits with some modifications. The rush to take advantage of its liberal provisions threatened a rapid exhaustion of petroleum reserves. Moreover, the importance of having a petroleum reserve for the use of the Navy forced Congress to curb the over-rapid exploitation. It was not until 1920, however, that the Mineral Leasing Act was passed, which provided for an orderly disposal of mineral resources on public lands. Under the provisions of the act, which applies to other minerals besides petroleum, such as coal, sulphur, phosphate, etc., a royalty of $12\frac{1}{2}$ per cent of production is paid to the government. The new arrangement, like others made previously, did not eliminate fraud, deceit and political corruption, as witness the notorious Teapot Dome scandal of 1924.[10]

The Engrossment and Concentration of Mineral Lands

Mining of minerals during the last two centuries, like timbering, has become a large-scale industry, requiring large acreages. This has led to a relatively rapid engrossment of mineral lands by single interests. Notwithstanding congressional efforts to guard against monopolization of mineral deposits on the public domain, concentration of large areas by private owners has gone on unabated, and the ownership of the most valuable deposits is now concentrated in a few hands, comprising mostly gigantic corporations.

The process by which this development has been accomplished is much the same as that experienced in the field of forest areas. As stated by Professor Gates: "American individualism, the belief that private interests could best and most usefully explore the mineral resources of the public domain, has been responsible for the transfer of the Calumet and Hecla copper of Michigan, the Anaconda's 'World's Richest Hill' lode in Montana, the Mesabi iron field in Minnesota and other valuable deposits to private ownership. Private enterprises rapidly developed

[10] For an analysis of the working of the Mineral Land Acts which shows their unsuitability to present conditions and the opportunities for fraudulent patents, see Marion Clawson, *op. cit.,* pp. 76–81, 303–6.

these and other natural resources and excited national pride in the growing industrial strength of the United States. Before long, however, the fear was aroused that monopoly was being established in the mining industry as in manufacturing, transportation, banking, and in land ownership, and that too much economic power and that too much wealth was in too few hands. Again, however, it was from the conservationist that the impetus came for government reservation of mineral lands and the practice of leasing."[11]

The Engrossment of Coal-Bearing Lands

Although coal mining in America began in colonial times, it was not until after the turn of the nineteenth century that coal became important as a source of fuel and energy. With this development came a scramble to possess coal-bearing areas, and a period of engrossment developed, particularly in the anthracite region of Pennsylvania. In this section occurred the earliest attempts to monopolize mineral resources in the United States; and the history of them, though constituting examples of individual enterprise, foresight, and progress, has been marked by what may be called depredation, notorious waste, and industrial conflict.

In the early decades of the 1800s, when the value of anthracite for heating and smelting purposes was demonstrated, what was considered wastelands in the mountainous regions of the Wyoming and Susquehanna valleys of Pennsylvania were eagerly acquired by a few individuals, and these acquisitions laid the foundation for the gigantic combinations of coal and transportation concerns in the United States.

The earliest recorded attempt to exploit coal lands is ascribed to Colonel Jacob Weiss, who lived near Mauch Chunk, in the Lehigh region of the anthracite area. Weiss in 1791 took a piece of coal, turned over to him by a hunter, to Philadelphia and showed it to some friends, among whom was Robert Morris, the financier of the Revolution, at this time heavily engaged in land-grabbing. These friends or-

[11] Paul Wallace Gates, "From Individualism to Collectivism in American Land Policy," in Chester McA. Restler, ed., *Liberalism as a Force in History*, p. 32.

ganized the Lehigh Coal Mine Company, an unchartered association which purchased ten thousand acres of coal lands.[12] Difficulties in transporting the coal to the market (Philadelphia), however, prevented the enterprise from becoming an immediate success; but in later years, through improvement of navigation on the Lehigh River, the enterprise received renewed vigor.

When it was proven that anthracite could be burned in iron furnaces, other capitalists, among whom were Josiah White, John Drinker, and Erskine Hazard, bought up coal lands in the same region and, by securing a charter for the Schuylkill Navigation Company and a lease of the property of the Lehigh Coal Mine Company, entered the coal-producing business. During the next three decades, and in fact continuing into the present century, the monopolization of the anthracite-coal lands went on, at times at a feverish pace. Beginning about 1812, William and Maurice Wurts, merchants of Philadelphia, bought up large areas of coal lands around Carbondale, Pennsylvania, at prices ranging from fifty cents to three dollars an acre, and a decade later succeeded in interesting New York capitalists in organizing the Delaware and Hudson Canal Company, a project to bring the coal to the New York market. This and other engrossing of coal lands by individuals and corporations, in combination with the construction, ownership, and operation of canals and railroads, led to monopolization of the anthracite-coal-bearing area by scarcely more than a half dozen corporations operating as a rule both as coal-producing and as transportation concerns.[13]

[12]See Eliot Jones, *The Anthracite Coal Combination in the United States,* p. 10.

[13]The principal anthracite-mining and railroad companies that developed from ownership and lease of lands are: the Reading Company, the Delaware and Hudson Company, the Delaware Lackawanna & Western Railroad, the Lehigh Coal and Navigation Company, and Coxe Brothers Company. Through congressional enactments and the operation of the anti-trust laws, the anthracite-mining operations (except in the case of the Delaware and Hudson Company) have been divorced from the transportation operations, with the result that the original mining companies or those subsequently created to take over the coal properties of the railroad companies are ostensibly owned by separate sets of stockholders. Jones, *op. cit.*

The Engrossment of Iron-Ore-Bearing Lands

The story of the engrossment of iron-ore-bearing lands follows a similar pattern to that of coal, but here the public domain was more largely involved. Congress, as we have seen, endeavored quite early to classify mineral lands separately in the public land distribution and provided for leasing arrangements, but, as in the case of almost all of the laws relating to the public domain, these efforts accomplished little. Certainly they did not prevent private engrossing of a large part of our most valuable resources, and much of it for fraudulent and detrimental purposes.

The acquisition and exploitation of iron-bearing areas are an example. Though originally conducted as a local industry on a small scale, modern iron mining, like that of coal and most other mineral production, has become essentially a large-scale industry and requires heavy capital investment. This development gives an incentive for ownership under a single control of the iron-ore-bearing lands. Moreover, the rapid expansion of the national territory and the creation of economical transportation facilities have, through the force of competition, altered from time to time the areas of iron mining and concentrated the main producing sections in regions where the ore can be mined most economically and most profitably.

This economic law is responsible for the engrossment and development of the Lake Superior iron region, which, for half a century, has produced the bulk of iron ore taken from American soil. Although the presence of iron in the region was known to the early settlers, it was not until 1844 that United States Government surveyors located the large iron-ore body there. Three years later, as we have seen (p. 208), Congress authorized the sale of a portion of these lands under liberal terms, but the region was largely neglected by speculators until just prior to the Civil War. One reason for this was the lack of means for transporting the ore, but in 1855 the ship canal around the rapids at Sault Ste. Marie was opened, affording relatively economical transportation by water to eastern iron and steel centers.

All this gave an impetus to engrossment of ore-bearing areas in the

Lake Michigan and Lake Superior ranges. In their competition for adequate ore supplies, the large steel-producing companies of the nation began a scramble to acquire both the ore lands and the railroads of the region. Some, like the Great Northern Railroad, which already held ownership of bearing lands, proceeded to add to its holdings. Individuals, also, like the Merritt Brothers, acquired large tracts,[14] but these in the main, by hook or by crook, came into the possession of the steel companies or their affiliates. At the end of the nineteenth century, just before the organization of the United States Steel Corporation, almost all of the important ore ranges in the Great Lakes area were monopolized by about a dozen steel companies, and there was hardly a handful of independent ore companies in active operation. In fact, one of the chief causes leading to the creation of the gigantic United States Steel Corporation was the monopoly advantage gained by its ownership or control, through leases, of most of the active iron-ore-producing region of the nation.[15]

Exploitation of Oil-Bearing Lands

Petroleum production, though of relatively recent origin, has rapidly become the most important mineral industry in the United States. Its output in commercial quantities began in 1859, when E. L. Drake, drilling for water near Titusville, Pennsylvania, "struck oil." The news of this discovery spread rapidly and led to a rush to acquire land in the region. Never before, except possibly during the California gold rush, was there such eagerness on the part of capitalists, speculators, and "get-rich-quick" seekers to exploit a natural resource. An adequate detailed account of the spreading out of the search for petroleum-bearing soil is not required here. It is the most spectacular episode in the economic history of the nation. Almost one half of the United States, exclusive of Alaska, is known to hold petroleum deposits, though not all of this is yet producing in commercial quantities.

[14] See *Seven Iron Men,* by P. H. De Kruif, for the story of the ore-land acquisitions of the Merritt Brothers.

[15] For a detailed account of the ore-land holdings and leases of the United States Steel Corporation, see the *Report of the Commissioner of Corporations on the Steel Industry,* 3 vols., Washington, 1911–13. See also Henry Raymond Mussey, *Combination in the Mining Industry.*

This rising tide of oil production, as it spread over the nation, covered much of the undisposed public domain. It has already been noted that as there was no specific legislation relating to the disposal of oil-bearing lands, the act of Congress of July 5, 1866 (30 U.S.C.A. 21), which related to precious metals, was applied. Under this act, lands valuable for mineral content could be claimed under regulations by location and discovery similar to the methods that prevailed in the mining regions of the Far West, and patents were issued for limited areas after the claims were proven. Around the turn of the last century, however, a strong conservation movement developed, and by the so-called Separation Act of July 17, 1914, a policy of reserving the mineral contents of public lands was adopted, the surface only being made available for homestead entry.

In 1908 the government became alarmed at the oil shortage, and an endeavor was made to withdraw the entire public domain from oil discovery under the 1866 mining law. Nothing along this line was accomplished, however, and oil prospecting on the public domain continued at an increasing rate. This brought a statement from the director of the United States Geological Survey, recommending a withdrawal of all oil-bearing public land from disposal, not so much to preserve these lands for the future as to prevent the waste of a valuable natural resource.[16] President Taft took such action, which was subsequently confirmed by Congress. However, it was not long before "oil shortages" developed because of mass production of the automobile and the growing use of petroleum for fuel following the gasoline scarcity that developed during World War I. This led Congress to pass the Oil Land Leasing Act of February 25, 1920 (41 Stat. 437), probably the most constructive piece of legislation relating to the public domain that has ever been enacted.

Under the act, applicants were granted a permit to prospect for oil upon limited areas of the public domain for a period of two years. If they discovered oil or gas they would receive a lease for twenty years with certain preferential rights of renewal and, as a reward for discovery, one fourth of the tract leased at a royalty of 5 per cent and the

---

[16] See U. S. Geological Survey Bulletin No. 623, p. 133.

balance at a sliding-scale royalty of from 12½ per cent to 33⅓ per cent. Power was given the Secretary of the Interior, under the act, to supervise closely the operations of the lessees, and provision was made to distribute a portion of the revenue from royalties to the states in which the leased land was comprised, to be used for road building and educational purposes.

The act, on the whole, has been successful. It has led to oil exploitation on the public domain at a moderate rate, without waste of natural resource, and it has obtained for the public at large a share of the revenue and wealth which would have been lost if the land had been disposed of freely or for a moderate cash compensation.

The Mineral Leasing Act of 1920 has been amended several times since its original passage. In its present form the act provides for two types of oil and gas leases, non-competitive and competitive. Non-competitive or "wildcat" leases are issued for tracts outside of known producing oil fields. Applicants for these leases are limited to an area of 15,360 acres in any one state and a maximum of 2,560 acres in a single lease. Such leases for prospecting are for five years at a nominal rental, and the drilling is supervised under regulations of the United States Geological Survey. If oil is struck, the lessee pays a royalty of 12½ per cent on oil or gas produced.

Competitive leases, so called, are issued for lands known to produce oil in commercial quantities. The leasing is done under competitive bidding, and the successful bidder must pay the royalty rate specified in the notice issued when the land is set up for bidding, together with a specified cash bonus to be paid when the lease is granted. The amount of the royalty and the cash bonus is based on the judgment of the experts of the United States Geological Survey. Despite the sharpness of the terms, compared with previous disposal practices, the number of lease applicants, though varying from year to year, has shown an increasing trend.[17]

[17]Clawson, *op. cit.*, pp. 304–5. For United States policy toward oil lands, see John Ise, *The United States Oil Policy.*

Chapter 19

Farm Tenancy and Its Problems

Land tenancy, as we have already shown, began in the United States in the earliest colonial period.[1] It is an outgrowth and relic of feudalism, which, despite opposition and condemnation, has persisted and spread even into the newly settled regions as the nation expanded and, as time goes on, threatens to develop to an extent that forecasts serious problems in the future. Under almost any system of individual ownership of large acreages, such as we have experienced in the United States and which has been a marked characteristic of land tenure from Roman times to the present, the working and exploitation of the use of the soil must necessarily be ceded to others by the direct owners. Landlordism, in fact, implies tenancy. It involved various systems of land rental, some of a political character as existed under feudalism, and some distinctively economic and commercial.

Under modern conditions, without feudalism, serfdom, or slavery, land tenancy has taken three principal forms: (1) tenancy under lease of land for cash or equivalent rental; (2) lease under a system or plan of division of the product; and (3) employment of a laborer or laborers to work the land under a plan whereby wages or other compensation is linked to a sharing of the crop or its proceeds.

The first is characteristic of land tenure in Great Britain and other leading European countries and is comprised in the quitrent system introduced in this country in the colonial era. It is, moreover, the com-

[1]For the story of the tenancy system in colonial Maryland, see *The Land System in Maryland, 1720–1765*, by Clarence P. Gould, pp. 67–72.

mon method of leasing urban land and buildings. The second system of leasing land on the basis of sharing the crop or its proceeds between lessor and lessee was common in France under the Old Regime and has become quite common in this and other countries. It is, in its nature, similar to the royalty-payment system in the exploitation of mineral deposits.

Under the third system—i.e., the "sharecropper"—the tenant is essentially an employee of the landowner. The latter, as a rule, supplies not only the land but also the improvements and equipment thereon. He pays no cash wages, though he may make cash advances to the worker, but compensates him for his services in a *pro rata* distribution of the proceeds from the sale of the crop. The worker of the land is thus called a "sharecropper" and, legally, is not considered a tenant.

Crop-share farming, powered by man and mule, was extensively adopted in the South immediately after the Civil War. The national economy has changed greatly since that time, but in some rural areas of the South and Southwest the system of crop-share farming has remained substantially unaltered. Man and animal power alone can no longer compete with the extended use of tractor power, although many leasing structures still function within the framework of an animal-power economy. Moreover, in proposals to raise incomes of "croppers" and tenants, little emphasis has been placed upon the interdependence of leasing arrangements and systems of farming.

Not infrequently, farm-leasing problems are examined largely in the setting of tenancy, but this approach leaves some of the basic economic issues unsolved. An appraisal of the factors affecting production indicates that many of the problems confronting tenants are also faced by other farm-tenure groups. Attaining maximum net returns from the working of the land has been difficult for tenants and others because of small farm units, too much reliance on hand labor, inadequate capital, and inefficient farm-management practices.

It is not necessary in carrying out the purpose of this work to enter into an analysis of the different features and refinements of land tenancy. Our aim is merely to trace its development, to point out its significance, economically, socially, and politically, and to forecast its trend.

Farm Tenancy and Its Problems

The evils or ill effects of land tenancy are well known. Numerous volumes have been written regarding it both in this country and abroad. In recent years in the United States it has become a matter requiring national and state legislation. However, it was not until the census of 1880 that the extent of farm tenancy in the United States became a matter of statistics. Since that time the enumeration of farm tenants has been improved, and each succeeding census until 1940 has shown an almost unbroken persistent growth in both the amount and proportion of farm tenancy. During the half century from 1880 to 1930 the total number of farmers in the United States increased from 4,008,907 to 6,288,648, a gain of 57 per cent. Tenants increased during the same period from 1,024,601 to 2,664,365, a gain of 160 per cent—obviously, the number of tenants increased more than two and a half times as fast during the period as did the number of owners and managers.[2]

Although some of this revealed increase in farm tenancy may be due to more accurate census reporting, there can be little doubt that farm tenancy in this nation, where for several centuries agricultural areas were ample, farm land relatively cheap, and much of it obtained freely from the public domain with little cash investment, has been intermittently on the increase. Moreover, under the ample mortgage-credit system prevailing throughout the nation, the capital outlay in acquiring productive land has been considerably reduced.

Since the census of 1940, when the growth and the evils of farm tenancy received widespread attention, the farm tenant population appears to be on the decrease. But this may be due to the favorable economic conditions of the period, for it is known that the rate of farm tenancy rises in periods of depression and falls during eras of prosperity.

Farm Tenancy before the Civil War

Despite the abundance and cheapness of agricultural land, farm tenancy was prevalent to a considerable degree before the Civil War. We have already seen that it had become both an economic and political problem in New York State, where it developed out of the colonial

[2]See Part VII of the *Supplementary Report of the Land Planning Committee of the National Resources Board*, p. 20.

land system there. It was taken up by the Wadsworths of Geneseo, who, unlike most of the large landholders in New York State, leased a large portion of their estate instead of disposing of it by sale.

Political opposition to land tenancy was manifest even in the South before the Civil War. Thus Thomas Hart Benton, an early senator from Missouri, expressed the view that "tenantry is unfavorable to freedom. . . . It lays the foundation for separate orders in society, annihilates love of country, and weakens the spirit of independence." He added, "The farming tenant has, in fact, no country, no hearth, no domestic altar, no household god. The freeholder, on the contrary, is the natural supporter of a free government; and it should be the policy of republics to multiply their freeholders, as it is the policy of monarchies to multiply tenants."[3]

In the southern states, owing to the existence of slavery, farm tenancy was undoubtedly the exception and not the rule, though we have little data regarding it. The profitableness of the slave-worked plantation made it uneconomical to divide up holdings and lease acreages to tenants. Moreover, farming of a single crop, such as cotton, on a small scale could hardly afford the means of livelihood of a cultivator who was subjected to the competition of the large slave-worked plantations. Accordingly, as stated by Enoch Marvin Banks, "In view of . . . the abundance of land in Georgia in the early decades of the last century, it is needless to say that no great amount of tenancy had arisen before 1860."[4]

In the mid-northwestern states, where practically all private acreage represented a part of the original national domain, and where actual ownership of land was made relatively cheap by the public land laws, land tenancy came into existence on a considerable scale. According to Paul Wallace Gates,[5] "A study of the early settlement of the prairie counties [of Indiana] reveals that responsibility for the high degree of tenancy, the large farms, the declining population, the poor tenant

[3]*Thirty Years View*, Vol. I, pp. 103-4.
[4]*Economics of Land Tenure in Georgia*, p. 82.
[5]"Land Policy and Tenancy in the Prairie Counties of Indiana," in *Indiana Magazine of History*, Vol. XXXV, No. 1, March 1939, p. 2.

homes, and the soil depletion is to be attributed in part to the operation of the land system in the nineteenth century."

It was pointed out as early as 1835 by Solon Robinson, an agriculturist of this region, that the "cash-sale system" of disposing of the public lands in unlimited areas was a prime cause of the above situation because it gave an opportunity to non-residents to obtain large bodies of land and let it out for lease to tenants.[6] It was in this period that eastern capitalists and manufacturers, particularly in New England, used their surplus cash to speculate in western lands.

It is noted by a writer on the early history of cotton manufacture in the United States that the files of New England cotton manufacturers contained numerous references to speculation in western lands.[7] When they failed to profit from such speculation and were unable to dispose of the land without great loss, they naturally sought to exploit it through lease to tenants. Thus landlordism became a detriment to early western development.

Professor Gates notes that among the Easterners who bought large tracts of western public land for the purpose of leasing were Daniel Webster, the Wadsworths of New York, Thomas Ludwell and Lee Brent of Virginia, and Romulus Riggs of Philadelphia.[8] Like so many others, Webster's project, for which he was compelled to borrow money, did not prove a success. However, several well-known capitalists of the times carried out their plans of dividing their lands among tenants. Among these was Henry L. Ellsworth, a member of the prominent Ellsworth family of New England, who in 1835 became United States Commissioner of Patents and in that capacity was impressed with the achievements of farm machinery as a means of large-scale farm cultivation. He saw opportunities for use of such machinery on the prairie lands of Indiana and Illinois. This led him, in company with others, to engross large acreages in the region. The Panic of 1837 did not deter him, and following the recovery he plunged more deeply into the pur-

[6]*Ibid.*
[7]See Caroline F. Ware, *The Early New England Cotton Manufacture*, p. 158.
[8]*Op. cit.*, p. 8.

chase of land. At the Crawfordsville, Indiana, land office between 1847 and 1852, he entered 73,500 acres, largely with military land warrants which he could buy from 65 cents to $1.10 per acre.[9] Other capitalists of this "Yale" group followed the same plan.

Ellsworth was bent on settling the land with tenants. In this he was partially successful. When he died in 1857, members of his family became heirs to over 110,000 acres in Indiana and Illinois, which was only a part of the holdings, since Yale University and Wabash College also received approximately 12,000 acres as a bequest. For almost a half century these heirs were engaged in selling and renting the land.

Contemporary with Ellsworth, others were engrossing large areas in the prairie region of the mid-Northwest. Among these were W. W. Corcoran, the Washington banker; Elisha Riggs and Romulus Riggs, his partner; Solomon Sturges; Alvah Buckingham; along with John Grigs, Isaac Funk, and a host of others—all absentee landlords, who endeavored to exploit their holdings, in whole or in part, through a system of land tenancy.[10]

Farm Tenancy after the Civil War

The ending of the slave-worked plantation system is responsible for the introduction of widespread farm tenancy in the South. Here, to a greater extent, it took the form of sharecropping more than in other territorial sections. As stated by James G. Maddox and Howard A. Turner of the Land Policy Section of the Agricultural Adjustment Administration:

> It is generally accepted, and hardly can be contested, that hundreds of thousands of tenant farmers appeared in the South in the years immediately following the struggle between the States. The slaves had their freedom, in that they were legally transferred from chattel to persons, but they were without land and equip-

[9] *Ibid.*, p. 11.

[10] For a more detailed list of these "frontier landlords," see Paul Wallace Gates, *Frontier Landlords and Pioneer Tenants*, "Land Policy and Tenancy in the Prairie Counties of Indiana" (*Indiana Magazine of History*, Vol. XXXV, No. 1, March 1939), "Cattle Kings in the Prairies" (*Mississippi Valley Historical Review*, Vol. XXXV, No. 3, December 1948), and other writings of the same author.

ment. The large landholders had their property and equipment, but they were without their former labor supply. The result of the compromise between the two groups was the development of tenant farming. The plantation owner furnished the land and equipment and the propertyless class furnished the labor. They shared in the proceeds of the crop produced. In these tragic years, when the South was not only conquered and its agriculture forced to readjust itself to free labor, but was also virtually bankrupt and had many areas devastated with respect to physical wealth and energetic manpower, the former slave was not the only one to become a tenant operator. Many whites were also forced to rent their land from others.[11]

The greatest amount of land tenancy or sharecropping exists in the cotton-growing area of the South. Georgia, Mississippi, Oklahoma, and Alabama are the most notable areas of the sharecropper. In these states there are more farms operated by tenants than by owners. The tenants in most cases, as has already been pointed out, are practically laborers with an uncertain stipend for their labor.

The Evils of Farm Tenancy

The spread of farm tenancy in the United States is no doubt due in large part to land engrossment arising from financial speculation and the consequent rising rental income from land. It is indeed a monstrosity of history that in a period of a century and a half a nation with a seemingly boundless area, largely arable, and with a relatively sparse population compared with Europe and Asia, and with land, until recently, distributed freely to settlers, should develop a "landless class."

Taking the nation as a whole, approximately one half of the farmers are tenants in one way or another. Tenant farming prevails in every section of the nation, and there is no evidence that the percentage will permanently decline. In fact, with the cyclical tendency for land values to increase, the proportion of tenant farmers is likely to rise, and the agrarian problems, which have wrecked older nations in Europe and Asia, promise to become serious here in our own blessed

[11]See Part VII of the *Supplementary Report of the Land Planning Committee to the National Resources Board*, p. 20.

land. It has been truthfully stated that "there has never been an attempt in this country to make a comprehensive analysis of all our land-tenure problems, or to evaluate the institution of rural tenancy as an integral part of our national agricultural economy. Most students of rural tenancy are, however, agreed that it is associated with, and perhaps the cause of, certain socially undesirable phenomena."[12]

Space permits only a discussion of a few of these.

One of the outstanding evils of rural tenancy is its discouragement of stability of farm occupancy. The tenant does not feel that he is fixed to the land he works. Thus the habit of migrating, which has dominated the American spirit since colonial days and which in earlier times was a useful force in the rapid settlement of the country, is enhanced. It is estimated that more than half of the farm tenants remain on the same piece of land less than two years. This has a bad effect, socially and economically, on both the farmer and the farm. It discourages farm improvement. It leads to careless farming. The tenant is apt to take little care to preserve the fertility and permanent productivity of the soil when he feels that he may move off the land when his lease expires. It is also a detriment to the making of adequate repairs and the employment and maintenance of efficient farm equipment. In European countries experience shows that when the peasant tills his own land he is more efficient and produces more. It is noted also that, particularly in the South, thousands of tenants move at the end of each harvest season.[13] Under such circumstances, the landlord must furnish supplies, machinery, and equipment, since tenants are not likely to haul such implements along with them. Poor methods of farming are thus inherent in the rural tenancy system.

Moreover, a migratory farm population is not conducive to high moral, political, or social standards. Migratory farmers, like migratory workers, are, on the whole, a shiftless, irresponsible lot. They have little interest in local and political affairs. The element of civic pride, the force that creates progressive communities, is absent in them.

The low economic status of many tenant farmers, particularly in the

[12] *Ibid.*, p. 37.
[13] *Ibid.*, Part VII, p. 39.

South and Southwest, intensifies the economic impact of agricultural and industrial depressions. When agricultural prices decline or when farm surpluses pile up, the tenants, whether sharecroppers or cash renters, are likely to suffer the extremes of poverty because of their lack of worldly goods. This was notable and significant during the agricultural depression of the 1930s, when the low condition of the sharecroppers became a national problem.

Another factor in the adverse situation is the demand and supply of efficient farm laborers. Tenant farmers are not likely to employ an adequate number of laborers on the farms they occupy, nor are they likely to pay a fair rate of wages. Since the employment of laborers is regarded by them as an expense that may not be recovered from the returns of the crop, and since farming, in itself, is essentially a risky undertaking, the tenants naturally evade as far as possible the employment of an adequate force of laborers. For these, as well as many other reasons—economic, political, and social—rural tenancy, particularly of the type where the tenant is dependent on his crops for a livelihood, should be eliminated as far as can be accomplished through national and local efforts. Henry A. Wallace, who as Secretary of Agriculture had a thorough knowledge of agricultural problems, well stated in 1935: "We have been talking about the evils of farm tenancy in this country for a great many years. It is high time that America faced the tenant situation openly and pursued a vigorous policy of improvement."[14]

The Bankhead-Jones Farm Tenant Act

On July 22, 1937, Congress, after extensive hearings on the unhappy farm tenant and sharecropper situation, finally passed the Bankhead-Jones Farm Tenant Act. The aim of this legislation was to afford the means needed to make the tenant farmer the actual owner of the land he tilled. Under the terms of the act, the Secretary of Agriculture was authorized to make loans and to insure mortgages in the United States and its territories in the amounts that would support a family-size farm

[14] A statement by Mr. Wallace before a subcommittee of the Committee on Agriculture and Forestry, U. S. Senate, 74th Congress, 1st Session.

to persons engaged in farming as an occupation. It was stipulated that no loan would be made for the acquisition, improvement, or enlargement of any farm unless it was of such size and type as the Secretary determined was sufficient to constitute an efficient family-type farm-management unit and to enable a diligent farm family to carry on successful farming of a type which the Secretary deemed could be carried on successfully in the locality in which the farm was situated.

This provision was aimed particularly to overcome the difficulty, as experienced by the southern cotton sharecropper, in making a livelihood from the produce of a small-acreage plot. At the same time, it sought to avoid making loans for an acreage in excess of the amount that could be successfully tilled by a single family. The act provided, in addition, for direct loans by the government and for federal insurance of tenant mortgage loans made through other sources. The act also provided for the setting up of county committees, with a majority of each comprising resident farmers, to assist and advise in making loans and mortgages. The duty of these committees consisted of: (1) the examination of applications for loans, (2) the appraisal of the farms involved, and (3) ascertainment of the qualifications of the loan applicant for receiving the loan. All loans made had to be certified by one member of the committee.

For the purpose of specifically carrying out the provisions of the act, a federal agency was created, the Farmers Home Corporation, to which the Secretary of Agriculture had power to delegate the duties assigned to him under the legislation. This agency was merged with other federal farm-credit agencies into one organization under the Farmers' Home Administration Act of 1946.

European Policy on Farm Tenancy

The problem of farm tenancy has been an economic and political scourge in many European countries, and they have been forced to deal seriously with the evil at various times. According to a statement prepared under the auspices of the Land Planning Committee of the National Resources Board, published in 1935,[15] "European countries

[15]*Op. cit.*, Part VII, p. 41.

have followed three general plans in their attempts to improve their tenancy situation. Some of the countries, such as England, for example, have accepted tenancy on privately owned land, and set about to improve the relationship between landlord and tenant by regulatory measures. Other countries, notably Ireland and Denmark, have pursued a policy of aiding tenants in becoming owners through a system of long-time loans from the government at a low rate of interest. Still a third procedure has been the promotion of state tenancy, under which plan the title to the land rests in the government and the tenant pays rent to the state for the use of the land instead of paying rent to a private landlord."

"The latter plan," says the Land Planning Committee in its report, "is too greatly at variance with present American ideals and principles to merit our consideration. Our policy should probably be developed through a combination of the first two schemes mentioned and should embody the following five objectives:

"1. To insure reasonable stability of occupancy among farm tenants.
"2. To eliminate excessive land speculation and irresponsible absentee ownership.
"3. To promote progress to ownership by farm operators who are competent to assume the responsibilities of an owner-operator.
"4. To create conditions of occupancy and land use favorable to soil maintenance and improvement.
"5. To stimulate a fuller identification of farm laborers and tenants with community life by reducing the number of migratory farm tenants and laborers, and by encouraging group activity among this class of our population."

Tenancy and Leased-Land Statistics

The percentage of the nation's farms operated by tenants was lower in 1950 than at any other time since 1880, when data on tenure were first collected. The percentage of farms under lease increased steadily from 1880, when 25.6 per cent of the farms were rented, until 1930, when 42.4 per cent were rented. The percentage then decreased slightly during the later depression years, being 42.1 per cent in 1935. By 1940, when the economy had recovered from the severe depression, the figure was 38.7 per cent. The greatest decline in recent years in the percentage of rented farms occurred during World War II. The proportion dropped then from the 38.7 per cent figure in 1940 to 31.7 per cent in 1945. The downward trend continued to 1950, with leased farms constituting only 26.8 per cent of all farms in that year, almost the same as the 1880 figure.

The recent decline in the number of rented farms has been accompanied by a decline in the percentage of land in farms under lease, which includes both land operated by tenants and land rented by part owners. The peak in the amount of rented land in farms for the entire country was reached in 1935, when 44.7 per cent of all farm land was under lease. The proportion declined to 35.4 per cent in 1950. This decrease, however, was not as large as either the decline in tenancy or the proportion of land operated by tenants.

Several causes have been responsible for the fluctuations in the proportion of rented units and in the total quantity of rented land since 1880. Several decades ago, cessation of the homestead programs ended the supply of free or cheap farm land. Throughout these years, population continued to increase at a rapid rate, which has resulted in an increase in a demand for agricultural products.

Before 1920 the demand for land increased and land prices rose—an increase in tenancy followed. After 1925 the number of tenants was augmented by a large number of former landowners, who found it impossible to maintain an equity in their land with the relatively low commodity prices and the credit arrangements prevailing at that time.

The marked change in economic conditions brought about by World War II enabled many farmers to improve their tenure position. The increase in land prices was not proportional to the increase in commodity prices. Military service and attractive non-agricultural employment removed many prospective land purchasers and tenants from the farm-land market. Moreover, since the war, favorable employment opportunities outside of agriculture have reduced the number of people required to produce the nation's food and fiber. The trend thus has been toward a more widespread owner operation of farms. But, as already noted at the beginning of this chapter, this may be merely a temporary development. As long as prosperous conditions continue and the demand for industrial workers rises, the motive to become tenant farmers is lessened. Should there be an unfavorable change in economic conditions, there is likely to be a reverse move back to agricultural occupations, and the number of tenant farmers may again be on the increase.

Several states, particularly in the Southwest, have passed legislation to alleviate the evils of farm tenancy; but, though helpful, they have not altered the fundamental conditions that make the farm tenant system economically and socially objectionable. As stated by Professor Spiegel in his book, *Land Tenure Policies at Home and Abroad:*[16]

> With few exceptions, the state laws adhere to the rules of the common law which does not secure adequate protection for the tenant and, in England, has been supplemented by the Agricultural Holdings Acts. Only a few similar attempts have been made in the United States, and the practical importance of these attempts is almost negligible. . . . It seems safe to say that state action did not succeed in improving the lease terms to a noteworthy extent. Hence, federal action seems necessary.

[16] Pp. 75–76.

Chapter 20

The Rise of Urban Real Estate Values

In no case is the unearned increment arising from land-rental value better illustrated than in the field of urban real estate. Here in the United States it has had an amazing opportunity to develop, since in no other country or section of the world have towns and cities grown up in so short a period of time. Even in colonial times, land in areas that were chosen as concentrated settlements was eagerly sought after. Because of the need of ports and of places for defense against savages, concentrated communities developed early, and population in these areas increased, as a rule, more rapidly than in outlying districts. This was due in part to the lack of adequate transportation facilities. The fact that in all the thirteen colonies the first settlements centered around one or more ports, which in time became the capitals of their respective administrations, is an indication of their importance to the economic and political life of the people. This laid the groundwork for the early growth of real estate values.

An illustration of the rapid rise of real estate values in colonial times can be noted in Philadelphia. William Penn, even before he arrived in America and soon after his grant was received from Charles II, ordered the city laid out at the junction of the Delaware and Schuylkill rivers. The lots (except those on the waterfront) were reserved for the first purchasers in England, whose names appeared on a parchment list of August 22, 1682. These drew for their lots. According to Alfred N. Chandler, "Heirs of holders of rights to such lots usually had difficulty in obtaining their plots, which soon became valuable, and recognition depended on payments for warrants, the survey, the return, the patent and its recording, besides many inconveniences."[1]

Regarding the success of his City of Brotherly Love, Penn wrote in 1683: "Within one year of my arrival, the value of the least desirable lots in Philadelphia increased to four times their value when first laid out, and the best lots were worth forty times, without any improvements thereon. And though it seems unequal that the absent should be thus benefited by the improvements made by those that are upon the place, especially when they have served no office, run no hazard nor as yet defrayed any public charge, yet this advantage does certainly redound to them, and, whoever they are, they are great debtors to the country."[2]

Real estate speculation was thus rife even in those early days, for, as Penn stated, there was "great buying of one another."

The story of Philadelphia's rise in land value is typical of that in other American towns and cities in the early days. "It seems ridiculous," writes Chandler, "that within only twenty years after the first white settlers arrived, all the land at Boston should have been privately appropriated," in referring to the privilege given by Boston to admit a carpenter named Palmer as an inhabitant "if he can get a house, or land to set a house upon." In neighboring Charlestown, John Greenland had a similar experience.[3]

Post-Revolutionary Boom Towns

In previous chapters the rage for town-jobbing and town-booming in the post-Revolutionary period has already been pointed out. To give the details of this development would require many pages, and it is proposed here merely to cite a few cases, particularly those which have reference to the rise in real estate values. Like all other fields of financial speculation, many of these ventures were failures—some at least to the immediate promoters, but with success to their followers. Others

[1] Chandler, *op. cit.*, p. 405.
[2] *Ibid.*, pp. 407–8.
[3] *Ibid.*, p. 99. For details of the growth in the value of town real estate in New England, see William B. Weeden, *Economic and Social History of New England, 1620–1789.*

were permanent disappointments. Whether the gains exceeded losses may never be revealed, but the almost steady and, in many cases, fabulous rise in urban real estate in most well-located American cities and towns is evidence that these values were not artificially created but, instead, were the result of the surging growth of population and the rapid agricultural and commercial progress that accompanied it.

Washington, the Federal City

Perhaps the most spectacular episode in American town jobbing is to be found in the creation of the city of Washington, then called the Federal City. As is well known, the framers of the Constitution provided that a site not exceeding ten miles square, separated from state jurisdiction and to be governed by Congress, should be selected as the nation's capital. Previous to the adoption of the Constitution, the Continental Congress had already passed a resolution authorizing a commission to lay out such a site at the Falls of the Delaware River. Robert Morris, then prominent in the affairs of the new Republic, sought to take advantage of the move and bought a tract of land, in all 2,500 acres, in the neighborhood. This site he named Morrisville, a name it still retains, though Morris lost it in 1798 when it was sold by the sheriff subsequent to the financier's bankruptcy in that year. It has only recently received attention as the location of the newest and largest steel-fabrication plant on the eastern seaboard.

While Morris was engrossing land in the prospective site of a federal city, the Constitution was adopted, and the First Congress was forced to battle over the selection of a site for the national capital. This was a perplexing problem, since sectional jealousy, then as now, prevailed in the nation's legislature, and no agreement could be reached on a proposed site. Robert Morris, who was then a senator from Pennsylvania, of course offered the Falls of the Delaware. But others could not see eye to eye with him, and it was not until after a compromise agreement between Hamilton and Jefferson—an early case of "log-rolling"—that a site was selected on the Potomac River, fourteen miles above Washington's home at Mount Vernon. Hamilton agreed to the selection of the site, and Jefferson, in return therefor, agreed not to oppose Hamilton's plan for the federal assumption of the debts of the states.

Congress appointed a commission to carry out the plan of erecting a federal district. Their chief problem was to acquire the land from the existing owners. These naturally demanded a high price. One of the principal owners was a Scotsman named Burnes, who was obdurate in holding out for favorable terms. It required a patriotic address by the Father of his Country to get the landholders to agree to sell out. He met them at Georgetown, a village located in the selected area, and in the course of his visit remarked "that the contention in which they seemed engaged, did not in my opinion comport either with the public interest or that of their own; that while each party was aiming to obtain the public buildings, they might by placing the matter on a contracted scale, defeat the measure altogether; not only by procrastination, but for want of the means necessary to effect the work . . . and that instead of contending they had better by combining more offers make a common cause of it."[4]

The proprietors then adhered to Washington's terms. They signed an agreement stating that "in consideration of the great benefit they were expected to derive from having the Federal City laid off on our lands" they conveyed in trust the whole of their lands upon condition that "the President shall have the sole power of directing the Federal City be laid off in what manner he pleased." The lots, it was agreed, were to be divided equally between the government and the owners, and those taken by the owners were to be paid for at the rate of $25 per acre.

As the commissioners appointed by Congress to lay out the city needed money to construct public buildings and improvements, they immediately offered their share of the lots for sale. So did the private owners. These were naturally desirous of securing the "windfall" that would come to them merely because of the placing of the site of the capital city on their lands.

Robert Morris, who at this time was engaged in a series of vast land speculations, along with two partners, John Nicholson and James Green-

[4]See *The Diaries of George Washington*, Vol. IV, p. 154.

leaf, were the largest purchasers of the "lots." The prices of lots ranged from $160 to $534. Whoever bought or held the lots was required to build on them, and there were also building restrictions. While the sale of lots was going on—and there was considerable disappointment regarding the sales—one of the first commercial panics with which the nation has been cursed occurred in the United States. The speculations of William Duer, Alexander Macomb, and other capitalists in New York, the reign of terror in France, the suspension of specie payments by the Bank of England—together, these "produced general stagnation of money contracts," as Jefferson wrote to the District Commissions. Morris and his partners were forced into bankruptcy. Samuel Blodget, Jr., another large speculator in Washington lots, followed in their wake. The construction of the "President's Palace," the capitol building, and other improvements was exceedingly slow, thus retarding the drift of population into the federal city. There was, accordingly, little incentive at the time to acquire real estate in the area. It was not until after 1800, when the federal government moved to the site, that some encouragement was given to the lot speculators, and even then the rise of land values was not as great as in Philadelphia, New York, and other cities, which were assuming a more significant role of commercial importance.[5]

Rise of Real Estate Values in the City of New York

The growth of real estate values in the City of New York undoubtedly has been the most spectacular of any metropolis in the world. Yet an adequate and authentic history of this development has never been written in a way to reach the general public. Perhaps it is the immensity

[5] A large early purchaser of Washington real estate was a wealthy and aristocratic East Indian trader named Thomas Law, who in 1794 decided to take up residence in America. While at Philadelphia, in conversation with President Washington, he became impressed with the prospects of the new national capital. He accordingly bought a number of lots there from the Morris-Nicholson-Greenleaf syndicate. Unlike these speculators, he succeeded in holding onto his purchases, though his real estate ventures caused him serious loss of fortune. In 1796 he married Elizabeth Parke Custis, a granddaughter of Mrs. George Washington. But the marriage was not a happy one, and a separation ensued in 1802. Law continued to reside in the national capital and became one of its most progressive and respected citizens.

and complexities of the rise in real estate values and the numerous transactions involved that have discouraged research along these lines.[6] Certainly it is impossible to give anywhere a nearly complete account in these pages. All that can be done is to comment briefly on the "high spots" comprised in the story of the principal owners of and operators in a two-century span of New York City history.

Trinity Corporation: Old Trinity Church in New York is reputed to own or have owned some of the most valuable urban real estate in the country. Its origin is an interesting story. A Dutch matron, Annetje Jansen (corrupted to Anneke Jans), came to America in 1630 with her husband, Roelof Jansen. They settled in New Amsterdam where Jansen, in 1636, obtained a grant of sixty-two acres of land covering a considerable portion of lower Manhattan, lying west of what now is Broadway, and extending as far north as Canal Street. Jansen died and Anneke married the clergyman, Dominé Everardus Bogardus. After Bogardus' death, Anneke had the Jansen grant confirmed by the English Government, and it was held by her and her heirs until 1671 when it was sold to Governor Lovelace. Lovelace was later disgraced. Thereupon the land passed to the Crown and in 1705 was granted by Queen Anne to Trinity as an endowment. Numerous suits were instituted by Anneke's heirs based on a claimed defect in the grant from them to Lovelace, but in all of these Trinity's title was upheld and today, after many grants by them of parts of the property to other institutions, and conveyances of additional portions for its own support, the church continues to enjoy the benefits of the remainder.[7]

John Jacob Astor's Holdings: One of the most successful engrossers of valuable land in New York City, as is well known, was the first John

---

[6] A popular account of the growth of real estate values in New York City may be found in the book of Arthur Pound, *The Golden Earth, The Story of Manhattan's Landed Wealth*. Extensive information regarding New York City real estate developments is also contained in the monumental work, I. N. Phelps Stokes, *The Iconography of Manhattan Island*.

[7] See Appleton's *Cyclopedia of American Biography*, Vol. I, p. 301.

Jacob Astor. Although his wealth originated from commercial enterprise, the foundation of the vast Astor Estate is the result of shrewd operations in real estate. Of course there were other capitalists of Astor's time who also accumulated fortunes because of the rise of the unearned increment in urban land values. Among them were John G. Wendel, Nicholas Emmerich, Henry Brevoort, Peter Goelet, Stephen Whitney, and a host of "old merchants of New York," as well as Stephen Girard and Jacob Ridgeway in Philadelphia, and Nicholas Longworth in Cincinnati. But Astor was the most astute of all, and his objective, as indicated by his will, was to create a permanent estate of his holdings for his heirs of succeeding generations. In executing this objective, he was successful.

Astor did not buy real estate for a profit on "turnover." He bought to hold indefinitely, to gain the profit arising from increasing rental values; and his descendants still live on the rentals of scores of lots and plots obtained at bargain prices by their ingenious and far-seeing progenitor. Land-poor individuals, institutions, and estates found him a willing purchaser of vacant and non-income-producing properties, provided he thought them cheap. He bought numerous lots from Trinity Corporation. He bought from distressed traders and merchants, from defaulting mortgagors, and when the real estate crash of 1837 came he had cash to buy at ridiculously low prices.

He did not care to sell until he obtained a price with which he could make a better investment. And he did not spend money on building and improving property unless he could reap the immediate reward of such expenditure. Occasionally he asked for and received grants of city land, and though political corruption or graft may have been at the bottom of some of these transactions, he generally offered some reward to the community, such as undergoing the expense of cutting streets, draining or filling in the donated plots or the surrounding areas. The Astor Estate is a typical example of how the unearned increment in land value can be garnered by private interests at the expense of the public at large.[7a]

[7a] Kenneth W. Porter, *John Jacob Astor, Business Man, passim.*

The Story of Chicago Real Estate

Chicago, as a "boom town," has almost as interesting a history as Washington and New York. It was not until the 1830s, however, that this metropolis attracted the attention of land-grabbers. However, as early as 1836 it was the fastest-growing metropolis in all Christendom. Chicago grew in population from 550 inhabitants in 1832 to over 5,000 in 1836, without including the perambulating speculators and real estate vendors. The value of taxable property in the same period rose from $19,560 to several millions. So utterly reckless had the city grown in this early period that the people "chased every bubble that floated on the speculative atmosphere. The more absurd the project the more madly was it pursued."[8] Specially improvised lake steamers, in the boom years 1835 and 1836, carried whole boatloads of land speculators to Chicago and Milwaukee, infected with what was then called "Michigan fever." So great was the demand for lots in this area that almost all northeastern Illinois was laid out in towns, just as almost seventy-five years later the whole coast of Florida was mapped out. Most of those who bought tracts in the region, even before seeing their plots, laid them out into city lots. The whole Chicago area became infested with "get-rich-quick strangers, capitalists, clerks, and even greedy clergymen."

The greatest stimulation to real estate speculation arose from the planning of a canal from Chicago to the Illinois River. The project was authorized by the Illinois legislature, which received a gift of federal land for the purpose. In 1836 the Illinois legislature ordered the trustees of the canal to sell "canal lots," though the exact route of the waterway was not yet definitely determined. The sale was hailed as a wonderful success. Single lots in Chicago brought from $9,000 to $21,400. Aggregate sales from June to September 1836 amounted to $1,359,465, of which $401,042 was received in cash.

But the coming of the Panic of 1837 in the next year led in nearly every instance to the abandonment of purchases. So great was the col-

---

[8] See Moses and Kirkland, *History of Chicago*, Vol. I, p. 98.

lapse that hardly an important purchaser carried his transaction to completion, preferring to forfeit the lots rather than complete the payments. Following the crash, lots that had been sold for more than $1,000 could not fetch $100 in specie.

The collapse of swollen real estate values in Chicago, as elsewhere, gave an opportunity for capitalists with funds to engross large plots in the urban areas. Among those in Chicago who reaped vast profits from such transactions were William Ogden, the first mayor of Chicago; Potter Palmer and Charles Butler of New York; Gurdon S. Hubbard, and several others. Ogden, in the interest of increasing the value of his Chicago real estate holdings, promoted railroads leading in and out of Chicago and was at one time president of the Chicago & North-Western Railroad.

Regarding his successful real estate operations after the 1837 debacle, Ogden wrote in his notebook: "I purchased in 1845 property [in Chicago] for $15,000 which twenty years thereafter [1865] was worth ten millions of dollars. In 1844, I purchased for $8,000 what eight years thereafter sold for three millions of dollars, and these cases could be extended almost indefinitely."[9]

Many similar enormous rises in real estate values in Chicago, St. Louis, and other pioneer metropolises, some of which laid the foundations for the wealthiest private estates in America, could be cited. It is stated by Homer Hoyt that the land value of the territory within the present city limits of Chicago increased from an estimated total of $1,400,000 in 1842 to $126,000,000 in the latter part of 1856, "an increase of eighty-fold in fourteen years."[10] St. Louis and New Orleans experienced a slower but somewhat similar rise in real estate values. Hardly a decade had passed since the United States acquired Louisiana Territory (in which these cities were located) when the combined wealth of a few individual newcomers exceeded the whole price paid for the region by the federal government. Most of this wealth was obtained

[9] See *William B. Ogden and the Early Days in Chicago,* by Hon. Isaac N. Arnold, Fergus Historical Series, No. 17, p. 21.

[10] *One Hundred Years of Land Values in Chicago,* p. 69.

in urban real estate speculation and town-jobbing. Speculators from the East, among whom were John McDonogh, Edward Livingston, and John B. C. Lucas, waxed wealthy in their real estate deals. Lucas acquired a large tract in St. Louis for which he paid $700. In a few years it was worth several millions. Like Nicholas Longworth in Cincinnati and Astor in New York, he did not sell, but left the tract to his heirs.

San Francisco Real Estate

It has been correctly stated that more fortunes have been made from land and real estate investments in California than in gold mining. After the United States took possession of this territory, land values rose, and with the further impetus given when gold was discovered there in 1848, land speculation became rife. Aside from dealings in the old Spanish grants, land speculation was first concentrated largely in the San Francisco area and later became prevalent in southern California in the neighborhood of Los Angeles.

It is quite conceivable that, even if gold had not been discovered in California just after the American conquest, real estate and land speculation would have flourished in the territory. Indeed, real estate speculation and the rise in urban real estate values in San Francisco began early in March 1847, two years before the gold rush. On March 10 of that year General Stephen Watts Kearny, American military commander of California, issued a proclamation granting the municipality of San Francisco the right and title of the Government of the United States and of the new territory to the beach and water-lots on the eastern part of the town. Within a week thereafter, this property was ordered to be sold and the proceeds used by the town authorities. In that year, also, an important section of the town was laid out into streets by the public authorities and the vacant area converted into town lots.

A public sale of these lots took place in 1847. Speculators and investors bought 200 lots at $50 to $100 each. As was customary in such cases where rapid town growth was desired, each purchaser was required to fence the lot and erect a building thereon within a year. Corruption prevailed in the disposal of the lots, and it is reported that the choice sites were secured by speculators "under the old regulations" or by private agreements with the city officials.[11]

In 1853, another great public sale of town lots took place. Values had advanced, but because the best selections had already been engrossed, prices were disappointing. At this time San Francisco was buzzing with the excitement of the gold discovery, and a "boom" was on. Advantageous locations were snapped up by astute buyers, and they demanded high prices when they offered the plots for resale. In the meantime immigration was rapidly adding to the population. "Squatting" became a general nuisance to the real estate owners. The squatters organized themselves into associations and resisted efforts to oust them. With "pre-emption" as a byword, the newcomers set up tents and cabins wherever they found a suitable vacant lot and defied dispossession.

There were further sales of "city lots." Members of the City Council and other privileged political favorites figured largely as buyers. The governor of the territory, hearing of the corruption, ordered the sales to be stopped. But this order was ignored by the City Council, who claimed the governor had no legal right to interfere. Among the city councilors who obtained choice parcels of real estate were Samuel Brannon, J. W. Osborn, William H. Davis, Gabriel B. Post, Talbert H. Green, and Rodman Price. The names of this delectable lot, remarks a historian, "are still perpetuated and honored by the people of San Francisco."[12]

There were obviously good reasons in this period for the rapid rise in real estate values in San Francisco, though of course speculation carried it beyond prudent heights. The town was the only good port accessible to the gold regions. It was the chief emporium for an immense back country where real money was sifted from the soil by the increasing hordes of prospectors. As a contemporary analyst noted: "In two years space, the financier doubled his capital, without risk to himself, and the accumulation went on in geometrical progression. But

[11] See Soule, Gihon and Nisbet, *The Annals of San Francisco*, pp. 180–84. Also Theodore H. Hittel, *A History of California*, Vol. III, p. 116.

[12] John P. Young, *San Francisco, A History of the Pacific Coast Metropolis*, Vol. I, pp. 186–87.

chiefly it was the holders of real estate that made the greatest fortunes."[13]

Although in 1854, because of overspeculation and local political corruption, a real estate depression occurred in San Francisco, real estate values after a few years continued to rise. Among those who made fortunes from real estate in the city were James Lick, founder of the famous Lick Observatory on Mount Wilson; Peter Smith, who through judgments obtained from non-payment of "city scrip," which he bought up in large quantities, obtained valuable tracts of city-owned land at ridiculously low prices; and David C. Broderick, United States senator from California from 1857 to 1859. The acquisitions of Smith and Broderick were validated by the courts. Their holdings included, besides beach and water lots, the public wharves and the city's valuable "underwater" lands. Today their monetary value is enormous.[14]

Los Angeles Real Estate

The "booming" of Los Angeles, now the largest city on the Pacific coast, began within three decades after that of San Francisco. In 1868 the former "pueblo," the seat of a Spanish mission, gave financial assistance toward the construction of the Los Angeles and San Pedro Railroad, which affords the town a commercial outlet to the nearest port. When shortly thereafter the Southern Pacific was planning a railroad from San Francisco by a southerly route to the East, the citizens of Los Angeles were desirous of having this line pass through their town. At this time the total population of the place was under six thousand. Collis P. Huntington, the promoter of the Southern Pacific, demanded a heavy price to comply with the request, but it was granted and the groundwork laid for a real estate boom. The Panic of 1873, however, caused a delay, and it was not until 1882 that the Southern Pacific tracks came into Los Angeles. In the meantime the Atchison, Topeka & Sante Fe Railroad also reached Los Angeles and instituted a rate war. All this led to a vast real estate fever in and around Los Angeles.

The speculative fever was induced largely by the influx of "develop-

[13]Soule, *op. cit.*, p. 498.
[14]Young, *op. cit.*, p. 192.

ers," who, taking advantage of the low rates of railroad fare resulting from the rate war between the Sante Fe and the Southern Pacific railroads, transferred their operations from the Middle West to the Pacific coast. These "developers" mapped out new mushroom "cities" all over Los Angeles County, some of them close to the limits of Los Angeles and some within the city itself. The boundaries of each new "city" almost overlapped those of its neighbors. The wooden street markers and the lot pegs gave them the appearance of a battlefield cemetery. Lots were offered in large and small quantities and were eagerly bought on the spot and sold at distant places. In the single year 1887 the value of real estate transactions recorded in Los Angeles approximated $100,000,000. But only a small part of this sum represented cash outlays, since the bulk of the sales were merely contracts to buy. As in similar transactions before and since, liberal credit was given lot purchasers. When the boom collapsed in 1889, most of these purchasers on credit forfeited their unpaid acquisitions.

Unlike the booms in Chicago and some other eastern cities, the Los Angeles boom of the 1880s was carried on by professional and unscrupulous town-jobbers, mostly from other sections. T. S. Van Dyke who published a history of the whole affair, derides the idea that it was analogous to any South Sea Bubble, or oil or mining-stock swindles. In the account of the speculation, he states:

> The actors in this great game were not ignorant or poor people, and from end to end there was scarcely anything in it that could be called a swindle. With few exceptions, the principal victims were men of means. Most of them, and certainly the most reckless of them, were men who in some branch of business had been successful—all had the amplest time to reverse their judgments and investigate the conditions. Some of the silliest of the lot were men who, during the first three fourths of the excitement, kept carefully out of it, and did nothing but sneer at the folly of those who were in it.[15]

The same might also be said of the Florida land boom of the 1920s. Many capitalists did not venture into the field until the boom reached

[15]*Millionaires for a Day: An Inside History of the Great Southern California Boom*, pp. 2–3.

its peak. But it cannot be said that most of the victims were people of wealth. Many of the poor and ignorant were losers in the venture.

During the 1920s, Los Angeles experienced another wild real estate boom. New developments were laid out over a large area surrounding the city, and lots were sold and as eagerly bought by speculators and home seekers at fabulous prices, akin to what happened in the same period throughout Florida. After the boom collapsed, however, the resulting depression in values was not as serious as in Florida.[16]

The collapse of the southern California land booms did not hinder the progressive rise in real estate values in the area. Today the county of Los Angeles is one large aggregation of cities and towns. But its rapid growth has been placed on a permanent foundation. It has advantages created by nature and human progress—the basis of sound land value. Its rapid growth, though accompanied by real estate boosting and town-jobbing, may be accounted for by the increase in population, commercial and industrial development, natural resources, and other factors to which the owners of the land as a class contributed very little but reaped the full benefit.

The growth of real estate values in San Francisco and Los Angeles can be matched to some extent by the rival cities of Tacoma and Seattle on Puget Sound. Though also fostered by real estate booms and the work of professional real estate "developers," the values have been created for the most part by favorable location for shipping and other transportation facilities, and by the importance as sites for commerce and industry. These advantages are not generally created by any single person or group of individuals. They are the work of nature, social progress, and the concentration of population.

Corporation Urban Engrossment

There are a few notable cases in the nation's history in which corporations engrossed large tracts of land to be held for other purposes than that relating to their business operations. From the earliest colonial times, industrial operations, such as mining, iron manufacture, and the like, followed the practice of creating villages or population

[16] See Marquis James, *The Biography of a Bank,* New York, 1954, pp. 235–36.

centers in which the operating concerns housed their offices and workers. The village of Hopewell, built around a forge in Pennsylvania, is a typical example. But in this there was no aim to reap the benefit of land rental. The practice was followed by a number of mining companies, who built and rented houses and maintained "company stores" for their workers. In most cases, however, the system has been abandoned, and it is noteworthy that the United States Steel Corporation, in the construction of Gary, Indiana, and in the planning of its new works at Morrisville, Pennsylvania, did not seek to monopolize the landownership in the area adjacent to their vast undertakings.

The most outstanding case of a large corporation creating a town and at the same time endeavoring to hold the title to the land within its boundaries intact was that of Pullman, Illinois. George Pullman, a wealthy Chicago car builder, in 1880 conceived a plan to locate his great car works near Chicago but withheld the selection of the site from public notice in order to ward off land speculators who would engross real estate in the area. He secretly bought 3,500 acres of land adjacent to Chicago at from $75 to $200 an acre. In 1883, after the new works were built, the land had risen to from $1,000 to $3,000 per acre, but Pullman would not dispose of any of it. Instead, his company, the Pullman Land Company, retained it and built "a model town," which was named Pullman, and, in addition to constructing homes, churches, and schools, erected its own gasworks, waterworks, and sewage-disposal plant. All these developments were retained by the Pullman Company and all rentals and charges accrued to it. Thus the venture was a real estate development as well as an industrial project. The town of Pullman remained an independent community in the Chicago area, "being surrounded on all sides by vacant land of lower value." The Pullman Land Company, however, by holding its land and not disposing of it, detracted from its development as a business center of Chicago. This center was developed elsewhere in areas where cheaper land could be obtained.[17]

Another somewhat though not entirely similar case of industrial real estate engrossment is that of Newport News, Virginia. The develop-

[17] Homer Hoyt, *op. cit.*, p. 135.

ment of this important southern seaport and industrial center was largely the work of Collis P. Huntington, California pioneer millionaire and railroad builder. Huntington, after the successful completion of his western railroad ventures, came East and acquired control of the Chesapeake & Ohio Railroad Company. In order to obtain a satisfactory tidewater terminus for this railroad, he conceived the idea of building a port in Hampton Roads, Virginia, on a site having a harbor sufficiently deep to accommodate large ocean steamers. The place selected was given the name of Newport News. A company, incorporated as the Old Dominion Land Company, was organized in 1880 to acquire the site. A "town boom" was started. Not only was the terminus of the Chesapeake & Ohio Railroad fixed at the place, but Huntington constructed one of the largest dry docks and shipbuilding plants on the Atlantic seaboard.

Undoubtedly the object of Huntington in creating the Old Dominion Land Company was to reap the profit from the rise in the value of the surrounding area which naturally would follow his construction of a railroad terminus and the shipbuilding enterprise. But there was no intention to withhold the land from sale, and lots and plots were readily disposed of. However, the Old Dominion Land Company continued to operate Newport News as a private venture until 1895, when a city charter was obtained from the state of Virginia. The president of the company at the time, in referring to the change to a municipal status, remarked in his annual report that, in the interests of the company, the charter was "reasonable as to its nature, care having been taken to avoid the imposing of extreme taxation or other burdens." At that time, the land company still owned 156 lots in the city and a 30-acre farm. In addition, it owned the Newport News Lighting and Water Company. Most of the company's lots had been sold on deferred payments, so with high taxes they were likely to revert to the company; but with a city charter, the expenses previously incurred by the land company in keeping the streets of the town in order would be borne by the taxpayers.

The amount of funds invested by the Old Dominion Land Company in its unique town-building venture was not large in the light of more recent similar land-speculation episodes. In 1891 its total capitalization was reported at $1,962,736. The cost of its real estate was put down as $1,585,299, while its buildings, including a hotel, cost an additional $1,118,564. But in 1930, when the company had wound up its affairs, the assessed valuation of taxable property in the city of Newport News, Virginia, was about $35,000,000. This is but one example of how enormously real estate values can be increased.

Another instance of a magnificent scheme of modern city building, with real estate speculation as the prime motive, was the promotion of Coral Gables during the Florida land boom of the 1920s. Coral Gables was originated by George Edgar Merrick, a Miami real estate operator. His first idea was to develop an exclusive inland suburb. However, as his plans developed and as the oncoming boom caused a rapid growth of Miami, the project was expanded to cover a sea-front community with forty miles of beach land. The aim was to make it a complete city, with business zones, workers' districts, and favorable locations for the rich and well-to-do. The whole project was a money-making scheme, similar to the town-jobbing of earlier days—and collapsed when the "Florida Bubble" burst.[18]

Summary

The foregoing account of the rise of urban real estate values is necessarily discursive and selective. The subject deserves a more definite and complete account, a research project well within the public interest, since, as already stated, in real estate the unearned increase in land values is so clearly demonstrated. Almost all economists are agreed that such values should accrue to the benefit of the people in common. But of course it has been argued that private property in land has been an indispensable instrument for the advance of civilization, and cupidity and progress frequently go hand in hand.

As the late Professor Frank Taussig has stated:

> There is no vested right in the indefinite future . . . with the rapid growth of modern cities and the unmistakable swelling of

[18] For a journalistic account of Coral Gables, see T. H. Weigall, *Boom in Paradise*.

site rents, a reservation of the community's rights with respect to urban land has met with steadily increasing recognition. The form in which this right is most likely to be asserted is that of a special tax on the newly accrued increase in site values. In strict theory, the whole of this increase might be taken through taxation. . . . But it is not likely, so long as the institution of private property remains, that there will be so drastic an application of the principle.[19]

And commenting on the taxation of site values in Germany and Great Britain, Professor Taussig had this to say:

In Germany, where so many movements toward social reform are being carried on in deliberate and well-planned fashion, the recent (1911) imperial legislation for taxing gains in site value did no more than appropriate thirty per cent of the increase. The hotly debated British tax of 1909 took twenty per cent. It may be that this is only a beginning, and those who oppose it will maintain that eventually everything will be taken. . . . But such objectives are urged against every proposal for social reform, and, if allowed, would prevent any disturbance whatever of the *status quo*. The day is gone by when they are felt to be insuperable. . . . The rights to property must approve themselves on examination in each particular case, and must submit to modification where a balance of gain for the public can be reasonably expected.[20]

[19]*Principles of Economics*, Vol. II, p. 103.
[20]*Ibid.*, p. 103.

Chapter 21

The Land and Taxes

The European Precedents

As since early times land was the principal form of wealth and income, it has been an object of taxation either directly or indirectly. According to the late Professor E. R. A. Seligman,[1] the ownership of agricultural land and real estate, along with other forms of property—i.e., the ownership of wealth in general—was regarded as a basis for the faculty of the individual to pay taxes. During the two centuries preceding the nineteenth century there gradually developed a system of classifying the items of wealth on the basis of their income production. This was not exactly a general income tax, such as we know it today, but was a step in that direction. It constituted merely the adoption of product or produce as things and not as a norm of taxation. It was still a tax on things and not on persons, and, in the process of assessing and levying the tax, no account was taken of the relative ability of the taxpayer to pay the tax. This system still prevails in most of the states of the Union, where real estate is assessed and taxed on a classification basis rather than on the actual income produced by each item assessed.

As the early American colonists came from England and were familiar with the tax systems of that country, the tax practices and theories that prevailed in Britain in the seventeenth and eighteenth centuries were naturally applied, as far as circumstances permitted, in the new settlements. In Britain, as in most other European countries, as stated in the previous paragraph, the early practice had been to levy

[1]*The Income Tax,* 2nd ed., pp. 12–15.

land taxes (including tithes) on the gross produce of soil. Later and gradually, the basis for the assessment was an assumed net product, thus making allowance for the expenses of cultivation.

Inasmuch as in those days it was highly impractical to calculate the net product of each individual parcel of cultivated land, the land had to be classified and the net product, actual or potential, fixed on the basis of the classification. As stated by Professor Seligman, although the method was undeniably a step in advance, it was not sufficient to create justice and equality in taxation. "The net produce of two farmers," as pointed out by Seligman, "after allowing for the expenses of cultivation, may be precisely the same but if the owner of one farm has purchased it on a mortgage, his final net earnings will be less than that of his neighbor. The net produce of a piece of property, in other words, is no necessary indication of the net revenue to the owner. The tax upon the thing, just because it is upon the thing, does not lend itself readily to the shifting conditions of the man who owns the thing; and yet the real ability of a person to pay taxes must be in some relation to his individual condition."[2]

While there is some difference of opinion regarding the foregoing argument, the tendency has been, as shall be shown later, to tax both improved and unimproved property on the basis of the tax being permanently fixed to the property. In other words, the tax is highly impersonal, the financial position of the taxpayer and his ability to pay not generally being taken into account. Thus the principle of a progressive tax has not been applied to land through progressive income taxation. Under a progressive rate of taxation, the net product or income from the land and its improvement, over and above the expenses of maintenance or cultivation, would be levied on the property but would be adjusted in order to be met by the individual taxpayer according to his financial situation.

Early Colonial Land Taxation

As Professor Richard T. Ely has stated in his pioneer work, *Taxation in American States and Cities:* "In the earlier days of the colonies there

[2] *Ibid.*, pp. 14–15.

was no great need for taxes. The mother country asked no assistance from them; quitrents satisfied the demands of the proprietor or the company, who in turn promised at least partial protection; fierce wars had not yet transferred the burden of defense to the shoulders of the people; the public wants of the colonists themselves were simple and easily supplied; there were few officials; and these were either wholly without compensation, or received but a few slight fees; and the chief and almost sole objects of their contributions were churches, schools and highways."[3]

Because of the scarcity of currency and the plentifulness of unoccupied land, it was the common practice in early colonial days to compensate officials and others for public services by grants of land. This had also been a practice in England but was limited to an endowment for extraordinary services to the state and was a relic of feudalism. In the colonies, however, it was applied to ordinary services. Thus Robert Lenthall, schoolteacher and minister, received 104 acres of land from Newport, Rhode Island, in 1640 and 100 acres were appropriated for a school "for the encouragement of the poorer sort."[4] Many other instances of this sort could be cited. In fact, as already indicated, the practice persisted even after the adoption of the constitution, when the federal government granted land to road builders and others performing services or encouraging land settlement.

As the early settlers had to undergo the expenses and the delays of clearing as well as cultivating the lands, as a rule, they were consequently in no position to pay taxes on the land. The colonies, therefore, for the most part resorted to other means of obtaining necessary revenues. Even in the case of quitrents, provision was generally made that no payments would be demanded until after a lapse of years. Among the revenue sources applied by the colonies were occupational or so-called faculty taxes, licenses, excises, fees, fines, and occasional lotteries.

However, it must not be assumed that land in the colonial period escaped taxation. At various times and in later years as an annual assessment, direct taxes were laid either in proportion to property held,

[3] P. 107.
[4] *Ibid.*

real or personal, or as a uniform charge in the nature of a poll or head tax. Individuals and companies were frequently taxed on the mass of their property—i.e., its estimated total value—but, as land was by far the chief item of wealth in the colonial period, it bore the lion's share of this direct taxation and in some of the colonies became the object of a special tax. Thus in Virginia a poll tax was the only direct tax levied for a considerable period. Because of its inequity and consequent burden on the poorer classes, it was replaced in 1663 by a land tax.[5] In course of time, when because of the burden of the inequitable poll taxes they were largely abandoned, the general property tax came into vogue and has continued (particularly as a source of revenue for local authorities) until the present day.

Land Taxation in the Early Federal Period

The American Revolution and the consequent formation of a federal government effected very little change, if any, in the systems or methods of taxation of the American states and local governments. There was no occasion for the states to alter substantially their tax laws, and the federal government refrained as far as possible from resorting to direct taxation, largely because of the constitutional provision which limited the method of such taxation to apportionment among the several states according to population.

The first important contemporary study of taxation in the early federal period was made in 1796 under the direction of Oliver Wolcott, then Secretary of the Treasury, who had been directed by Congress to prepare a plan for laying and collecting federal taxes, with reference to the levying of a direct tax. Wolcott pointed out the diversity among the states both as to the objects and principles of taxation and the methods of assessing, apportioning, and collecting the taxes. In seven states he found a uniform capitation or poll tax, whereas in other states no such tax existed. "Land was taxed in one state according to quantity, in another according to quality, and in a third not at all." As pointed out by Professor Ely, the diversity of the principles and methods of obtaining state revenues at the time was undoubtedly due to the relatively

[5] *Ibid.*, p. 111.

light burden of taxation in those days. There were both laxity and neglect in the collection of the state taxes, while the localities, counties, and towns found sufficient revenues from indirect rather than direct sources to carry out their public services.

As an indication of the early laxity in land taxation, the new state of Tennessee in 1796 had a provision in its constitution which stated that "all lands are liable to be taxed, and they shall be taxed uniformly, so that no 100 acres shall be taxed higher than another, except town-lots. No freeman shall be taxed higher than 100 acres of land, and no slave higher than 200 acres. No article of manufacture shall be taxed except to pay expenses of inspection." A similar system of taxing land prevailed in Vermont at this early period.[6] Here we have a case of inequitable land taxation which very likely came into being because of the large landholdings of individuals who undoubtedly controlled or influenced legislation of the period.

Professor Ely in his book, *Taxation in American States and Cities*, already quoted, presents a table indicating the various sources of state revenues in 1796. This table reveals that all except one of the fifteen states then in the Union had a land tax, though four also had a general property tax. Thus there is evidence that land and real estate taxation had already become a source of state and local revenue after the Revolution. The dependence on land as a source of direct taxation is to be expected in a period when land constituted the principal item of private wealth in the community.

In giving details of taxes on land in 1796, Professor Ely discloses a variety of methods of taxation. "In Vermont all lands which had been improved two years and were within enclosure, and in North Carolina all lands, excepting town lots, which were assessed according to valuation, were taxed uniformly according to quantity. In Rhode Island and New York lands, together with all other property, real and personal, were taxed according to estimated valuation. They were assessed in Massachusetts and New Hampshire according to their products or supposed annual rents. A peculiarity of this tax in the latter state was the arbitrary and variable size of the acre. It was not a certain number of

[6] See Frederick A. Wood, *The Finances of Vermont*, p. 19.

square rods, but was a sufficient quantity of orchard land to produce ten barrels of cider, or of arable land to produce twenty-five bushels of Indian corn, or of mowing land to produce a ton of hay. A quantity of land sufficient to support a cow one year was regarded as four acres. In Connecticut no regard was had for the value of lands in their assessment, but all were assessed uniformly according to the mode of cultivation or condition, each kind being placed in the list at a fixed rate; as for example, meadow lands at $2.50 per acre. Taxes were levied on land in Pennsylvania according to a triennial valuation, in Virginia according to a permanent valuation.

"The average or relative value of lands in different counties or districts was fixed by law in Maryland and New Jersey, and this average value multiplied by the number of acres therein became the basis of taxation. Within the counties or districts, lands contributed to the total sums assessed to them in proportion to their value. Lands in Kentucky, except town-lots, were divided into three classes according to quality, and, in South Carolina and Georgia, lands were taxed uniformly by districts or classes, whether cultivated or not. Delaware had no direct tax on land, but a tax was levied on the income from land in a general income tax."[7]

Land Taxation Merges into the General Property Tax

From the beginning of the nineteenth century through the period of the Civil War and thereafter, the nation witnessed an industrialization that diversified and intensified the various forms of property and wealth. This acted to decrease the dependence on land as a source of public revenue, and it did actually decrease the relative burden on land as its value increased more rapidly than the general tax load. Nevertheless, as the aggregate weight of taxes increased, state and local governments, and particularly the latter, came to rely more and more on the taxation of land and improvements. Under this so-called "general property tax," which supposedly levied on real and personal property alike, real property, owing to its tangible nature which defied concealment, tended to bear a relatively greater burden, and personal property,

[7] *Op. cit.*, pp. 119–20.

whether productive or non-productive, fell comparatively in importance as a revenue source. In practically all states and municipalities, the proportion of revenue accruing from personal property under the general property tax has been declining for years, with the result that in many states and local taxing bodies the assessment of personal property has been abandoned and the old special land and house taxes have been restored. Thus land, and the improvements thereon, is still the fertile source of revenue to the states and their subdivisions.

But the general property tax today, comprised largely as a tax on realty, is not an equitable or logical tax. In most cases it taxes both the land and the improvements thereon at the same rate. Although it taxes both productive and unproductive property, it penalizes productive improvements by placing on them a tax burden. Moreover, it permits the holding of real estate from productive use with the prime motive of gaining the rise in future rental value; i.e., the unearned increment.

For this reason alone, agricultural lands and land sites not put to productive use, or held merely for speculative purposes, should bear a higher tax rate than the tax levied on real estate improvements. Even the late Professor Seligman, who strongly decried the taxing of unproductive property, supported this principle. In his *Essays in Taxation*, he writes:

> The great element of reason in the demand for the taxation of unproductive property is to be found in the assessment of real estate. It is an undoubted fact that real estate is often held for speculative purposes and that it is the duty of the community not to encourage such speculation by exempting vacant lands from taxation. The owner expects to reap from the future value of the land, whether he sells or keeps it, a sum more than sufficient to recompense him for his outlay and intervening loss of interest and profit. He is prospectively earning an annual revenue from the land, whose present unproductiveness is technical rather than real. It is thus perfectly logical to tax unproductive real estate, even though the basis of taxation be product rather than property. It is the estimated, rather than the actual, product that is taxed.[8]

[8] 1st ed., p. 58.

The most notable case of holding real estate in an unimproved condition for purposes of profit is, as stated previously, that of John Jacob Astor. As there noted, Astor as early as 1800 pursued a policy of utilizing his mercantile gains in the purchase of land just beyond the city limits. He gradually sold this land at an advanced price and used the proceeds to buy more extensive tracts somewhat farther out. Much of this land was held unimproved by the Astor Estate for upward of a century. In the meantime, as New York City rapidly expanded because of increase of population, the land advanced in value manyfold, undoubtedly far in excess of the taxes paid and the compound interest on the original investment.

The benefits derived by individuals and corporations in holding land in an unimproved condition for profit at the expense of the public and as hindrance of economic progress have been recognized by economists and social philosophers for several centuries, and, as shall be pointed out in the following chapter, ways and means of offsetting the evil have been proposed. It has been widely discussed in American as well as European economic literature, but as yet little action of a positive nature has been taken to meet the problem. Possibly constitutional limitations, wherein the tax laws require conformity to certain methods of assessment for tax purposes, have been the greatest impediment in correcting the evil through political action.[9]

Taxation of Improvements

The means most commonly attempted in several American states to discourage landholdings for speculative purposes was to tax bare land value at a higher rate than the buildings and improvements made on the land. The distinguishment of buildings from the land itself in tax assessments has been followed in a few states from quite an early period. Thus at the beginning of the last century Kentucky taxed land without regard to improvements. Ohio, another new state, in 1825 enacted a law which provided that land should be valued "without taking into consideration the value of the actual improvements made

---

[9] For a discussion of this topic, see H. G. Brown, *The Economic Basis of Tax Reform*.

thereon."[10] A few other states made attempts to follow out this principle. Thus it was early recognized in the development of American taxation systems that citizens should not be made to pay a penalty for adding wealth to the country. Yet, in spite of this, the general tendency for many years following the Civil War was to apply the "general property" principle, wherein all property, real and personal, improved and unimproved, productive and unproductive, was taxed at a uniform rate.

The Incidence of Land Taxation

Although it is not the intention in these pages to enter into economic theories of taxation, the fact that the taxation of land and its improvements has become almost the exclusive tax on tangible wealth in America requires some discussion of the shifting and final incidence of such taxation. The question here is whether the tax on land or urban real estate (i.e., land and its improvements) is borne by the owner or the tenant or is divided between them. This question cannot be definitely answered, since various circumstances alter the results. As stated by the late Professor Seligman, who had devoted years to the study of the subject:

> If our general property tax were actually enforced, then beyond all doubt the real estate tax would be entirely borne by the owner. But it is precisely in the American cities that the general property tax has become practically a real property tax. In other words, city real estate bears, if not the exclusive, at least the greater, weight of municipal taxation. In proportion as the city houses are taxed at a far higher rate than other capital, the main condition under which the tax may be shifted to the occupier is present. If we take the small American towns where the investments are mainly local, and where personal property is reached to a fairly good degree, then it is very probable that the real estate tax is not shifted to the occupier. But the larger the city and the greater the chances of investment in outside capital, the less will be the proportion of personalty taxed and the greater will be the possibility of a shifting of a part of the real estate tax.

[10] See Ely, *op. cit.*, p. 135.

And Professor Seligman concludes:

> It may be said in short that while the real estate tax falls on the owner in case of stationary or declining population, a considerable portion of the tax is shifted on the tenant in the normal case of a prosperous town or city district under the present administration of our property tax. When we reflect that in the city of New York over three fourths [probably greater now] live in tenement houses, we are thus forced to the conclusion that a large burden of our American local taxation is today borne by those least able to pay. The question as to how far these may again be able to shift the tax on others is a part of the large question of the tax on property, profits or wages.[11]

Proposals for Taxation as Remedies for the Land Question

Since equitable landholding and land taxation are bound up together, the solving of the problem of the land question may be approached through reforms in taxation. Two proposals have been presented. One is to tax land under a progressive-rate system, such as has been applied to the income tax. The other is the absorption of the economic rent of land through taxation, as proposed by Henry George. Both proposals may be applied simultaneously, as neither interferes or offsets the other, and no valid inequities would be involved. The application of a progressive rate of taxation to individual landholdings would naturally act as a damper on the monopolization and accumulation of land—an evil which has existed in civilized nations for centuries and which has been the cause of widespread discontent in many countries from Roman times to the present day. That it has not yet been seriously felt in the United States is due largely to the general abundance of land, its relative cheapness, and its rapid and widespread distribution. But it is undoubtedly manifest that with the continuous population growth and the encroachment of metropolitan and urban areas on tillable land, as well as the appropriation of large areas for industrial, mining, forestry, and even agricultural uses, land- and home-ownership are becoming more and more restricted to a relatively small segment of the nation's total population.

[11] *Op. cit.*, pp. 233-34

As yet no serious effort has been made to tax land on a rising progressive rate in accordance with the size and value of individual holdings. Many economists tell us such progressive taxation is impractical. The matter has been discussed, however, in several areas, and such a proposal has been made in California. The effect of such a tax may be problematical and its practicability may not undergo the test, but it should be remembered that "impracticability" was applied by critics and statesmen when Great Britain inaugurated the income tax in 1799.

The progressive rate of income taxes, which is almost universal throughout the civilized world, has been an important factor in promoting a redistribution of wealth and, if properly applied in relation to size and value of individual landholdings, could aid further in promoting this social reform. Moreover, the advantage of such a tax lies in its relative non-shiftability and inherent justice. There is no avenue by means of which the progressive rate could be transferred to others, whether tenants or consumers. Where large landownership arises from the nature or form of business operations, such as mining, forestry, or even agricultural enterprise, of course the progressive tax rate would not apply.

It is interesting to note that, probably because of the influence of Thomas Jefferson, the first federal direct tax law, enacted by Congress on July 14, 1798, provided for a progressive tax rate on land and improvements, the rate increasing with the value of the property assessed. According to the terms of the act, a tax was to be levied "upon every dwelling house, which, with the out houses appurtenant thereto, and the land whereon the same were erected, not exceeding two acres, shall not be valued at more than one hundred, and not more than five hundred dollars, the tax rate to be one tenth of one per cent." This rate was increased progressively, ranging from three tenths of one per cent on houses valued at more than $500, up to one per cent on houses valued above $30,000. This progression applied only to dwelling houses; agricultural lands could be assessed by the individual states at rates sufficient to make up their portion of $2,000,000—the estimated receipts from the direct tax levy.[12]

[12] See Timothy Pitkin, *A Statistical View of the Commerce of the United States of America*, pp. 309–10.

Land-Value Taxation

In taxation under equitable principles, it should be made clear that there is a difference between land and "real estate"; i.e., the bare land as such and the improvements made thereon. The former obtains its value because of its situs or fertility, which is a combination of natural advantages or the result of human progress. Its value, therefore, can be attributed to no single individual or group, but to peculiar circumstances in which all the populace plays a part. However, if capital and labor are applied to the land, such as erecting buildings and adding other improvements thereto, those that furnish the capital and labor create additional wealth. If such additions to wealth are taxed—and they are the sources of employment and sustenance to the commonwealth—then those who create wealth and give employment are penalized, while those who hold property which is the bounty of nature, intended for common use, suffer no penalties as long as the rise in value of such property more than compensates for the taxes levied thereon. Thus it is made manifest, and the theory is becoming widespread, both in this country and abroad, that, in taxation, the value of the land as distinguished from the value of the improvements thereon should be taxed exclusively or at a higher rate.

The arguments of those who support this theory have been well summarized by Dr. Harry Gunnison Brown:

> The point of view of those who favor public appropriation of the annual rental value of sites and natural resources is that taxes should be so levied as to further the common welfare. . . . They stress the fact that the *annual rent* of land is a geologically- and socially-produced value; that the individual is not responsible for it and that it is socially undesirable for the private individual to enjoy it. . . . They call attention to the fact that not to take the economic rent of land as a first source of public revenue compels drawing more heavily on the earnings of labor and of thrift. And they conclude that a society in which the annual rent of land . . . is taken in taxation for public needs would be a far better society for the ordinary person to live in than the economic society we now have.[12a]

[12a]"Anticipation of an Increment and the 'Unearned Decrement' in Land Values," *The American Journal of Economics and Sociology*, Vol. 2, pp. 343–58.

The principle of the public appropriation of the annual value (or economic rent) of land has had widespread support ever since it was proposed so forcefully by Henry George in 1879. Indeed, it was put forward in some form or other by George's predecessors in land reform (notably Thomas Spence and John Stuart Mill). Here again there is a problem of "practicability." Can the return from the natural and inherent powers of the land be distinguished from the return received from its improvements? In most of our states the distinction already is being made in the periodic valuations of properties for tax purposes. But, assuming the difficulty to exist—as in some instances it must—this does not mean it is impossible to fix a criterion.

It should be noted as an argument against the impracticability of taxing the value of land in lieu of improvements, that such taxation has been in operation in widely separated areas for almost a half century. It has been applied in modified and different forms in Denmark, Australia, New Zealand and South Africa, and, in the United States, in Pittsburgh, Pennsylvania; Fairhope, Alabama; and Arden and Ardentown, Delaware. In quite another way, during the same period, "land-value increment taxes" were put into operation in Germany. These were taxes levied at the time a property was sold on the increment in the capitalized value of land.

Regarding the experience with land-value taxation in Australasia, Yetta Scheftel, writing in 1916 in her prize-winning book, *The Taxation of Land Value*, states:

> In no case has there been a repeal of the tax except to extend its operation; in other words, after its adoption, however great the opposition may have previously been, the levy of the tax ceased to be a party measure. Indeed, the opponents of the tax seem to have become reconciled to its existence. Secondly, the adoption of the tax by one state after another, by the local bodies, and recently by the federal government of Australia, argues in its favor and for its expedience in that country.[13]

Concerning the application of the principle of increment-value taxation in Germany, which was used by various local governing bodies

[13] P. 120.

comprising the principal cities from 1904 until the end of World War I, and was adopted to some extent by the national government under the name of *Wertzuwachssteurer* (value increase tax), Dr. Frederic C. Howe, in his book *European Cities at Work,* published in 1913, states:

> Community after community adopted it until in April, 1910, the tax had been introduced into towns and cities with an aggregate population of 15,000,000. Nor is there any substantial protest against it, in spite of the fact that real estate interests are active in city politics as well as the provision of the Prussian law that one half of the members of the city council must be owners of real estate. The tax meets with all but universal approval.[14]

Summary

In summing up the question of land-value taxation, I can hardly do better than cite a paragraph from the philosophical work of Professor George Raymond Geiger, entitled *The Theory of the Land Question.*

> Land value is not an industry-produced value. Its creation is an automatic and gratuitous social act, and its disposition in terms of taxation can have no negative effect on the processes that produce wealth. In fact, a tax on land values acts as a definite stimulant for production. The tragic paradox is that our present species of revenue-getting is largely one of self-mutilation. Society cripples itself by the continued sapping of wealth. It seems to do this deliberately, for always have there been theorists to point to the social fund of land value as a source of relief from this self-crippling.[15]

[14] P. 195.
[15] *Op. cit.,* p. 192. For treatises and discussions relating to the taxation of land-rent values, see Harry Gunnison Brown, *The Economics of Taxation; The Economic Basis of Tax Reform;* Yetta Scheftel, *The Taxation of Land Value;* Thomas G. Shearman, *Natural Taxation.* For contrasting views, see Seligman, *Essays in Taxation,* Chap. III; John Rae, *Contemporary Socialism,* Chap. XII; and W. H. Mallock, *Property and Progress.*

Chapter 22

The Progress of Land Reform in the United States

The Pioneers in Land Reform

The land-reform movement in Western civilization began in the eighteenth century in France and England. In the period during which the American colonies were making preparations to throw off the British yoke there came into existence a general intellectual movement for political and economic liberalism. It was marked by the writings of Voltaire, Rousseau, and the Encyclopedists, along with "the economists"—i.e., the physiocrats in France—and was closely followed up by British and Scottish radicals of the period, among whom may be included William Blackstone, John Locke, Thomas Spence, William Ogilvie, Thomas Paine, and a host of other minor or less known philosophers and reformers. The rise of the science of economics, then called "political economy," aided the movement.

Space does not permit an elaboration of the theories of these writers, but, in the main, their philosophy was based on the doctrine of natural law, according to which the earth and the fullness thereof was the common property of mankind, in which all human beings should participate equally. The impact of the Industrial Revolution during the last half of the eighteenth century, along with the economic deterioration and distress which accompanied the separation of a large part of the population from owning or tilling the soil, fostered the movement. It formed an outlet for the widespread dissatisfaction with economic and political conditions.

Undoubtedly the most original and radical of the early land reformers was Thomas Spence. Spence was of Scottish origin but was born in Newcastle, England, in 1750, where he progressed from a self-taught workman to a tutor and lecturer. Possibly through the influence of the French physiocrats he became interested in economic problems and published from time to time a number of pamphlets dealing with various phases of the subject. On November 8, 1775, he delivered a lecture on land reform before the Newcastle Philosophical Society. In this address he enunciated a plan of expropriating the landlords, having their lands taken over by the parishes, which would, in turn, lease separate parcels to farmers for a moderate rental. This rent, Spence held, would be sufficient to meet the expenses of both the local and national governments, and therefore no other imposts would need to be levied. Thus Spence may be regarded as a forerunner of Henry George and an original proponent of the "single tax." Spence in 1796 published his lecture in pamphlet form and was indicted in 1801 and tried in London for sedition.

Another Scotsman, William Ogilvie, professor of humanities in Kings College, Aberdeen, who was born in 1736 and died in 1813, published anonymously in 1782 *An Essay on the Right of Property in Land with Respect to Its Foundations in the Law of Nature*. Like Spence, he argued that land was the common property of mankind and that "no individual can derive from his general right of occupancy a title to any more than an equal share of the soil of this country. He proposed a tax be imposed on barren lands and so regulated as to encourage the proprietor in its immediate cultivation, and if he failed to do this, to oblige him to turn it back to the community. In line with the physiocratic doctrine he held "no scheme of taxation can be so equitable as a land tax."[1]

Early American Land Reformers

The physiocratic principles imbued by Spence, Ogilvie, Filangieri (an Italian), and others who wrote and lived in the late eighteenth century had only a slight influence on the American continent. Though there is evidence that John Locke's ideas had gained followers in the colonies

[1] George R. Geiger, *The Philosophy of Henry George*, pp. 146–52.

and influenced such men as William Penn, Thomas Jefferson, John Adams, Thomas Paine, and other pre-Revolutionary statesmen, these, with the possible exception of Thomas Paine, did not preach the doctrine of common ownership of land or a single tax on land. Jefferson, however, as we have already indicated, was opposed to private engrossment of land.

The indifference to land reform in the early days of the Republic may be due to the fact that most of the intellectual men of the colonial and post-Revolutionary periods were landowners, and since land in the country was relatively cheap and could be easily obtained by purchase or otherwise, they could see no argument for common landownership. Thus, though both Benjamin Franklin and Thomas Jefferson were conversant with physiocratic doctrines, they never came out openly for the "natural right to land" or the principle of a tax on the unearned increment.[1a] Franklin had been engaged in a huge land-speculation project just before the Revolutionary War, and Jefferson, who was opposed to land speculation, openly declared that in America "there was land enough for all."[2] Thomas Paine, however, did adopt the "natural right to the soil" doctrine, and in his pamphlet, *Agrarian Justice,* proposed a plan for land redistribution.

Immediately following the Revolution, the intellectual segment of American society, particularly those who were interested in economic and political affairs, came under the influence of the British classical economic writers. The first American edition of Adam Smith's *Wealth of Nations* appeared in 1796. It is this work which the late Professor Dunbar of Harvard University holds influenced Alexander Hamilton in his economic ideas. It should be remembered that Hamilton swayed early American economic and financial policies for several decades after

[1a] However, in his *Fruits of Solitude,* written in 1693, William Penn stated that "if all men were so far tenants to the public that the superfluities of gain and expense were applied to the exigencies thereof, it would put an end to taxes, leave not a beggar, and make the greatest bank for national trade in Europe."

[2] Jefferson, it must be admitted, did favor the idea that if "in any country [there are] uncultivated lands and unemployed poor, it is clear that the laws of property have been so far extended as to violate natural right." Geiger, *op. cit.,* p. 191.

the Revolution, and there certainly was nothing in Hamilton's expressed ideas that would make him an agrarian or "free soiler."

In 1817, David Ricardo published in England his *Political Economy*, in which he enunciated the economic law of rent. The work attracted some interest in the United States, for it was republished in Georgetown, D.C., soon after its appearance in England. The work received the attention of American economists—most of whom, however, took issue with the ideas expressed therein. It is proposed in a few following paragraphs to review these discussions in so far as they relate to land and land taxation.

The Land Question and Early American Economists

Aside from their endeavors to refute the Ricardian theory of rent, American economists during the first half of the nineteenth century evinced little interest in land problems. This, as already stated, is undoubtedly due to the relative plentifulness of arable land in the country during this period. Despite the numerous discussions in Congress and elsewhere regarding the disposal of the public domain, it is rarely mentioned in the economic literature of the period, and little aid or advice was obtained from contemporary economic scholars.

The economist who in his writings during this period discussed most often land as a factor in economic life was Henry C. Carey. Carey, a prolific writer, staunchly denied the Ricardian theory of rent, mainly on the assumed ground that the poorest lands were first cultivated and the better-quality soils came into use as land became scarcer. However, he did take notice of the concentration of landholdings both in the United States and abroad. In his *Principles of Social Science*[3] he states:

> With the growth of commerce, the development of the powers of the earth, and the creation of local centers of action, land becomes divided, and the little farm of a half a dozen acres is made to yield a larger quantity of raw materials than before had been obtained from hundreds or from thousands of acres. . . . Property in land then becomes consolidated, the tenant-at-will and the day laborer replacing the little and independent proprietor so much regarded by Adam Smith. So was it, as we have seen, in

[3] 1883, Vol. II, p. 215.

Italy and Greece, and so is it now in all the countries in which commerce has been subdued by trade. So it is in these United States, the little land owner of New York gradually giving place to the great proprietor of thousands of acres of land, cultivated by men whose tenure is fully proved by the inferior character of the houses in which they live.... The rural population there declines. ... Such, too, is the tendency of Ohio, and such must it become, in succession in all the Western States.[4]

Despite this gloomy picture of the deterioration of the soil (written in 1856), Carey offered no remedy. He apparently accepted the situation as a natural and progressive economic development.

Among the early American economists who, though not agreeing entirely with Ricardo's theory of rent, supported the principle of rising land values owing to the relative scarcity of fertile land resulting from an increasing population, was George Tucker (1775–1861), a professor of moral philosophy and political economy at the University of Virginia. In a small book entitled *The Laws of Wages, Profits, and Rent Investigated,* published in Philadelphia in 1837, he wrote:

> When it is known from past experience, as it commonly may be, that although there is at the time a superabundance of land for the wants of population, this will not, by reason of the natural increase of mankind, continue to be the case; sagacious and provident individuals are desirous of acquiring land, not for its present, but for its future value.... Most of the public lands which are sold for a dollar an acre would be valueless if it were not for the value which the future increase in population will be certain to impart to it.
>
> It thus happens that land may bear a price in the market, when it would yield no rent.... But this superabundance of land cannot be permanent. By the natural increase of population and consequent increased demand for fertile land ... the relation between them is gradually undergoing change.... It is in this change of relation between the quantity of fertile land, and the numbers who derive sustenance from it, that we find the origin of rent, and the main cause of its progressive increase.[5]

Tucker, in the concluding portion of his work, expresses opposition

[4] *Ibid.,* Vol. II, p. 216.
[5] Pp. 94–95.

to nationalization or collective ownership of land. He concludes:

> The well-being and even the safety of society is clearly on the side of the present conditions of things, in which the land is the property of one portion of the community, and the other has to rely on their capital or industry . . . to procure their just products of the soil. . . . Nor could we alter this distribution without incurring far greater evils than we prevent. All that can reasonably be required from social regulation is that every one should be free to place himself in one class or the other, according to his means and inclination, or to turn his capital into land, or to turn his land into capital, as suits him best.[6]

Though early American economists dealt lightly with the question of land reform, we have already seen from a previous chapter that there was some agitation among radical labor leaders for the establishment of the "natural-right" idea relating to land. As early as 1821 the Philadelphia labor publication, *Mechanics Free Press,* first recommended that "Public Lands be reserved as a donation to the citizens of the United States," under leases free from rent, and all tracts unoccupied for a given period were to revert to the government.[7] It has already been noted that in 1829 Thomas Skidmore, a printer active in the then Workingman's Party, published a book in New York entitled *Rights of Man to Property.* In this volume he advocated that all landed property be equally divided, by a credit on the state's books, and put up at auction in parcels, purchasable on credit terms. He proposed abolishing hereditary property in land, and on the decease of a person holding land, such property was to revert to the state as a social dividend. It was these proposals which George Henry Evans adopted in his land-reform articles in the *Working Man's Advocate.*

Labor and the Land Question

From the Civil War and until the appearance of Henry George's *Progress and Poverty* in 1879, the attention of most American economists centered on the tariff and currency problems. The question of

[6] *Ibid.*, pp. 177-78.
[7] Cited in J. R. Commons and H. L. Sumner, *Documentary History of American Industrial Society,* Vol. V, pp. 43-45.

land and its rent was neglected. The question, however, was kept alive in the political circles and the labor press. Horace Greeley, the editor and politician, joined hands with George Henry Evans, the land reformer, in agitation for liberal settlement laws. In this movement we have in America a revival of the older ideas of Spence, Ogilvie, and Paine. Evans' and Greeley's activities have already been covered in a previous chapter, and there is no need for further elaboration here. But to give an idea of the nature and extent of the agitation, the following text of a handbill widely distributed in 1848 is offered:

> Are you an American citizen? Then you are a joint owner of the public lands. Why not take enough of your property to provide yourself a home? Why not vote yourself a farm?
>
> Are you a party follower? Then you have long enough employed your vote to benefit scheming office seekers. Use it for once to benefit yourself: Vote yourself a farm.
>
> Are you tired of slavery—of drudging for others—of poverty and its attendant miseries? Then, vote yourself a farm.
>
> Would you free your country and the sons of toil everywhere from the heartless, irresponsible mastery of the aristocracy of avarice? . . . Then join with your neighbors to form a true American party . . . whose chief measures will be first to limit the quantity of land that any one may henceforth monopolize or inherit: and second to make the public lands free to actual settlers only, each having the right to sell his improvements to any man not possessed of other lands.[8]

The trade-union movement, which was rapidly developing at this time, added to the fires of "free land" agitation. "Vote yourself a farm" became a popular shiboleth of organized labor and was a standard item in programs laid out in workers' conventions. The labor press was unanimously for a liberalization of the disposal of the public domain. The agitation was effective and was largely influential in the passage of the Pre-emption and Homestead Acts of 1842 and 1862, respectively.

[8] Quoted from *The Armies of Labor*, by Samuel P. Orth, pp. 48–49. For a brief account of the attitude of early American labor unions toward landownership and land reform, see Richard T. Ely, *The Labor Movement in America*, Chap. III.

As noted in a previous chapter, a prominent advocate of land reform in the mid-nineteenth century was Gerrit Smith. Elected to Congress in 1848, Smith introduced in the House of Representatives on February 21, 1854, a set of resolutions (see pages 179-80 for the full text) in which it was denied that Congress had a right to dispose of the public land either by gift or sale. In a speech delivered in presenting the resolutions, Smith expressed his beliefs thus:

> I admit that there are things in which a man can have absolute property, and which without qualification or restriction, he can buy and sell, or bequeath, at his pleasure. But I deny that the soil is among these things. What a man produces from the soil he has an absolute right to. He may abuse the right. It nevertheless remains. But no such right can he have in the soil itself. If he could he might monopolize it. If very rich he might purchase a township or county; and in connection with half a dozen other monopolists he might come to obtain all the lands of a state or a nation. Their occupants might be compelled to leave them and to starve, and the lands might be converted into parks and hunting grounds for the enjoyment of the aristocracy. Moreover, if this could be done in the case of a state or nation, why could it not be done in the case of the whole earth?[9]

There were more of that period when Gerrit Smith, Evans and Greeley, and a number of other radical reformers were agitating against land monopoly. They had their counterparts in Great Britain, where the land problem was more severe and where the debates on the repeal of the Corn Laws were in progress. It was the period when Richard Cobden, John Bright, Herbert Spencer, Dove, and the two Mills (father and son) held sway and economic and political reforms were violently agitated. These movements overseas were bound to have repercussions on this side of the Atlantic, and added to the fire of popular discontent.[10]

Among the agitators of the late pre-Civil War days was an obscure Wisconsin tailor named Edwin Burgess. In a series of letters written to

---

[9] Quoted from Geiger, *op. cit.*, p. 195.

[10] For a discussion of the relation of the early labor movement in the United States to land reform, see Norman Ware, *The Industrial Worker, 1840–1860*, especially Chaps. XIV and XV.

the Racine *Advocate* in 1859-60, he attacked, among other evils, land monopoly and land robbery and proposed that "all taxes should be put on land." Thus Burgess is hailed as a forerunner of Henry George, though it is well established that George never heard of him until after he had put forth his proposal for collecting the economic rent of land in *Progress and Poverty*. Neither did the general public learn much of Burgess, though his letters were collected and published in a book by W. S. Buffham of Racine as *The Edwin Burgess Letters on Taxation*.[11]

The Coming of Henry George

After the passage of the Homestead Act in 1862, the clamor for "free land" abated somewhat, and despite the liberal land grants to railroads and colleges and the abuses under the Swamp Land and Timber Land Acts, little attention was directed toward the land question. In the meantime, a native of Philadelphia, Henry George, who had given up a seafaring career and settled in California, where he became a printer, newspaper reporter, and editor, began to indulge in literary work. In July 1871 he published at his own expense a 48-page pamphlet entitled *Our Land and Land Policy, National and State*. He had become impressed by the existence both in the East and West of the shocking contrast between "monstrous wealth and debasing want" that existed side by side, and was convinced that the cause of it was largely due to the speculative rise in the value of land. He noted in this progressive rise the presence of an unearned increment, which more than a generation previously David Ricardo and Thomas Malthus had called attention to in expounding the economic theory of rent and which was elaborated by John Stuart Mill and other economists in their writings.

In this first essay on the land question George proposed a solution to the problem. He argued that the imposition of a tax which would absorb the unearned increment would not only eliminate a social injustice but would also provide ample revenue for governmental pur-

[11]See George R. Geiger, *op. cit.*, p. 156-58.

poses. This proposal was in contrast to that of land nationalization, which at this period was being vigorously put forward by John Stuart Mill, the English philosopher and economist, in the program of the British Land Tenure Reform Association.

Following the publication of *Our Land and Land Policy*, George continued his newspaper work, entered politics in California, and was active in reform movements of the time. He eagerly increased his knowledge of economic problems, particularly those relating to land, and was deeply impressed by the conditions of poverty in Ireland, Great Britain, and other European countries, where large landholdings and land tenancy were the rule. He gained a reputation in California as an economist, and in March 1877 he was asked to deliver an address on political economy at the University of California.

A few months thereafter he began the writing of his most notable work, *Progress and Poverty*. This masterpiece, because of interruptions owing to lecture engagements and other personal problems and difficulties, was not completed until March 1879. While preparing the text, George consulted numerous works on economics, history, and philosophy, and his knowledge in these fields has been characterized as a marvel of ingenuity.[12] He succeeded after some difficulty in having the book published in a limited edition of five hundred copies in San Francisco in 1879, and late in January of the next year it was put out by the well-known publishers, D. Appleton & Co., in New York. In the meantime George was undergoing financial difficulties which forced him to seek a position in New York City, where he was to reside for the remainder of his career.

The publication of *Progress and Poverty* in New York proved to be a phenomenal success, and it became one of the best sellers in American book history. It attracted attention of scholars, statesmen, and the general public both in the United States and abroad. It was soon translated into several languages, and editions appeared in England and on the European continent. Edition after edition appeared. Numerous societies and organizations were formed to foster and carry

---

[12] See Francis Nielson, *Modern Man and the Liberal Arts*, Chap. III, The Robert Shalkenbach Foundation, New York, 1947.

out the ideas expressed in its pages. The "single tax" slogan was heard everywhere throughout the land.

As stated by Professor Geiger, "The popular interest in *Progress and Poverty* perhaps is not difficult to explain. The country was in the grip of violent labor agitation which followed the widespread industrial depression of 1873 to 1877, and which had flamed out in the riots and bloodshed of the great railroad strike of the latter year. An unmistakable labor class consciousness was now at the point of crystallizing. . . . It was a period of industrial upheaval, a day when labor sensed its growing importance, and George's book could not have appeared at a more favorable time for its popular reception. Its prophetic fervor and almost holy sincerity, together with the practical and simple suggestions it offered, could hardly have failed to impress the workingman and the thinker interested in social reform."[13]

The influence of Henry George on economic writing both in America and abroad was tremendous. The unearned increment in land value had already been acknowledged and upheld by most economists and sociologists. Taxing the economic value of land, however, met with opposition, but this opposition was based on practical rather than theoretical grounds. As stated by David A. Wells, a leading American economist of the period:

> There can be little doubt that the desire for greater simplicity in taxation is generally felt, and in part put into practice. The mass of various kinds of imposts, added without any system or real connection or relation one to another, has often resulted in so large a number of charges on Government account as to defeat itself. The French taxes at the end of the last century, with their added fault of inequality and injustice in distribution, led naturally to the theory of a single tax—the *impôt unique* of the Physiocrats—which did not become a fact, yet registered the protest against the multiplicity and crying oppressiveness of the remains of

[13] Geiger, *op. cit.*, pp. 56–57. Richard T. Ely, a prominent American economist in his day, writing in 1886, has this to say regarding George: "One may object to Henry George's teaching—as I do most decidedly—and rejoice at the good which his works are doing in stimulating the thoughts and the generous aspirations of the people. It would, indeed, not be an easy matter to over-estimate the educational value of 'Progress and Poverty.' " *The Labor Movement in America*, p. 126.

the feudal dues and fiscal experiments undertaken under the stress of an empty treasury. So it has been noted at the present time that where an opportunity has offered there is a tendency in European countries to simplify their taxes. . . .

There is an earnest movement in favor of a single tax on the value of land, exclusive of other real property connected with it. As involving a question of abstract justice the proposition has much in its favor, but it cannot be denied that practical obstacles oppose its adoption. The recent commission on taxation in Massachusetts thus treats of it: "It proposes virtually a radical change in the ownership of land, and therefore a revolution in the entire social body. In this form of taxation all revenue from land alone is to be appropriated—that is, the beneficial ownership of land is to cease. Whether or not this system, if it had been adopted to the outset and had since been maintained, would have been a public advantage may be an open question, but it would certainly seem to be too late now to turn to it in the manner proposed. In any event, it involves properly not questions of taxation, but questions as to the advantage or disadvantage of private property in land."[14]

Another prominent American economist, a contemporary of Wells, General Francis A. Walker, discusses in considerable detail the theories of Henry George in his well-known book, *Land and Its Rent* (1883). In this volume General Walker states:

> What is original in Mr. George's work is the enormous importance assigned to rent as an element in the distribution of wealth. No other writer ever attributed to rent anything approaching the same degree of importance. We have seen Mr. [John Stuart] Mill, weighed down by a sense of injustice of allowing the large increment of the land to pass to the landlord, propose that the State should assert the right of the community, as a whole, to this body of wealth: but Mr. Mill never dreamed of advancing the theory that rent necessarily, in the progress of society, absorbs the entire gain in productive power, and even more than that gain, leaving the laboring classes actually worse off by reason of every successive improvement in the arts of the social order. . . . Mr. George looks upon rent as a conscious evil, which, growing by what it feeds upon, draws into itself all

[14] *Theory and Practice of Taxation*, pp. 633–34.

the vital forces of the community. . . . If Mr. George is right here, he had discovered a principle of supreme importance, the neglect of which should put every professional economist to the blush.[15]

Thus General Walker, though disagreeing with a number of doctrines and assertions of George, and even asserting "that we have nothing to learn from Mr. George about either land or rent"[16] acknowledges the importance of his views as a factor in the progress of economic principles and a prophecy of "a new economic dispensation."

Despite the opposition of many of his contemporary economists and the political attacks on his land-reform theories, Henry George maintained his popularity through several decades and gained many followers.[17] He himself was opposed to making the collection of unearned increment a national political issue. In a letter to Leonard Tuttle, secretary of the Delaware Single Tax Association, dated July 30, 1895, he wrote: "I have been loath to advise the concentration of single-tax effort in any particular state for the reason that I have held that to command the general support of single taxers the movement should originate in the locality and would be certain to be generally supported as it showed strength. The movement in Delaware seems to be of this kind, and to be worthy of the support of single taxers generally. I have already sent a contribution to its funds and hope to do more."[18]

[15]Pp. 196–98.
[16]*Ibid.*, p. 181.
[17]Among the followers of Henry George in the last three decades of the last century was Terrence V. Powderly, the head of the powerful Knights of Labor. Regarding this, Norman J. Ware wrote:

"Land reform was his major ideal. 'In my [Powderly] opinion,' he said 'the main, all absorbing question of the hour is the land question. . . . Give me the land and you may frame as many eight-hour laws as you please, yet I can baffle them all and render them null and void.' . . . 'Miners,' he said, '. . . instead of asking for more pay should agitate the question, Who owns the coal lands.' A wage program he considered 'short sighted work.' He was interested in the Irish Land League, and represented the agrarianism of G. H. Evans combined with Irish anti-landlordism. He believed not only that no more public lands should be given to corporations and speculators, but those already distributed should be restored to the people. He spoke for Henry George in 1886 in the mayoralty campaign but he was not a single-taxer and the Order [i.e., the Knights of Labor] paid little attention to his reform ideas." *The Labor Movement in the United States*, pp. 88–89.

[18]This letter is in the possession of the author.

The Influence of George on Land Reform and Taxation

Though the adoption of a plan to take the economic rent of land and "untax" improvements on land, as advocated by George, was never proposed in any national or state political convention, the proposal has been instrumental in aiding in land and tax reforms. This influence extended beyond the bounds of the United States and, in fact, had a greater effect in foreign lands than our own. Schemes of land-value taxation, and land-value-increment taxation, as already noted, have been put into practice not only in the newer countries, such as Australia, New Zealand, and South Africa, but also on the European continent in Denmark and Germany and, to some extent, in Great Britain.

Henry George's theories of land reform, in view of their large following consequent to the publication of *Progress and Poverty,* can also safely be said to have had a beneficial influence on the improvement of the land-tenure systems of the United States. Although these changes have not been pronounced, there has been a livelier public interest in land affairs, particularly in the matters relating to the disposition of the public domain. It may be said also to have influenced state laws relating to land tenure, land taxation, and landownership concentration. As stated by Geiger: "Henry George must be considered as part of a great tradition that extends far in the past and includes in its ranks many great names. That tradition is more important than the work of any one man. Whether consciously or not, George borrowed from and contributed to that stream of thought; he has become an integral part of it. Therefore, unless one is overconcerned with the difficult questions of originality and influence, it perhaps does not matter too much just what place the individual, Henry George, did occupy in that history of land taxation. That is to say, the collection of land values for social purposes, no matter how opportunistic or locally conditioned it appears, cannot be divorced from social and economic theory, cannot be cut off from the whole concept of the unearned increment."[19]

By way of summation of Henry George's philosophy, it should be borne in mind that he was not a radical in his ideas. These ideas were not revolutionary. Under his proposed plans, land would still be owned

---

[19] *Op. cit.,* p. 384.

in fee. He was opposed to land nationalization and communism. He merely proposed a means of recovering from private interests the portion of property values in land which, in his belief, were derived from the community at large and applying the proceeds to meet public needs. He held that his plan of absorbing the economic rent through taxation would improve the general welfare and lead to social betterment. He argued that such a system would create pressure to put unused land on the market and that it would tend easily and naturally to pass into the hands of those who actually would use it. Thus a curb would be placed on land speculation. Moreover, by thus putting additional land to use, added employment would be created and poverty could be abolished. Since the problem of unemployment is of great concern to this and future generations, the propositions of Henry George should command more public attention than ever before.

Chapter 23

Landownership: What of the Future?

We have told the story of land acquisition and distribution in the nation—a phase of American history largely neglected. We now come to the point of summation, with a look into the future.

It should be quite evident from the foregoing pages that land policies in America have followed no stable pattern, despite the efforts from colonial times to distribute the land liberally among the inhabitants. Never before in the history of civilized man has land been so abundant and so rapidly and indiscriminately distributed as in these United States! Never before was there a greater opportunity to correct the evils of land acquisition and ownership that have pestered mankind from the days of the early Roman Empire down to the present! Yet little has been accomplished along these lines.

We have seen that the early colonists followed the tenets of the antiquated land systems of Europe. They retained feudalist principles at the very time that feudalism was on the way out. Instead of taking steps toward land reforms in a vast area untrammeled by traditions and antiquated statutes, they even attempted to return to the old systems of tenures which for centuries were the prime causes of political and economic unrest and which still hamper human progress.[1]

---

[1] Commenting on the land policy of the United States, Richard Jones, an English economist, writing in 1831, has this to say:

"The United States of North America, though often referred to in support of different views, afford another remarkable instance of the power vested in the hands of the owners of the soil, when its occupation offers the only means of subsistence to the people. The territories of the Union still unoccupied, from the Canadian border to the shores of the Floridas, from the Atlantic to the Pacific, are

Though, as already noted, feudal ideas of landownership and control met with opposition in most of the colonial settlements and did not succeed, the Revolution brought few if any fundamental changes in land tenure. True, primogeniture and entail were abolished by most of the states, and quitrents gradually disappeared, but the British laws and traditions of landlord and tenant, and the inequitable principles followed in land acquisition, land use, and land taxation were continued without significant changes.

Bungling Administration of the Public Domain

No better illustration could be cited as historical proof of a bungling and ineffective land policy than the administration and distribution of the public domain. The history of it is replete with good intentions almost completely nullified by political indifference, fraud, and corruption. Perhaps it was the immensity of the task of administrating the distribution of vast areas of unsettled territory that brought about this situation. The newly organized federal government, like several of the individual colonies before it, could not master the task. The impulse toward land engrossment, so widespread throughout our history, outwitted all moves for equitable land distribution.

---

admitted in law and practice to be the property of the general government. They can be occupied only with its consent, in spots fixed on and allotted by its servants, and on the condition of a previous money payment. That government does not, it is true, convert the successive shoals of fresh applicants into tenants, because its policy rejects such a measure. Its legislators inherited from the other hemisphere at the outset of their career the advantages of an experience accumulated during centuries of progressive civilization: they saw that the power and resources of their young government were likely to be increased more effectually by the rapid formation of a race of proprietors, than by the creation of a class of state tenantry. It has been suggested that they may have acted unwisely in overlooking such a mode of creating a permanent public revenue. Had they perversely entertained the will to do so, unquestionably they had the power. Their rapidly increasing numbers could have been sustained only by the spread of cultivation. As fresh settlements became necessary to the maintenance of the people, the government might have made its own terms when granting the space from which alone the population could obtain subsistence; and this without parting with the property of the soil. Had this been done, the career of the nation, essentially different from what it has been, would more closely have resembled that of the people of the old world." *Peasant Rents*, pp. 6–7.

The first quarter century of the public land policy, despite the congressional acts and reforms in administration recommended by both Jefferson and Hamilton, was wavering and highly unsatisfactory. It was not until 1812 that a definite and unified policy was adopted for public land distribution. In that year the General Land Office was established. Its administration, as we have already shown, has been notably lax and inefficient, and political corruption and collusion have pervaded its history for more than a century. It can be said without much doubt or hesitation that no phase of federal government activities bears greater marks of ineptitude and disgrace than the General Land Office's operations, despite the endeavors of the Congress and the administrators to rectify the shortcomings.

It should be borne in mind also that during this period land dealing was the principal business in America. In fact, land-grabbing, real estate gambling, and town-jobbing have marked American business annals almost from the time of Columbus to the present day. So great at times have been their force that adequately to forestall or retard them, under our system of land tenure, seemed out of the question.[2]

---

[2] Regarding the contrast between conditions of landownership in Britain and the United States, the English economist, James E. Thorold Rogers, writing in the early 1870s in his book, *Cobden and Modern Political Opinion*, pp. 92–93, states:

"There is no reason to interfere between the parties to the contract for a lease of lands in Broadway or in the neighbourhood of Boston, although the causes which operate to create rent are as dominant in these parts of the American Union as they are in London or Manchester, and are quite as much illustrations of the unearned increase of land as any which could be quoted from our immediate experience. The fact is, the American Union is so wide, that if individuals are unwilling or unable to purchase or rent land in the immediate neighbourhood of great commercial activity, they can, without abandoning the political and social habits of their country, and the numberless associations which such habits bring with them, seek a spot where they can bargain to greater advantage, or obtain virgin soil at a nominal price. Nor, again, is the American Union, or indeed any other civilised country, hampered and restrained by a system which gives an opportunity to the worst faults of a monopoly by fostering every means for accumulating and retaining land. Men do not grumble at the injustice of nature, but they are irritated irreconcilably by the injuries of law. Nay it is one of the misfortunes which are sure to ensue from erroneous legislation, that it always begets a disposition to remedy one wrong by another . . . to cry out that it is too late to reform a process, and that immediate necessity requires fundamental change."

What of the Future?

Though it is not regarded as a function of the historian to look into the future, it is only by reference to the past that significant trends can be traced. And it is the task of statesmen to look to these trends and prepare in advance to foster or impede them, as the case demands. The history of landownership, land distribution, and land use in the United States certainly should offer a background for future decisions and actions.

Sounding a warning along these lines, the English economist, Augustus Mongredier, writing in 1882 in his book, *Wealth Creation,* stated:

> It is a fact that there is a limit to the supply of land—it is a fact the world's population is fast increasing and therefore using up that supply—and it is a fact that, as the demand becomes greater while the supply remains the same, a proportionate rise in value must ensue. Reason how we may, and infer what we may, those facts have to be confronted. Is it wise to adjourn the consideration of the pinch till the pinch itself shall come?[3]

It is frequently stated in many quarters that we have no land question in the United States. By this it is inferred that we are not burdened by the problem of inequitable land distribution such as has oppressed Europe, Asia, and other parts of the civilized world. Land here has been abundant, it has been made available, it is easily transferable, and it is comparatively widely distributed. Contrasted with conditions in the older nations, where land engrossment, serfdom, and tenancy have created economic distrust and political dissatisfaction and upheavals, and still constitute pressing problems requiring solution, this is undoubtedly true. But, on the other hand, as the preceding chapters should show, we have had waves of land engrossment, speculation, inequities, abuses, and depressions, which have led to political discontent. And no change in this tendency is yet in the offing.

Land Reform and International Problems

As already stated, the problem of land reform has existed in most nations throughout the world for centuries. It has led to peasant re-

---

[3] P. 253.

volts, to political upheavals, to parliamentary reforms and national constitutional changes. On the European continent and in Great Britain, steps to solve the problem have been and still are being taken. Since World War II, measures for relief and betterment have also been taken in Asian, African, and Latin-American nations. The question has been placed on the agenda of the United Nations.

The United Nations General Assembly, at its fifth session, in 1950, when it considered the problem of land reform, expressed the view that the agrarian conditions which persisted in many underdeveloped countries and territories constituted a barrier to their economic development because such conditions reduced agricultural productivity and were a major cause of low standards of living for the populations of those countries and territories. The General Assembly then stated its conviction that "immediate steps should be taken to study the extent to which existing agrarian conditions hamper the economic development of underdeveloped countries" and adopted certain recommendations for action by governments.

At its thirteenth session, in September 1951, the Economic and Social Council had before it a report, *Land Reform: Defects in Agrarian Structure as Obstacles to Economic Development,* prepared by the United Nations in co-operation with the Food and Agriculture Organization. After a detailed discussion, the Council adopted a resolution which recommended that governments institute appropriate land reforms in the interest of landless farmers and those with small and medium-sized holdings, and further recommended that governments should take, from among a wide range of other recommendations, such further measures as were appropriate to the circumstances of their countries.

The prime mover of these actions was the United States of America. In presenting the matter before the General Assembly, Isador Lubin, United States representative in the Economic and Social Council of the United Nations, at Geneva, Switzerland, on September 3, 1954, stated:

> We in the United States recognize that the attainment of peace and stability depends to a considerable degree on immediate and

positive steps to correct systems of land tenure which exploit the workers on the land, steps which will remove inequitable taxes on farm lands and agricultural products, eliminate unreasonably high rents and exorbitant interest rates on farm loans. We are of the firm conviction that peace and stability in many parts of the world will require the elimination of those economic and social practices which work extreme hardship on rural people.[4]

Mr. Lubin, in supporting his motion, listed the actions taken by Congress to provide for landownership and to alleviate the conditions of distressed farmers, but he proposed no enduring or positive remedies which actually would mean land reform—reform in landownership as a whole—to cover the entire nation, rural and urban. Yet he added in his remarks: "To be successful a program of land reform requires a conviction not only among people who live on the land but also among the public officials, and national leaders, of the need both to adopt consistent long-range land policies and to undertake programs necessary to sustain such policies year after year."[5]

Should We Have Land Reform?

There is no tangible evidence that we have a consistent long-range policy of land reform, as advocated by Mr. Lubin, or, if we should have such a policy, that programs would be undertaken "to sustain it year after year." Most of the farm-support legislation is in the nature of relief measures. They do not go to the basis of the problem. They do not uphold the principle that land is not an economic commodity, despite its economic value. Land cannot be reproduced. Like air, it must be made accessible. Its quantity and its situs are fixed. It thus lends itself readily to monopolization—even when held in limited quantity. Thus genuine land reform requires permanent action to offset the continuous tendency throughout the ages for private or public owners to engross large acreages in both rural and urban areas. "Latifundia," which the geographer Pliny says destroyed Italy, did not come at once to Italy under the Roman Empire. It developed because conditions

---

[4]See *Land Reform, A World Challenge,* Department of State, Washington, D.C., p. 31. United Nations, Economic and Social Council, *Official Records,* Sept. 3, 1951, pp. 492–96.

[5]*Ibid,* p. 35.

were favorable to it. It was difficult to uproot these conditions. "It can happen here"—unless farsighted moves are taken to prevent it.

It is evident from historical precedent in both this country and in foreign lands that the present wasteful land system cannot remain unchanged indefinitely. In times of economic distress there will be renewed clamors for land reform. New and radical schemes of land distribution and land use will be put forth. There is a danger, therefore, in delays in dealing with the land question as it exists today or as it may assume some unexpected form in the future. If history teaches us anything, it teaches us that destructive social and political movements can be forestalled or allayed by the timely adoption of reasonable reforms. An ounce of prevention is worth a pound of cure.

On this point the following statement written by the English author, Charles William Stubbs, is interesting. In his book, *The Land and the Laborers,* published in 1884, he states:

> A wide extension of proprietorship in the soil is . . . the strongest bulwark of national safety. Those who talk about the danger of Radical and Socialist ideas, appear to forget, that when a social commune was erected in Paris in 1871, there were five million land owners in France ready to take the side of public order, and to enforce the conservative view with regard to the right of property. Have we such conservative view with regard to the right of property? Have we such conservative safeguard in England? I venture to say that the seven hundred and ten land owners who are proved by the new Doomsday Book to hold one-quarter of the whole land of England could not stand for a moment against the breath of revolution. I have no desire to be an alarmist. But I do most solemnly believe that the concentration of land in large estates, and the consequent accentuation of the contrast between the rich and the poor, is full of danger for the future, and is, in fact, a direct provocative of social revolution. *Latifundia perdidere Italiam* was the verdict of the historian Pliny on the ancient empire of Rome. God grant that it may not be the verdict of some future historian on the fall of Imperial England![6]

We can take an example from Britain, where land reform for three or more centuries has been a permanent, not an intermittent, problem,

[6] P. 33–34.

as in the United States. In addition to various parliamentary acts, such as the Small Holdings and Allotment Act of 1908 and similar subsequent measures, the government has adopted and modified plans for the use of the land under which a right is retained to share in the increment to land value regardless of the causes. These acts are now known as the "Town and Country Planning Acts." The aim and purpose of these Acts are to ensure that the limited land resources of the nation are used in such a manner as to maximize welfare and give to the people as a whole a part of the unearned increment accruing from rising land values. This legislation is far from perfect but this, at least can be said of it, it is an indication that land and the uses thereof are recognized as a public responsibility to be administered in behalf of public welfare.[7]

The Dangers That Confront Us

As already stated, it is the function of true statesmanship to foresee political, social, and economic problems long before they become acute and intolerable and to take steps to forestall them. This has not always been done in America. It required a devastating civil war to settle the slavery question. It may in time require a social conflict of a similar nature to solve the oncoming land question. Such conflicts have occurred and are still occurring in other civilized countries. Witness the revolutions in Mexico and other Latin-American countries, where the slogan, *Tierra y Liberdad* (Land and Liberty) has been the favorite outcry of insurrectionists. In very few cases in ancient or modern times have there been political uprisings that have not had their roots in the demand for land reforms.

Until now we have escaped serious episodes of this nature, largely because of the relative abundance of land. But this situation is changing. For almost a half century, free land, capable of private profitable use and occupation, has practically disappeared. Moreover, the nation has been thrown back on its frontiers. It cannot advance its limits through new territorial acquisitions. At the same time, population is

---

[7] For a recent account of the British Town and Country Planning Acts, see Ben W. Lewis, *British Planning and Nationalization*, Chap. 7.

rapidly increasing, and despite technical progress in agriculture, the pressure of population on the food supply—already experienced by older nations—is merely a matter of time. Moreover, industrialization, combined with the growth of vast urban areas, is decreasing the already occupied arable land. Urban growth and development create a land-tenancy problem, notwithstanding the remarkable improvement in transportation facilities and construction progress. The housing problem, which is already upon us, is merely a forerunner of the land question. The billions of taxpayers' dollars now being expended in slum clearance and in providing decent living quarters at reasonable rents are an indication that land is a natural monopoly, and, unless social and political action is taken to offset its engrossment in the hands of a few, similar measures of relief will be required for land employed in agricultural and industrial uses.[8]

What Are the Remedies?

For several centuries statesmen, philosophers, reformers, as well as economists and sociologists, have proposed reforms in the system of landownership and distribution. We have already seen in a previous chapter proposals comprising measures ranging from a mere change in the methods of land distribution, use, and taxation of land to the extreme demand for complete land nationalization. It is not the intention here to cover the whole field on this inquiry again. However, by way of summary, the following proposals will be briefly reviewed: (1) absorption of the economic rent of land and simultaneously untaxing im-

---

[8] Writing on the general indifference to the land problem, Geiger, in his book, *The Theory of the Land Question,* remarks on page 5: "This chronic refusal to see the land problem in anything but a restricted and archaic perspective may well be one of the contributing factors to our modern economic incoherencies. Surely it is an indication of myopia to cast about for social patterns and to plan political structures without so much as a glance at the very obvious basis of economic life. There are programs and programs, all of them seemingly founded on the proposition that industry and capital and finance are ethereal essences floating about balloon-like and deigning no commerce with the ground. There are books and books on economics, every week a new batch. In how many of them will you find the word 'land' mentioned in the indexes? Perhaps Chesterton complained correctly when he found that the man in Bedford is not conscious of Bedfordshire. Our urban populations have virtually forgotten that we all live on the land."

provements (i.e., primarily buildings) on land as advocated so earnestly by Henry George as a matter of justice; (2) progressive taxes on land; (3) limitation of private landownership; (4) social control of land use; and, finally, (5) land nationalization. Each of these will be considered in turn.

Absorption of the Economic Rent of Land and Untaxing Improvements

This, in brief, is the proposal of Henry George. The principle is based on the Ricardian theory of rent, a theory which, despite the attacks made upon it, has survived and is widely acknowledged by most modern economists as well as those of the old-time classical school. And it has had its practical application also. We have seen that several European cities have adopted the principle in one form or another. It has been applied also tentatively in modified form in Australia, New Zealand, and South Africa, and to a slight extent in this country. Moreover, it is an integral concept in the several British Town and Country Planning Acts, which have been from time to time enacted as measures of land reform. In the United States, despite the widespread popularity of Henry George's doctrines since the publication of *Progress and Poverty* in 1879, it has never been wholeheartedly applied, though it is embedded in the federal "capital-gains tax." The separate classification of land value from the value of improvements thereon in the general property tax laws, which has gained headway in states and municipalities, is a partial recognition of the Henry George doctrine, and this gives promise of eventually capturing the unearned increment in realty taxation.[9]

In the course of time the practical difficulties attached to fixing the monetary value of economic rent may be overcome. If we are to have justice in taxation, then any equitable program of taxation should con-

---

[9] It is interesting to note that the late Professor E. R. A. Seligman, who was not particularly impressed with the Henry George theory, looked with some favor on an unearned-increment tax to absorb the increase in real estate value owing to public improvements. (See Seligman's *Reform of Municipal Taxation*.) Such a tax was also proposed by Edward H. Spengler, a pupil of Professor Seligman, in his monograph, *Land Values in New York in Relation to Transit Facilities*, p. 135.

tain the "windfall" principle; namely, values gained by the taxpayer that are unearned or fortuitous or due to chance or social progress should bear a much higher rate than values arising out of labor or the personal efforts of the individual.

The argument for this form of taxation is expressively stated by Professor George Raymond Geiger in his excellent study entitled *The Theory of the Land Question,* already mentioned in the previous pages.

> Land values are social benefits, the privileges that result from the interaction of social forces, and therefore they are peculiarly a basis and a source of taxation. Ground rent represents the degree to which society has co-operated to produce values; it is a measure of social progress. The rent of land is a measure of the unearned privileges that accrue to the owner of land through political and economic organization; and therefore it seems consummately fitting that such rent be applied to defray the expenses of the political organization. Indeed, this benefit criterion seems to be the only ethical basis for the existence of taxation. Taxation, just as everything else, must be justified and not merely accepted, and the one sure justification appears to be that social fiscal requirements be met out of a social product. At least there is a supreme neatness in the application of economic rent to the category of taxation. Here is a fund that no individual has been instrumental in creating, yet now it reverts to individuals. Taxation is intended for social purposes, yet in our present economic arrangements, society depends upon the contributions (rather sacrificial offerings) of individuals out of individual earnings, without attempting significantly or appreciably to tap the fund that society, itself has produced.[10]

The Progressive Tax on Land

By a progressive tax on land we mean the taxation of land at a progressive rate, based on the amount or the value of land held in single or pseudo-single ownership. The objective here would be a discouragement of large concentration of landholdings by individuals or small groups of individuals or by corporations. It is interesting to note that even in the early days of the Republic the opposition to land engrossment by individuals led to a proposal of such a progressive tax.

[10] *Op. cit.,* pp. 184–85.

As already stated, Thomas Jefferson made such a proposal. It is also noteworthy that the first direct tax levied by the federal government in 1798 was a tax, the rate of which on urban land was graduated in accordance with the acreage held by the taxpayer. But as time went on, this system disappeared and, except for "homestead exemptions"—i.e., exemption from tax of a fixed value of land and improvements as an aid to small holders—the writer has been unable to find any tax laws of the states which vary the rate of taxation in accordance with the value or the extent of the acreage taxed. But as stated by Marshall Harris: "Intense interest is found in at least one state and among liberal thinkers as to the advisability of following Jefferson's suggestion by increasing real estate taxes on large landholdings, probably in geometrical progression, as they become larger."[11]

According to Professor Henry William Spiegel, in a discussion of taxation and land tenure:

> In the United States there is ample evidence that small properties are burdened with the property tax to a higher degree than large and higher-priced properties which tend to be underassessed. While this example points to an unintentional effect of taxation, which may facilitate concentration of land, absentee ownership, and tenancy, there are various instances of intentional effects of tax policies upon land tenure. The progressive land tax of New Zealand, in force from 1891 to 1931, provided for differentiation according to size of estate, character of tenure, and residence of owner. It is generally recognized that taxes of this type contributed to the breakup of many large estates and to the decrease in absentee ownership in New Zealand and Australia.[12]

Regarding foreign experience with taxation of land at progressive rates as a measure to impede accumulation of land and to break up large estates, the recent United Nations publication, *Progress of Land Reform*, states:

> In countries where agriculture is the leading industry and where taxes levied on farm land or farm produce make an important, though declining, contribution to government revenue, there has been a tendency in recent years to replace flat rates by

[11]*Origin of the Land Tenure System in the United States*, p. 348.
[12]*Land Tenure Policies*, p. 35.

a progressive system with exemptions and rapidly rising rates. In New Zealand, "since 1936 land tax has been levied at graduated rates . . . The graduation was designed to encourage subdivision of large holdings into smaller and separately owned farms, but owing to the substantial increase in recent years in farming income in proportion to the land tax payable, the effect of land tax graduation in relation to the question of subdivision is now almost negligible." In India, "small landholders are given a favourable treatment under the Agricultural Income Tax which has been introduced in recent years in a number of States, such as Assam, West Bengal, Bihar, Orissa and Uttar Pradesh, as the tax is levied at a progressive rate and complete exemption is allowed in cases of incomes below the prescribed limit." In Brazil, some States levy a progressive tax on land values or areas. The Egyptian land tax was made progressive in 1942. In Portugal, a progressive supplementary tax was introduced in 1946; in Lebanon, a progressive tax on agricultural income was introduced in 1951; and in Pakistan, an agricultural tax is paid, at progressive rates, in the Punjab, East Bengal and the North-West Frontier Province. In Poland, land tax, "the only tax paid by peasants in People's Poland, is progressive."[13]

Thus it appears that a progressive tax on land is not only feasible but has been put into practice in various countries as a means of providing land reform.

Limitations to Landownership

There were suggestions to limit individual ownership of land in colonial times, and proposals along this line were made from time to time as land engrossment became a feature of the nation's economy. Both Thomas Jefferson and John Adams seemed to favor it. It was one of the doctrines of the *Working Man's Advocate* under the editorship of Evans. But largely because of constitutional limitations, no political action toward this end was ever directly taken in the United States. However, in the course of time, the states enacted laws limiting the acquisition of land by corporations to an amount which is necessary or reasonably incidental to carrying out the purposes of their

[13] Pp. 262–63.

creation.[14] Exceptions have been made, largely in the interest of banks and insurance companies, where land is acquired through the collection or liquidation of debts. But even in this case, as regards banks, insurance companies, and similar institutions, a number of states require the disposal of unessential realty within a limited period or under certain conditions, such as the attainment of a sales price covering the cost of acquisition. From time to time, owing to foreclosures, banks, insurance companies, and similar organizations have become heavy owners of real property, and if allowed to continue this ownership they could become the chief landed proprietors of the nation.

Some evidence of this was presented in the hearings before the Temporary National Economic Company in 1940, when Mr. Glenn Rogers, manager of the Farm Loan Division of the Metropolitan Life Insurance Company, stated that this company "is the largest farmer in the United States, owning approximately 1,430,000 acres of farm land," comprising 7,531 farms, and representing an investment of approximately $80 millions. In addition to this, the company owned urban property, the value of which reached high proportions. Most of these property holdings have been liquidated in accordance with the requirements of the state insurance laws. In more recent years, life-insurance companies have added substantially to their holdings of industrial and commercial real estate through the technique of "sale and lease back" to responsible corporations.

In addition to the restrictions on ownership of landed property by profit-making corporations, a few states have enacted legislation limiting landownership by religious corporations, and a Kansas statute of recent date provides that no corporation shall be granted a charter and no foreign corporation shall be given permission to engage in agriculture or horticulture, except cattle raising.[15]

Beginning in the colonial era, the laws of various states restricted ownership of land to citizens. The "comity clause" of the Constitution (Article IV, Section 2), whereby the citizens of each state shall enjoy all the rights, immunities, and privileges of citizens in the several states,

[14]Spiegel, *op. cit.*, p. 11.
[15]*Ibid.*, p. 12.

has been interpreted by the United States Supreme Court to cover the right of individuals to acquire and possess property, but the Court does not interpret this clause as extending this right to corporations. A corporation is not considered a citizen under the "comity clause," and states are not required to give corporations chartered by other states rights and privileges that they may grant to their own citizens or corporations.

During the period of rapid land engrossment in the western states, a number of foreign individuals and corporations, organized specifically for this purpose, acquired large tracts of land. This led several of these states to enact legislation prohibiting or restricting foreign landownership. Of course such legislation is hampered by treaty obligations of the federal government, which, together with the Constitution, can override or annul state legislation.

Social Control of Land Use

It is apparent from the preceding pages that land, from time out of mind, has been regarded as a distinct species of property, subject to definite laws and traditions regarding its tenure, its use, and its control. The legal concept of eminent domain is an Anglo-Saxon inheritance that has never been denounced or altered, and the extension of its application under the police power of the state and under changing social conditions seemingly has no bounds. The constitutional fathers adopted the principle *in toto*, despite the high regard they held for property rights and their efforts to afford such rights full protection. Thus there has been a tendency in most civilized nations to restrict the rights of landownership and, through public control, to regulate the utilization of types of land resources such as forest, water, and mines, along with zoning provisions and other use limitations. All these developments have been upheld by court decisions, and there is good ground for holding that restrictions on the ownership and use of real property will expand and be intensified.

There is no better example of the rapid progress of this tendency than in Great Britain. Previous to the first decade of the twentieth century there was practically no outstanding act of Parliament seeking to regulate or control the use of land, though there were cases where cities and towns adopted planning and layout patterns. Landlords, as a rule, exercised full and untrammeled control over the use of their properties. Vast estates could be converted into sporting parks, and needed agricultural areas could be neglected with impunity. As stated by Dr. George G. Sause, Jr., of Lafayette College, in his doctoral thesis, *Land Development-Value Problems and the Town and Country Planning Act of 1947,* "government intervention was regarded not only as an undesirable encroachment on individual liberty, but also a hindrance to national progress."[15a] As a result, co-ordinated long-term planning of the use of land was entirely absent, "and the result was uneconomic, unhealthy and inconvenient congestion in certain areas, suburban sprawl, loss of agricultural land and the defacing of the countryside."

But this laissez-faire policy has been abandoned. In 1909 the British Parliament enacted the first of a series of Town and Country Planning Acts. It has been an underlying principle of these laws that individual plots of land are not to be considered as isolated units which are the concern solely of their owners, but as parts of a larger whole in which the neighborhood and community or the entire nation have a legitimate interest. Privately held land could be appropriated by the community, and in the process of compensating owners the unearned increment could be partially, if not wholly, confiscated, while at the same time land benefited by public improvements could be assessed on the value thereof. It is thus conceivable, as time progresses and the land-reform problems of Great Britain develop further, that complete nationalization of land use in that tight little island may be an eventuality.[16]

Aside from legal enactments relating to public lands, and the passage of local zoning laws, little has been accomplished in the United States in regulating, controlling, or promoting the use of privately held landed property. Indeed, there has been little if any agitation for it, aside from

[15a] Doctoral dissertation submitted at Columbia in 1952. Available in the library of Columbia University in typescript or microfilm.

[16] Space does not permit the consideration of similar developments in other European countries under pressure of land reform. Reference, however, may be made to the recent publication of the United Nations, Department of Economic Affairs, *Progress in Land Reform.*

the crop-allotment principle embedded in the agriculture price-support acts. The idea, it is frequently stated, is opposed to the American tradition of individual freedom. Moreover, there appears at present to be no pressing need for such reform. This view is set forth by Professor G. S. Wehrwein, a prolific student of land economics, who wrote in 1939:

> In our anxiety to control erosion, prevent the destruction of forests or to curb speculation we seem to accept uncritically the policies of Europe without recognizing fundamental differences. It is one thing to formulate land-use policies for a nation with abundant resources and approaching a stationary population and quite another for a nation with limited resources but which insists on stimulating population increase for reasons which cannot be separated from the social philosophy, ideology and nationalistic ambitions of that nation. . . . There is something admirable about American land tenure, a free system which has permitted landless laborers and penniless immigrants to climb the agricultural ladder.[17]

But what of the future? Can we escape history? The experience of every European nation—in fact, all civilized peoples—has been a tendency of pressure of population on subsistence, a relative scarcity of arable land, a tendency to develop slum areas in cities and towns, and a trend toward concentration of landownership. Some of these developments, we have already shown, are upon us. Others are likely to come sooner than many think. We already have overcrowding in cities and towns. The public is paying the landlords dearly to overcome or ameliorate the housing shortage. The federal, state, and city governments have been forced into the business of creating housing facilities and in affording urban and rural mortgage credit. Taking a long-range view, we can have, in the not-too-distant future, either strict social control over the use of land or, as an alternative, land nationalization.

Land Nationalization

We have already shown that land nationalization as a philosophic objective has been advocated for more than two centuries. It was not until the 1870s, however, when it was proposed by the eminent British

[17] Quoted from Spiegel, *op. cit.*, p. 4.

philosopher and economist, John Stuart Mill, that it was given a practical significance. It has been seriously advocated in various forms in Great Britain by such prominent writers as Alfred Russel Wallace, Lord Addison, Lord Astor, and B. Seebohm Roundtree. In the United States it has also had supporters—both Socialists and non-Socialists—though they have been less outspoken than the English advocates and have been received generally with almost universal non-acceptance or indifference.

The reason for this indifference lies in the American tradition. This was noted by Alexis de Tocqueville more than a century ago. In his famous work, *Democracy in America,* he wrote:

> In no country in the world is the love of property more active and more anxious than in the United States; nowhere does the majority display less inclination for those principles which threaten to alter, in whatever manner, the laws of property.[18]

De Tocqueville was undoubtedly impressed by the rage for land speculation and land engrossment which has prevailed throughout this nation's history. It has its basis not so much in human greed or cupidity as in the individualist ideal of self-independence. Property, particularly landed property, is the means of obtaining freedom from individual serfdom and want. Its trend toward enhancement in value as society progresses gives an added impetus to obtaining its possession and profitable use. Accordingly, any suggestion of land nationalization has met with indifferent popular reception on these shores.

Nor is land nationalization a valid and practical remedy in solving the land question. American experience has shown how inept the government can be as a landlord. In no field of political administration have there been more wasteful and inefficient actions. Even the Socialists and other proponents of radical creeds in this country have not forcefully adopted land nationalization as an important plank in their political creeds. Henry George, in his radical land-reform principles, held aloof from any idea of land nationalization. In *Progress and Poverty* he wrote: "I do not propose to purchase or to confiscate private property in land. The first would be unjust, the second needless."

[18] Part II, Book 3, Chap. 21.

Selected Bibliography

General Works

Abrams, Charles. *Revolution in Land*. New York: Harper & Brothers, 1938.
Anderson, B. *The Farmer Seeks Jeffersonian Democracy*. Baltimore: King, 1943.
Brodrick, George Charles. *English Land and English Landlords*. London: The Cobden Club, 1881.
Ely, R. T., and Wehrwein, G. E. *Land Economics*. New York: The Macmillan Co., 1940.
Finlason, W. F. *History of the Law of Tenures of Land in England and Ireland*. London, 1870.
Fisher, Joseph, and Birkbeck, Wm. Lloyd. *The Land Question*. New York: Humbilt Publishing Co., n.d.
Garnier, Russell M. *History of the English Landed Interest, Its Customs and Its Laws*. London: Swan Sonnenschein, 1908.
Geiger, George Raymond. *The Theory of the Land Question*. New York: The Macmillan Co., 1936.
Gonner, E. C. K. *Common Land and Inclosure*. New York: The Macmillan Co., 1912.
Gras, N. S. B. *A History of Agriculture in Europe and America*. 2nd ed. New York: Crofts, 1940.
Johnston, V. Webster, and Barlowe, Raleigh. *Land Problems and Policies*. New York: McGraw-Hill Book Co., 1954.
Jones, Richard. *Peasant Rents*. 1931 reprint. New York: The Macmillan Co., 1895.
Pollock, Sir Francis. *The Land Laws*. 3rd ed. London: Macmillan, 1896.
Propyn, J. W. (ed.). *Systems of Land Tenure in Various Countries*. London: The Cobden Club, 1876.
Sakolski, A. M. *The Great American Land Bubble*. New York: Harper & Brothers, 1932.
Sato, Shosuke. *History of the Land Question in the United States*. Baltimore: The Johns Hopkins Press, 1886.
Spiegel, Henry W. *Land Tenure Policies at Home and Abroad*. Chapel Hill: University of North Carolina Press, 1954.
Timmons, John, and Murray, W. G. (eds.). *Land Problems and Policies*. Ames: Iowa State College Press, 1950.
Walker, Francis A. *Land and Its Rent*. London: Macmillan, 1883.
Whittaker, Sir P. T. *Ownership, Tenure and Taxation of Land*. London: Macmillan, 1914.
Wicksteed, Charles. *The Land for the People*. London: Swan Sonnenschein, 1894.

World Land Reform. *A Selected Bibliography.* U. S. Department of Agriculture Library Inst. 55. Washington, D.C.: Government Printing Office, 1951.

Primitive Landownership

Baden-Powell, B. H. *The Origin and Growth of Village Communities in India.* London: Swan Sonnenschein, 1899.

——————. *Land Systems in British India.* 3 vols. Oxford, 1892.

De Coulanges, Fustel. *The Ancient City.* Boston: Lee & Sheppard, 1874.

——————. *The Origin of Property in Land.* 2nd ed. London: George Allen & Unwin, 1927.

Finley, M. J. *Studies in Land and Credit in Ancient Athens, 500-200 B.C.* New Brunswick: Rutgers University Press, 1952.

Gomme, George Laurence. *The Village Community.* New York: Scribner & Welford, 1890.

Hodge, Frederick W. (ed.). *Handbook of the American Indians, North of Mexico.* Washington, D.C.: Bureau of Ethnology, Smithsonian Institution, Bull. #30, 1907-10.

Lacombe, Paul. *L'Appropriation du Sol. Essai sur la passage de la Proprieté Collective à la Proprieté Privée.* Paris: Armand Colin, 1912.

Laveleye, Emile de. *Primitive Property.* Translated by G. R. L. Marriott, with an introduction by T. E. Cliffe Leslie. London: Macmillan, 1878.

Letourneau, Charles. *Property, Its Origin and Development.* London: Walter Scott, Ltd., 1892.

Liversage, V. *Land Tenure in the Colonies.* Cambridge: Cambridge University (Eng.) Press, 1945.

Loure, R. H. *Primitive Society.* New York: Liveright, 1920.

Maine, Sir Henry. *The Early History of Institutions.* 4th ed. London: John Murray, 1890.

——————. *Ancient Law.* 4th Am. ed. New York: Henry Holt & Co., 1906.

——————. *Village Communities.* London: John Murray, 1871.

Maurer, George L. von. *Einleitung zur geschichte der Mark-Hof-Dorf und Stadtverfassung.* Berlin: C. Keiser, 1854.

Meek, C. K. *Land Law and Custom in the Colonies.* 2nd ed. London: Oxford University Press, 1949.

Morgan, L. H. *Ancient Society.* New York: Henry Holt & Co., 1878.

Neilson, Francis. *The Eleventh Commandment.* New York: Viking Press, 1933. Reprinted by C. C. Nelson Publishing Co.

Seebohm, Frederic. *Tribal Custom in Anglo-Saxon Law.* London: Longmans, 1911.

Schaefer, Henry. *Hebrew Tribal Economy and the Jubilee as Illustrated in Semitic and Indo-European Village Communities.* Leibsig, 1922. (New York: Stechert.)

Sheddick, V. *Land Tenure in Basutoland.* London: Commonwealth Relations Office, 1954.

Lands in the Colonial Period

Abernethy, Thomas P. *Western Lands and the American Revolution.* New York: Appleton-Century, 1937.

Akagi, Roy Hidemichi. *The Town Proprietors of the New England Colonies.* Philadelphia: University of Pennsylvania Press, 1924.

Albion, Robert G. *Forests and Sea Power.* Cambridge: Harvard University Press, 1926.

Alvord, Clarence. *The Mississippi Valley in British Politics.* Cleveland: Clark, 1917.

Andrews, Charles McLean. *Essays in Colonial History.* Presented to Charles McLean Andrews by his students. New Haven: Yale Univerity Press, 1931.

Ballagh, James C. "Introduction to Southern Economic History; The Land System," in *Report of the American History Association for 1897.* Washington, D.C.: Government Printing Office, 1898.

Banks, Enoch M. *Economics of Land Tenure in Georgia.* New York: Columbia University Press, 1905.

Batchellor, Albert Stilman (ed.). *The New Hampshire Grants.* New Hampshire State Paper Series. Concord: E. N. Person, Public Printer, 1895.

Bond, Beverley W., Jr. *The Quit-Rent System in the American Colonies.* New Haven: Yale University Press, 1919.

Cameron, Jenks. *The Development of Governmental Forest Control.* Baltimore: Johns Hopkins University Press, 1928.

Chandler, Alfred N. *Land Title Origins, A Tale of Force and Fraud.* New York: Robert Schalkenbach Foundation, 1945.

Dorr, Henry C. "The Proprietors of Providence," in *Publications of the Rhode Island Historical Association.* New Series, Vol. III. Providence, 1895-96.

Egleston, Melville. *The Land System of the New England Colonies.* Baltimore: The Johns Hopkins Press, 1886.

Ford, Amelia C. *Colonial Precedents of Our National Land System, as It Existed in 1800.* Madison: University of Wisconsin Press, 1910.

Gould, Clarence P. *The Land System in Maryland.* Baltimore: The Johns Hopkins Press, 1913.

Harris, Marshall. *Origin of the Land Tenure System in the United States.* Ames: Iowa State College Press, 1954.

Harrison, Fairfax. *Virginia Land Grants.* Richmond: Old Dominion Press, 1925.

Higgins, Ruth Loring. *Expansion in New York, with Especial Reference to the Eighteenth Century.* Columbus: Ohio State University Historical Studies, No. 14, 1931.

Mark, Irving. *Agrarian Conflicts in Colonial New York, 1711-1775.* New York: Columbia University Press, 1940.

Sullivan, James. *History of Land Titles in Massachusetts.* Boston, 1801.

Woodard, Florence May. *The Town Proprietors of Vermont.* New York: Columbia University Press, 1936.

The Public Domain

American State Papers, Class 8. *Public Lands.* 8 vols. Washington, D.C.: Gales & Seaton, 1833-60.

Clawson, Marion. *Uncle Sam's Acres.* New York: Dodd Mead & Co., 1951.

Cole, Arthur H. "Cyclical and Sectional Variations in the Sale of Public Lands, 1816-1860," in *Review of Economic Statistics,* Vol. IX. Cambridge: Harvard University Press, 1927, pp. 41-53.

Donaldson, Thomas. *The Public Domain.* H. Exec. Doc. 47, 46th Cong., 2nd Session, Pt. 4. Washington, D.C.: Government Printing Office, 1884.

Dunham, Harold Hathaway. *Government Handout, A Study in the Administration of the Public Land, 1875-1891.* New York: published by the author, 1941.

Gates, Paul Wallace. *Frontier Landlords and Pioneer Tenants.* Ithaca: Cornell University Press, 1945.

──────. *The Wisconsin Pine Lands of Cornell University, A Study in Land Policy and Absentee Ownership.* Ithaca: Cornell University Press, 1943.

──────. *Fifty Million Acres: Conflicts over Kansas Land Policy, 1854-1890.* Ithaca: Cornell University Press, 1954.

──────. "The Disposal of the Public Domain in Illinois," in *Journal of Economic and Business History.* Vol. III, Feb. 1931.

──────. "Land Policy in the Prairie States," in *Journal of Economic History.* Vol. I, May 1941.

──────. "The Struggle for Land and the Irrepressible Conflict," in *Political Science Quarterly.* Vol. 66, June 1941.

──────. "From Individualism to Collectivism in American Law Policy," in *Henry Wells Lawrence Memorial Lectures.* Vol. III. New London: Connecticut College, 1953.

──────. "The Homestead Law in an Incongruous Land System," in *American Historical Review.* July 1936.

──────. "Federal Land Policy in the South, 1866-1888," in *Journal of Southern History.* Aug. 1940.

──────. "Southern Investments in Northern Lands Before the Civil War," in *Journal of Southern History.* May 1939.

──────. "The Role of the Land Speculator in Western Development," in *Pennsylvania Magazine of History and Biography.* July 1942.

Haskins, Charles Homer. *The Yazoo Land Companies.* New York: The Knickerbocker Press, 1891.

Hibbard, B. H. *A History of the Public Land Policies.* New York: The Macmillan Co., 1924.

Hill, Robert T. *The Public Domain and Democracy.* New York: Columbia University Press, 1910.

McLendon, S. G. *History of the Public Domain of Georgia.* Atlanta: Foote, 1924.

Moody, William Godwin. *Land and Labor in the United States.* New York: Scribner, 1883.
Orfield, M. N. "Federal Land Grants to the States with Special Reference to Minnesota," in *Minnesota University Studies in Social Science.* Vol. II, St. Paul, 1915.
Paxson, Frederic L. *History of the American Frontier.* Boston: Houghton Mifflin Co., 1924.
Peffer, E. Louise. *The Closing of the Public Domain, Disposal and Reservation Policies, 1900-1950.* Stanford: Stanford University Press, 1951.
Phillips, William A. *Labor, Land and Law.* London: T. Fisher Unwin, 1886.
Robbins, Roy M. *Our Landed Heritage, the Public Domain, 1776-1936.* Princeton: Princeton University Press, 1942.
Stephenson, George M. *The Political History of the Public Lands from 1840 to 1862.* Boston: R. G. Badger, 1917.
Treat, Payson Jackson. *The National Land System, 1785-1820.* New York: E. B. Treat & Co., 1910.
Yard, Robert S. *Our Federal Lands, a Romance of American Development.* New York: Scribner, 1928.
Zahler, Helene Sara. *Eastern Workingmen and National Land Policy, 1829-1862.* New York: Columbia University Press, 1941.

Texas Public Land

Barker, Eugene C. (ed.). *The Austin Papers.* Pts. I and II, published as Vol. II of the *Annual Report of the American Historical Association,* 1919 and 1922. Washington, D.C.: Government Printing Office, 1924 and 1928.
———. Pt. III. Austin: University of Texas, 1927.
Bishop, Curtis K. *Lots of Land.* Austin: Steck, 1949.
———. *History and Disposition of the Texas Public Domain.* Austin: The State of Texas, 1945.
McKetrick, R. *The Public Land System of Texas.* Wisconsin University Bull. #905. Madison, 1918.

Railroad and Canal Land Grants

Ackerman, William K. *Early Illinois Railroads.* Chicago: Fergus Printing Co., 1884.
———. *Historical Sketch of the Illinois Central Railroad.* Chicago, 1891.
Daggett, Stuart. *Chapters on the History of the Southern Pacific Railroad.* New York: Ronald Press, 1922.
Gates, Paul Wallace. *The Illinois Central Railroad and Its Colonization Work.* Cambridge: Harvard University Press, 1934.
———. "Land Policy of the Illinois Central Railroad," in *Journal of Economic and Business History.* August 1931.
Greever, William S. *Arid Domain. The Santa Fe Railway and Its Western Land Grant.* Stanford: Stanford University Press, 1954.

Haney, Lewis H. *A Congressional History of Railways.* 2 vols. Madison: University of Wisconsin, 1908 and 1910.
Hedges, James B. *Henry Villard and the Railways of the Northwest.* New Haven: Yale University Press, 1930.
McAllister, W. A. *A Study of Railroad Land Grants in California.* Los Angeles: University of Southern California, 1940.
Oberholtzer, Ellis Paxon. *Jay Cooke, Financier of the Civil War.* 2 vols. Philadelphia: G. W. Jacobs & Co., 1907.
Overton, Richard C. *Burlington West. A Colonization History of the Burlington Railroad.* Cambridge: Harvard University Press, 1941.
The Pacific Railroad, *Congressional Proceedings in the 37th, 38th and 41st Congress.* West Chester, Pa.: F. S. Hickman, 1875.
Putnam, James William. *The Illinois and Michigan Canal, A Study in Economic History.* Chicago: University of Chicago Press, 1918.
Sabine, Edwin M. *The Building of the Union Pacific.* New York.
Sanborn, John Bell. *Congressional Grants of Land in Aid of Railways.* Madison: Wisconsin University Bull., Economics, Political Science and History Series, Vol. II, Nov. 3, 1899.
Smalley, Eugene V. *History of the Northern Pacific Railroad.* New York: G. P. Putnam's Sons, 1883.

State Land Policies and Problems

Cheyney, Edward Potts. *Anti-Rent Agitation in the State of New York.* Philadelphia: University of Pennsylvania, 1887.
Cowan, Helen I. *Charles Williamson; Genesee Promoter.* Rochester Historical Society, 1941.
Christman, H. *Tin Horns and Calico.* New York: Henry Holt & Co., 1945.
Ellis, David M. *Landlords and Farmers in the Hudson-Mohawk Region, 1790-1850.* Ithaca: Cornell University Press, 1946.
Evans, Paul Demand. *The Holland Land Company.* Buffalo: The Buffalo Historical Society, 1922.
Livermore, S. *Early American Land Companies, Their Influence on Corporate Development.* New York: The Commonwealth Fund, 1939.
McNall, Neil A. *An Agricultural History of the Genesee Valley, 1790-1860.* Philadelphia: University of Pennsylvania Press, 1952.
Murray, David. "The Antirent Episode in the State of New York," in *Annual Report of the American Historical Association.* Vol. I, 1896, pp. 139-73.
Nevins, Allan. *American States during and after the Revolution, 1775-1789.* New York: The Macmillan Co., 1924.
Turner, Orsamus. *Pioneer History of the Holland Purchase of Western New York.* Buffalo: The Buffalo Historical Society, 1849.

Forest and Mineral Land Policies

Hopkins, W. C. *Stability of Forest Land Ownership.* New Haven: Yale University Press, 1941.

Ise, J., Jr. *The United States Forest Policy.* New Haven: Yale University Press, 1920.

———. *The United States Oil Policy.* New Haven: Yale University Press, 1926.

Jeffers, D. S. *The Influence of the Philosophy of Free Land Upon the Forest Policy of the United States.* Ph.D. thesis. New Haven: Yale University, 1935.

Jones, Eliot. *The Anthracite Coal Combination in the United States.* Cambridge: Harvard University Press, 1914.

Lewis, Elmer A. (compiler). *Oil Land Leasing Act of 1920, with Amendments and Other Laws Relating to Mineral Lands.* Washington, D.C.: Government Printing Office, 1955.

Mussey, Henry Raymond. *Combination in the Mining Industry, A Study of Concentration in Lake Superior Iron Ore Production.* New York: Columbia University Press, 1905.

Salo, Sara J. *Timber Concentration in the Pacific Northwest, With Special Reference to the Timber Holdings of the Southern Pacific Railroad, the Northern Pacific Railroad and the Weyerhaeuser Timber Company.* Ann Arbor: Edwards Brothers, 1945.

Social Science Research Council. *A Survey of Research in Forest Land Ownership.* A Report of the Special Committee in Forest Economics. New York: Social Research Council, 1939.

United States. *Report of the Commissioner of Corporations on the Steel Industry,* Part I. Washington, D.C.: Government Printing Office, 1911.

———. *Report of the Commissioner of Corporations on the Lumber Industry,* Part II—*Concentration of Timber Ownership in Important Selected Regions.* Washington, D.C.: Government Printing Office, 1914.

United States Forest Service. *A National Plan for American Forestry.* A report prepared for the Forest Service, U. S. Department of Agriculture, in response to Sen. Res. 175, 72nd Cong. Sen. Doc. #12. Washington, D.C.: Government Printing Office, 1933.

United States National Resources Board. *National Land Resources Requirements, Problems and Policy.* Pt. VIII of the Supplementary Report of the Land Planning Committee to the National Resources Board. Washington, D.C.: Government Printing Office, 1935.

Wirth, Fremont P. *The Discovery and Exploitation of the Minnesota Iron Lands.* Cedar Rapids: Torch Press, 1937.

Farm Tenancy

Black, J. D., and Allen, R. H. "The Growth of Farm Tenancy in the United States," in *Quarterly Journal of Economics.* Vol. 51, May 1937.

Gates, Paul Wallace. *Frontier Landlords and Pioneer Tenants.* Ithaca: Cornell University Press, 1945.

———. "Land Policy and Tenancy in the Prairie States," in *Journal of Economic History.* Vol. I, May 1941.

Goldenweiser, E. A., and Truesdell, L. E. *Farm Tenancy in the United States.* U. S. Census Bureau Monograph 4. Washington, D.C.: Government Printing Office, 1924.

Hibbard, A. H. "Tenancy in the United States," in *Quarterly Journal of Economics.* Vol. 26, Feb. 1912.

———. "Farm Tenancy in the United States," in *Annals of the American Academy of Political and Social Science.* Vol. 40, March 1912.

McNall, Neil A. *The First Half-Century of Wadsworth Tenancy.* Ithaca: Cornell University Press, 1945.

Schuler, E. A. *Social Status and Farm Tenure—Attitudes and Social Conditions of Corn-belt and Cotton-belt.* Social Research No. IV, U. S. Dept. of Agriculture. Washington, D.C.: Government Printing Office, 1938.

Turner, H. A. *A Guide to Farm Tenure Data in Census Publications.* Washington, D.C.: U. S. Bureau of Agricultural Economics, 1948.

———. *The Ownership of Tenant Farms in the United States.* Washington, D.C.: U. S. Bureau of Agricultural Economics, 1926.

United States Special Committee on Farm Tenancy. *Report Submitted by the President to Congress.* 75th Cong., 1st Sess., House Doc. 149. Washington, D.C.: Government Printing Office, 1938.

———. *Farm Tenancy Report of the President's Committee.* Washington, D.C.: Government Printing Office, 1937.

United States Bureau of Agricultural Economics. *Trends in the Tenure Status of Farm Workers in the United States since 1880.* Washington, D.C.: Government Printing Office, 1948.

Urban Land Values

Arner, G. B. L. "Land Values in New York City," in *Quarterly Journal of Economics.* Vol. 45.

Bartholomew, Harland. *Land Uses in American Cities.* Cambridge: Harvard University Press, 1955.

Grebler, Leo. *Experience in Urban Real Estate Investment, An Interim Report Based on New York City Properties.* New York: Columbia University Press, 1955.

Hoyt, Homer. *One Hundred Years of Land Values in Chicago.* Chicago: University of Chicago Press, 1933.

Porter, Kenneth W. *John Jacob Astor, Business Man.* 2 vols. Cambridge: Harvard University Press, 1931.

Pound, Arthur. *The Golden Earth, The Story of Manhattan's Landed Wealth.* New York: The Macmillan Co., 1935.

Spengler, Edwin H. *Land Values in New York in Relation to Transit Facilities.* New York: Columbia University Press, 1930.

Woodbury, C. (ed.). *Urban Redevelopment Problems.* Chicago: University of Chicago Press, 1953.

Land Taxation

Adams, Henry Carter. *Taxation in the United States, 1789-1816*. The Johns Hopkins University Studies in Historical and Political Science. Second Series. Baltimore: The Johns Hopkins Press, 1884.

Brown, Harry Gunnison. *The Economics of Taxation*. New York: Henry Holt & Co., 1924.

———. *The Economic Basis of Tax Reform*. Columbia, Mo.: Lucas Bros., 1932.

———. *Two Essays on the Taxation of Unearned Incomes*. Columbia, Mo.: Lucas Bros., 1921.

Brown, Harry Gunnison et al. (eds.). *Land-Value Taxation Around the World*. New York: The Robert Schalkenbach Foundation, 1955.

Ely, Richard T. *Taxation in American States and Cities*. New York: Thomas Y. Crowell & Co., 1888.

Fillebrown, C. B. *The A B C of Taxation*. New York: Doubleday, Page & Co., 1916.

Marsh, Benjamin C. *Taxation of Land Values in American Cities, The Next Step in Exterminating Poverty*. New York, 1911.

Post, Louis F. *The Taxation of Land Values*. Indianapolis: Bobbs-Merrill, 1915.

Scheftel, Yetta. *The Taxation of Land Value, A Study of Certain Discriminatory Taxes on Land*. Boston and New York: Houghton Mifflin Co., 1916.

Schwab, John C. *History of the New York Property Tax*. Baltimore: American Economics Association, 1890.

Seligman, Edwin R. A. *Essays in Taxation*. 9th ed. New York: The Macmillan Co., 1921.

Stalker, Archibald. *Taxation of Land Values in Western Canada*. Montreal, 1914.

The Single Tax

Barker, Charles Albro. *Henry George*. New York: Oxford University Press, 1955.

Buffham, W. S. (Printer). *The Edwin Burgess Letters on Taxation*. Racine, Wis., n.d.

Dawson, William Harbutt. *The Unearned Increment, or Reaping without Sowing*. London: Swan Sonnenschein, 1890.

Fillebrown, C. B. *The A B C of Taxation*. New York: Doubleday, Page & Co., 1916.

———. *Thirty Years of Henry George*. 3rd ed. Boston, 1915.

George, Henry. *Progress and Poverty*. New York: The Robert Schalkenbach Foundation, reprinted 1956.

———. *The Science of Political Economy*. New York: The Robert Schalkenbach Foundation, reprinted 1953.

———. *The Land Question, etc.* New York: The Robert Schalkenbach Foundation, reprinted 1945.

Johnson, E. H. "Methods of Taxing the Unearned Increment," in *Quarterly Journal of Economics*. Vol. 24, 1909-10.
Johnson, J. F. "The Proposed Increment Tax for New York," in *Quarterly Journal of Economics*. Vol. 27.
Post, Louis F. *The Single Tax*. Cedar Rapids, Ia., 1889.
Shearman, Thomas G. *Natural Taxation*. 3rd ed. Garden City: Doubleday, Page & Co., 1915.
Young, Arthur N. *The Single Tax Movement in the United States*. Princeton: Princeton University Press, 1916.

Land Reform

Anonymous. *On Land Concentration and Responsibility of Political Power*. London: Kegan Paul, Trench & Co., 1886.
Beer, M. (ed.). *The Pioneers of Land Reform, Spence, Ogilvie, and Paine*. New York: Alfred Knopf, 1929.
British Information Services. *Town and Country Planning in Britain*. New York, 1955.
California, Commission on Immigration and Housing. *Report on Large Land Holdings in Southern California*. Sacramento: State Printing Office, 1919.
Cox, Harold. *Land Nationalization*. 2nd ed. London: Methuen, 1906.
Cox, Samuel S. *Free Land and Free Trade*. New York: G. P. Putnam's Sons, 1880.
Dawson, William Harbutt. *The Unearned Increment, or Reaping without Sowing*. London: Swan Sonnenschein, 1890.
Ely, R. T. "Landed Property as an Economic Concept," in *American Economic Review*. Vol. 7, Supplement, March 1917.
Fels, Mary. *Joseph Fels, His Life Work*. New York: B. W. Huebsch, 1916.
Frothingham, Octavius B. *Gerrit Smith, A Biography*. New York: G. P. Putnam's Sons, 1879.
Garrison, William Lloyd, the Younger. *Gerrit Smith and Land Monopoly*. Chicago: Public Publishing Company, 1906.
Geiger, George Raymond. *The Philosophy of Henry George*. New York: The Macmillan Co., 1933.
———. *The Theory of the Land Question*. New York: The Macmillan Co., 1936.
George, Henry. *Social Problems*. New York: The Robert Schalkenbach Foundation, reprinted 1949.
Gibbons, John. *Tenure and Toil, or Rights and Wrongs of Property and Labor*. Philadelphia: J. B. Lippincott & Co., 1888.
Gregory, John G. *The Land-Limitations Movement*. Vol. II, No. 14. Milwaukee: Publication of the Parkman Club, 1897.
Harlow, Ralph Volney. *Gerrit Smith, Philanthropist and Reformer*. New York: Henry Holt & Co., 1939.
Jones, Richard. *Peasant Rents*. 1831 reprint. New York: The Macmillan Co., 1895.

Mill, John Stuart. *Papers on Land Tenure* in "Dissertations and Discussions," Works of John Stuart Mill. Vol. V. New York: Henry Holt & Co., 1875.
Mitchell, C. Clyde. *Land Reform in Asia, A Case Study*. Washington, D.C.: National Planning Association, Pamphlet 78, 1952.
Muirhead, James F. *Land and Employment*. London: Oxford Press, 1935.
Simpson, Stephen. *The Workingman's Manual, A New Theory of Political Economy*. Philadelphia: T. L. Bonsal, 1831.
Skidmore, Thomas. *Rights of Man to Property*. New York: A. Ming, Jr., 1829.
Stamp, L. Dudley. *The Land of Britain, Its Use and Misuse*. London: Longmans, 1955.
Stubbs, C. W. *The Land and the Laborers*. London: Swan Sonnenschein, 1891.
Tannebaum, Frank. *The Mexican Agrarian Revolution*. New York: The Macmillan Co., 1929.
Thackeray, S. W. *The Land and the Community*. New York: D. Appleton & Co., 1889.
United Nations. *Progress and Land Reform*. Analysis of replies to a United Nations questionnaire. New York: United Nations, Department of Economic Affairs, 1954.
———. *Land Reform: Defects in Agrarian Structures as Obstacles to Economic Development*. New York: United Nations, Department of Economic Affairs, 1951.
United States Department of Agriculture. *World Land Reform, A Selected Bibliography*. U. S. Department of Agriculture Library List 55. Washington, D.C.: Government Printing Office, 1951.
———. Department of State. *Land Reform, A World Challenge*. U. S. Department of State Publication 4445. Washington, D.C.: Government Printing Office, 1952.
———. National Resources Board. *Certain Aspects of Land Problems and Government Land Policies*. Pt. VII of the Supplementary Report of the Land Planning Committee of the National Resources Board. Washington, D.C.: Government Printing Office, 1935.
Wallace, Alfred Russel. *Land Nationalization*. London: Swan Sonnenschein, 1896.
Warriner, Doreen. *Land and Poverty in the Middle East*. London: Royal Institute of International Affairs, 1948.
Wilson, Alexander J. *Reciprocity, Bi-metallism and Land-tenure Reform*. London: Macmillan, 1880.
Wisconsin, University of. *Conference on World Land Tenure Problems, Proceedings*. Madison: University of Wisconsin Press, 1951.

Note: For a detailed bibliography of writings since 1900 relating to landownership, see U. S. Department of Agriculture, *Bibliographical Bulletin*, No. 22. Washington, D.C.: Government Printing Office, 1953.

Index

Aborigines, land tenure among, 7-8

Absentee ownership: in American colonies, 25-26, 43, 45; prevalence of, 142; rise of in West, 132-33

Adams, John, land views of, 45, 186

Addison, Lord, and English land reform, 17

Allen, Ethan, and Vermont squatters, 191

American colonies: failure of quitrent system in, 41-42; first settlements made by chartered trading companies, 18; land-grabbing a general practice in, 21; nature of land system in, 46; motives and methods of land distribution in, 42-43, 45; objectives of land systems in, 43-44; speculation in, 46-58; and western land grants, 48-52. *See also* under names of states

American Land Co., 134; canal-lot investment of, 159

American and Sharon Land Co., 171

Arden, Del., and taxation of unearned increment, 260

Ardentown, Del., and taxation of unearned increment, 260

Astor, John Jacob, real estate holdings of, 235-36, 255

Austin, Moses: on fraudulent land sales in Louisiana, 106-7; granted land by Mexican Govt., 149; and Louisiana Territory claim, 109

Austin, Stephen F.: land speculation of, 119; and New Madrid Claims, 120-21; and Texas colonization, 149-50, 152, 154

Australia, and taxation of land values, 260

Baldwin Corp., 171

Baltimore, Lord. *See* Calvert

Baltimore, Md., system of quitrents in, 38

Baltimore & Ohio Railroad, 158

Bankhead-Jones Farm Tenant Act (1937), 225-26

Baring, Alexander, and speculation in Maine lands, 80

Barlow, Joel, and Scioto Project, 90

Barlow, Raleigh, on disposal policies of public domain, 147

Beard, Charles A., cited, 67

Beaubien, Carlos, and Maxwell Grant, 146

Benton, Thomas H.: claims tenantry unfavorable to freedom, 220; and Louisiana land-grant controversies, 108

Berkeley, Lord John, 36

Berkeley's Hundred, Va., 34

Biddle, Nicholas, "money monopoly" of, 100

Bingham, William: and land warrants, 77; and purchase of Maine lands, 80

Bingham's Million Acres, Me., 80, 194-95

"Bonanza farms," origin of, 170-73

Bond, Beverley: on abolition of quitrents in Pennsylvania, 196; on beneficial result of quitrent system, 196-97; on failure of quitrent system in colonies, 41-42

Boone, Daniel, 108

Boston Ten Towns, 70 n.

Boudinot, Elias, and Symmes' Miami Purchase, 91

Briggs, Joseph, cited, 97-98

Brodrick, George, on landlordism, 16-17

Burgess, Edwin, proposes single tax, 269-70

Burr, Aaron, 73; criticism of, 75-76; and De Bastrop Claim, 113, 114-15

Butler, Charles, and American Land Co., 134

California: and discovery of gold in, 143, 208-9; exploitation of timber lands in, 202; landed estates in, 144-45; Mexican land grants in, 143-45; real estate as source of large fortunes, 239

California Lands Commission, 144

Calvert, Cecil (1st Lord Baltimore), 38

Canton Co., 158

Carey, Henry C., on concentration of landholdings, 265-66

Carey Act (1894), 137-38

Carondelet, Baron de, and Spanish claims in Louisiana, 111, 113

Carteret, Sir George, 36

Cass, Gen. George W., and "bonanza farms," 170-71

Castro, Henry, and colonization of Texas, 151

Index

Central Pacific Railroad of California, 165
Charles II, of England: and New Jersey grants, 36, 37; and revocation of military tenure, 35
"Chartered companies," nature of, 18-20
Cheney, B. P., and "bonanza farms," 171
Cherokee Strip, Okla., "opening" of, 139
Chicago, history of land boom in, 237-39
Chesapeake & Ohio Railroad, and development of Newport News, 245
Chillicothe, O., as center of land speculation, 99, 100
Cincinnati, O., site selected by Symmes, 95
Civic freedoms, emergence of theory of, 44
Clamorgan, Jacques, and Louisiana land claims, 110-12
Clamorgan Grant, La., 110-12
Clamorgan Land Assoc., 112
Clark, Daniel, and Spanish grants in Louisiana, 116-17. *See also* Gaines, Myra Clark
Clark, George Rogers, expedition of, 102
Clawson, Marion: on abuses in timberland distribution, 202; on disposal of public domain to railroads, 173-74; on land acts, 138, 140-41
Clay, Henry, defends national land policy, 129
Cleveland, O., laid out by Connecticut proprietors, 95
Coal lands, engrossment of in Pennsylvania, 211-12
Cobden, Richard, and English land reform, 17
Cole, Arthur H., on influences in fluctuations of land sales, 183
Connecticut: and claim to Western Reserve, 92-93; overcrowding population in, 57; method of land taxation in early federal period, 253; and Mohawk Valley claim, 70; restricts land alienation, 28
Connecticut Land Co., 93, 95
Connecticut Western Reserve, 92-93
Constable, William, and Macomb Purchase, 75
Constitutional Convention: and controversy over taxing powers of federal government, 67-68; land a factor in, 64-67

Continental Congress: and Mohawk Valley dispute, 70; not concerned with land questions, 63-64
Cooke, Jay: on commercial advantages of Duluth, 168; interest in Northern Pacific Railroad, 168-70
Cooper, Lord Ashley, and Carolina grant to, 39
Copper lands, engrossment of, 210
Coral Gables, Fla., promoted by land speculation, 246
Cortlandt Manor, N.Y., 32
Crédit Mobilier, 167
Crown-Zellerbach Corp., timber-land holdings of, 204
Cutler, Manasseh, and Ohio colonization scheme, 87, 88, 89, 90

Dalrymple, William, and "bonanza farms," 170
Davis, John P., on regulated companies, 18
Dayton, Jonathan: and Macomb Purchase, 75; and selection of site for Dayton, 96; and Symmes' Miami Purchase, 91
Dayton, O., selection of site for, 96
Deane, Silas, on need of western land, 57
De Bastrop Claim, La., 113-16
De La Guerra. *See* La Guerra, de.
Delaware: entails in, 63; method of land taxation in early federal period, 253; primogeniture modified in, 61
Denmark, and taxation of land values, 260
Desert Land Act (1877), 137
Douglas, Stephen A., opposes Illinois Central grant, 159-60
Drake, E. L., discovery of oil by, 214
Duer, William: and Scioto Project, 88, 89, 90, 91; and Maine holdings, 80, 194
Duluth, Minn., Cooke's plans for, 168
Dutch West India Co., and colonization of New York, 30
Dwight, Timothy, on Virginia military warrants, 77

East India Co.: chartered, 20; compared with Plymouth and Virginia companies, 21
East Jersey, under Carteret, 36
East Jersey Co., 37

Easton, Rufus, and Louisiana land claims, 109
Economic rent. *See* Rent, economic
Edgar, John, and western land-grabbing, 103
Elkins, Stephen B., and Mexican grants in New Mexico, 145-46
Ellis, David, on anti-rent movement in New York, 189, 190
Ellsworth, Henry L., western land engrossment by, 221-22
Ely, Richard T.: on colonial land taxation, 249-50; on methods of obtaining state revenue, 251-52, 252-53
England: absentee ownership in, 25-26; creation of "landless" classes in, 45; decadence of tenure theory in, 35; effects of disintegration of feudalism in, 45; feudal system in, 12-13, 14, 15, 16; Poor Laws, 14; progress of feudal land tenure in, 13-17. *See also* Great Britain
Engrossment: biblical admonition against, 5; of public domain, 98-101, 131-33; role of land companies in, 133-35
Entail: abolished in U.S., 60-61; in colonies, 62, 63; a feature of feudal land tenure in England, 14, 15, 16; Jefferson's objection to, 62; law and custom of after Revolution, 61
Escott, T. H. S., on trend toward landownership in Great Britain, 17
Ethiopia, feudalism in, 12
Europe, feudal system in, 11-17
Evans, George H., advocates land reform, 177-78, 267, 268

Fairhope, Ala., and taxation of unearned increment, 260
Farming, crop-share system, 218
Farm tenancy. *See* Tenancy, farm
Fell, Jesse, land-jobbing ventures of in Illinois, 162
Feudalism: advantage of in England, 14; basis of, 12; breakdown of, 15; economic and political foundation of, 12; effects of disintegration of in England, 45; fee ownership contrasted with, 14-15; growth of in Europe, 11-17; land-allotment feature of in England, 23; origin and growth of in England, 12-13
Fiske, John, 61
Fletcher vs. Peck, 79

Florida, land boom in, 242-43, 246
Flower, George, influence of on British speculation in western lands, 104
Fordham Manor, N.Y., 32
Forests: abuses of under timber acts, 201-3; advantages of public ownership of, 204-6; exploitation of in U.S., 199-201; national system established, 203
Fort Duquesne (Pittsburgh), 49-50
Fort Orange, N.Y., 31
France, land-reform movement in, 262-63
Franklin, Benjamin: land speculations of, 264; on right to private property, 45; and Vandalia Co., 55-56
Franklin, William, and settlement of Illinois country, 56
"Freemen," origin of, 15
French and Indian War, 50; and western land acquisitions, 53

Gaines, Myra Clark, and litigation over Louisiana claims, 116-18
Galveston Bay and Texas Land Co., 151-53
Gary, Ind., constructed by U.S. Steel Corp., 244
Gates, Paul W.: on effects on land engrossment by private capitalists, 141-42; on engrossment of mineral lands, 210-11; on landlordism, 132, 133; on land tenancy in mid-Northwest, 220-21; on Pre-emption Act of 1841, 130
Geiger, George R., 3; on influence of H. George, 272, 275; on question of land-value taxation, 261, 287
General Land Office, 138, 139; function of, 125; inefficiency in, 279
Genesee, Lords of. *See* Wadsworths
Genesee Country, N.Y., 72
Geneseo, N.Y., and Wadsworth purchase, 73
George, Henry, 26, 182; distinguishes land as entity distinct from improvements on, 44; influence of *Progress and Poverty,* 271-72; on land monopolization in California, 143-44; land-reform proposals of, 270-72; opposed to land nationalization and communism, 276, 294; philosophy of, 275-76; on relation between depressions and speculative land booms, 183, 184; taxation of land values proposed by, 259
Georgia: colonial land policy of, 40-41; proprietorship system abolished, 61;

method of land taxation in early federal period, 253; and Yazoo claim, 77-79
Georgia Yazoo Co., 78
Germany, and taxation on unearned increment, 260-61
Girard, Stephen, and De Bastrop Claim, 113, 115-16
Gold: impact of discoveries in California, 208-9; legislation concerning valid claims, 209
Gorges, Sir Ferdinando, original Maine grants to, 192
Gorham, Nathaniel, and land purchases in New York, 71, 72
Great Britain: agitation for economic and political reforms in, 269; land-reform movement in, 17, 262-63; problems of land reform in, 283-84; progress in control of land use, 291-92; system of landlordism in, 16-17; trend toward landownership concentration in, 16-17. *See also* England
Great Northern Railroad, and speculation in iron-ore land, 214
Greeley, Horace: advocates limited landownership as antidote to speculation, 162; advocates reform in national land system, 180, 268; critic of public land policy, 135; urges land reform in New York, 190

Hamilton, Alexander, influence of economic and financial policies of, 264-65
Harris, Marshall, on Jefferson's opposition to primogeniture and entail, 62
Harrison, William Henry: suggests change in national land policy, 94; on Virginia's western claims, 102-3; and western land-grabbing, 103
Hebrews, ancient, regarded land as heritage of God, 5
Henderson, Richard, promotes settlement of Kentucky, 52
Henry, O., on corruption and fraud in Texas, 148
Henry, Patrick, land deals of, 51, 52, 55
Holbrook, Darius B., and Illinois Central Railroad, 159-60
Holland, as leading trading nation of Europe, 31
Holland Land Co., and Genesee Country, 72
Homestead Act (1862), 166, 180, 181; fraud and abuses resulting from, 139-43; labor's influence in passage of, 268; provisions of, 136-37

Hopewell, Pa., creation of, 244
Howe, Frederic C., on unearned-increment tax in Germany, 260-61
Hulbert, Archer B., on Ohio Co. of Associates, 89-90
Huntington, Collis P.: and development of Newport News, 245; promoter of Southern Pacific Railroad, 241

Illinois: absentee landlordism in, 132-33; canal projects and land speculation, 159; and grants to railroads, 160; settlement of, 56; spread of land-jobbing to, 101
Illinois Central Railroad: capital gain from land sales, 164; land grant to, 158-63; speculative interest in, 160-63
Immigration, European, beginning of, 104
"Inclosures," in England, 14
Indiana, lead mines in, 207; spread of land-jobbing to, 101
Indian Line, 51
Indians: driven out of western lands, 102; effect of on colonial settlements, 22, 23, 31; and Georgia-South Carolina land dispute, 77; and western land disputes, 49-50
Ireland: absentee ownership in, 25; rise of "rack renting" in, 25
Iron-ore lands, engrossment of, 210, 213-14
Iroquois Indians: in New York, 70; pre-emption of land of, 71; land tenure among, 7-8

Jackson, Andrew, on cost and revenue of public domain, 125; issues "Specie Circular," 127
Japan, feudalism in, 12
Jarrot, Nicholas, and western land-grabbing, 103
Jefferson, Peter, land deals of, 51
Jefferson, Thomas: denounces Georgia's Yazoo grants, 78; on fraudulent land practices in Louisiana, 107-8; influence of on land-tenure reform, 61-63; and Kentucky Territory, 52; on King's usurpations, 55; land views of, 45, 62, 186, 264; and Livingston's Louisiana claim, 118-19; proposal of on distribution of public domain, 86
Johnson, V. Webster, on disposal policies of public domain, 147

Johnson, Sir William, 51; and settlement of Illinois country, 56
Joint stock company, development of, 20
Julian, George W., 145; land theories of, 181-82
Justice, ancient concept of in relation to landownership, 5, 6

Kearny, Gen. Stephen W., and sale of public land in California, 239
Kennebec Purchase, Me., 47, 192
Kentucky: methods of land taxation in, 253, 255; settlement of, 52
King, Rufus, on danger of property requirement for congressmen, 65
Knox, Gen. Henry, Maine grants of, 80, 194

Labor, and "free land" agitation, 268
La Guerra, de, claim, Calif., 144
Land: allotment of in Massachusetts Colony, 24-25, 26, 27; a chief item of wealth in colonies, 67; in Constitutional Convention, 64-67; and the Continental Congress, 63-64; industrialization decreased dependence on as source of public revenue, 253; as different from real estate, 259; distribution of in colonies, 23, 24, 29, 33-35, 42-43, 45; economic rent of, collection of, 62-63, 259-60, 275; entity distinct from improvements on, 44; essential to existence, 4; a factor in westward movement, 57-58; leased, statistics on, 227-29; monopoly of by town proprietors, 27; nationalization of, as a land-reform remedy, 293-94; origin of question of in America, 26; philosophic concepts of in colonial era, 44-45; progressive tax on, 287-89; as a question of economic justice, 4; remedies for, 285-94; reform in taxation as solution to question of, 257-58; restraints on alienation of in New England colonies, 27-28; and Revolution, 59-68; role of in human progress, 10; social control of use of, as reform measure, 291-93; a source of revenue to state and local governments, 254; status of in primitive society, 3; status of in colonies, 35; taxation of improvements on, 255-56; tenure of among aborigines, 7-8. *See also* below
Land, state: disposal of after Revolution, 69-81, 71-73; defects in system of, 80-81
Land companies, role of, 133-35; southern, 48-51. *See also* names of companies
Land and Its Rent (Walker), 273
Land-grabbing: curbed by Revolution, 56-57; a general practice in colonies, 21; in Kentucky, 52; as motive in establishment of colonies, 45; in Tennessee, 52-53; by southern land companies, 48-51
Land-jobbing: in California, 143; in Louisiana, 108; opposition to in New York, 75-76; spread of, 101
Landlordism: a detriment to early western development, 221; in England, 43; Gates on, 132, 133; a hindrance to agriculture and urban development in Britain, 16; implies tenancy, 217; in Ireland, 43; and pre-emption acts, 131-33; prevalence of, 142; system of in Britain, 16-17
Landownership: by aliens in N.Y., 73; in colonial era, 18-32, 33-58; effect of Revolution on status of, 55; European background of, 11-17; future of, 277-94; and land disposal in local politics, 185-98; political and philosophical aspects of, 1-10; as early pre-requisite for voters and congressmen, 64-65, 66; proposed remedies for, 285-94
Land reform: and early American economists, 265-67; early pioneers in, 263-64; in England, 15-17; important to peace and stability, 281-82; influence of George on, 275-76; and international problems, 280-82; necessity of, 282-84; progress of in U.S., 262-76; proposed remedies for, 285-94; "safety-valve" theory of, 182-84; U.N. resolution on, 281
Land speculation: in colonies, 28, 46-58; a factor in economic depressions, 183-84; and railroad grants, 165-74; after Revolution, 81. *See also* under cities and states
Lane, Ebenezer, 156
Lehigh Coal Mine Co., and exploitation of coal in Pennsylvania, 212
Lexington, Ky., land speculation in, 100
Lick, James, and San Francisco real estate, 241
Licking Land Co., 96
Limantour Claim, Calif., 144
Livingston, Edward, and Louisiana land claim, 118-19

Livingston, John, 71
Livingston Manor, N.Y., 32
Locke, John: and "Fundamental Constitutions," 39, 197; philosophy of, 44, 45, 63, 262
London Co., 33, 34
Longworth, Nicholas, land deals of, 101
Los Angeles, land speculation in, 239, 241-43
Louisiana Purchase, 106
Louisiana Territory: antedating of Spanish claims in, 106-9; purchase of, 106; Spanish land claims in, 110-23; squatter claims in, 109-10
Loyal Co., and western land grants, 49, 50
Lubin, Isador, on importance of land reform to peace and stability, 281-82; on requirements of land-reform program, 282
Lynch, Col. Charles, and De Bastrop Claim, 114

Macomb, Alexander, and purchases of state land, 74-76
Madison, James, philosophy of, 65-66, 67
Maine: colonial land distribution in, 29; early land speculation in, 47-48; entails in, 63; Massachusetts claims to, 79-80; squatter conflicts in, 192-95
Maison Rouge Claim, La., 116
Manhattan Island, first settlements on, 30, 31
Marietta, O., founded by Ohio Assoc., 95
Mariposa Estate, Calif., 144
Martin's Hundred, Va., 34
Maryland: disintegration of manorial system in, 61; King's taxing power waived in, 35; land system in, 38-39; method of land taxation in early federal period, 253; quitrents abolished in, 196
Mason, George, and landownership as prerequisite for voters and congressmen, 66-67
Mason, John, original grantee of New Hampshire land, 29
Massachusetts: and claim to Maine District, 79-80; disposal of state lands by, 71-73; entails in, 63; and Kennebec Purchase, 47; land speculation in after Revolution, 76, 77; ethod of land taxation in early federal period, 252; and Mohawk Valley claim, 70; town system of land allotment in, 25
Massachusetts Bay Co., 24-25, 29
Massie, Gen. Nathan, and Chillicothe town-jobbing venture, 99
Maxwell, Lucien B., 145-46
Maxwell Grant, N. Mex., 145-46
Maxwell Land Grant and Railroad Co., 146
McArthur, Gen. Duncan, land speculations of, 99
McCormick, Daniel, and Macomb Purchase, 75
McCulloch, Hugh, and land speculation in Maine, 195
McDonogh, John, land dealings of, 122
McMaster, John B., on Scioto Project, 91
Mechanics Free Press, advocates donation of public lands to U.S. citizens, 267
Merchant adventurers, 19-20
Merrick, George E., promoter of Coral Gables, 246
Mesabi, Minn., engrossment of iron fields in, 210
Mexico, land tenure in primitive society, 8-9
Miami (O.) Purchase, 91-92, 95
Mill, John Stuart: and English land reform, 17; proposes land nationalization, 294
Mineral lands: early legislation on disposal of, 207; conservation movement, 215-16; engrossment and concentration of, 210-14; exploitation of oil-bearing lands, 210, 214-16; and discovery of gold, 208-9; U.S. policy of leasing, 207-8
Mineral Leasing Act (1920), provisions of, 216
Minnesota, rise of land values in, 172
Miranda, Guadelupe, and Maxwell Grant, 146
Mississippi, land purchases in, 134
Mississippi Co., 53
Missouri, and New Madrid Claims, 120-21
Mohawk Valley, N.Y., dispute over pre-emption of, 70
Moody, William G.: advocates land reform, 181; on objections to "bonanza farms," 171
Morhouse, Abraham, and De Bastrop Claim, 113-14
Morris, Gouverneur, land views of, 65, 66

Morris, Robert: and exploitation of coal lands, 211-12; and Genesee Country, 72; and land companies, 133; and land speculation in Washington, D.C., 232, 233-34; and land warrants, 76-77, 80
Morrisania, Manor of, N.Y., 32
Morrison, William, and western land deals, 103
Morrisville, Pa., development of, 244
Mt. Carmel and New Albany Railroad of Indiana, 158

Natural rights, emergence of theory of, 44
Neri, Philip Henry, 113-16
Nevada, exploitation of timber lands in, 202
New England: basis for land distribution in, 23; boundary disputes in, 24; colonial land practices in, 22-30; and quitrent system, 41; "town settlements" in, 22-25; primogeniture modified in, 61; problems of land disposal in, 191-95
New Hampshire: and dispute over New Hampshire Grants, 191; land distribution in, 29-30; method of land taxation in early federal period, 252-53
New Hampshire Grants, controversy over, 29, 30, 191
New Jersey: early history of, 36-37; land exploitation in, 36; methods of land taxation in early federal period, 253; primogeniture modified in, 61
New Madrid Claims, Mo., 120-21
New Mexico: land tenure among Pueblos, 8; and Mexican grants, 143, 144, 145-47
Newport News, Va., development of, 244-45
New York: and alien ownership of land, 73; anti-rent movement in, 189-90; colonial land system in, 30-32; disposal of state land in, 69-70; and dispute over New Hampshire Grants, 30, 191; Dutch holdings after Revolution, 72-73; land reform in, 187-90; laws against primogeniture, 31; method of land taxation in early federal period, 252; and Mohawk Valley claim, 70; Ogden and Macomb purchases, 74-76; and Phelps-Gorham dispute, 71, 72

New York City: rise of real estate values in, 234-36; sale of public domain in, 85
New York Genesee Land Co., 71, 72
New Zealand, and taxation of land values, 260
Nicholson, John, and land warrants, 76-77
North Carolina: colonial proprietorship system abolished, 61; land distribution in, 39; method of land taxation in early federal period, 252; quitrent system in, 197
North Dakota: "bonanza farms" in, 170; rise of land values in, 172
Northern Pacific Railroad: background of, 167-70; land policies of, 172, 173; and origin of "bonanza farms," 170-73; reorganized, 172
Northwest (Old). See Northwest Territory
Northwest Improvement Co., 173
Northwest Ordinance (1787), 63-64, 82-87
Northwest Territory: government established, 88; land speculation in, 97, 99, 100, 101-3, 103-4; land disposal in, 82-83, 85. See also Northwest Ordinance

Ogden, Samuel, and N.Y. land purchases, 75
Ogden, William B., and canal project in Illinois, 159
Ogilvie, William, and land reform in England, 17, 262, 263
Oglethorpe, James, founder of Georgia, 40
Ohio: colonization schemes in, 87-92; and Connecticut's claim to Western Reserve, 92-93; federal land offices in, 94; land speculation in, 95-97, 99, 100; method of land taxation in, 255-56
Ohio Co. of Associates: colonization scheme of, 87, 88, 89-90, 95; and Northwest grant, 83; sale of public domain to, 87-91; and western land grants, 49, 50
Oil Land Leasing Act (1920), 215-16
Oil lands, exploitation of, 214-16
Oklahoma, and "opening" of Cherokee Strip, 139
Old Dominion Land Co., 245-46
Omaha Indians, land tenure among, 8

Oregon, exploitation of timber lands in, 202
Otis, Gen. Harrison G., and Bingham's Million Acres, 194
Our Land and Land Policy (George), 270, 271

Pacific Railroad Act, 165
Paine, Thomas, philosophy of, 178, 262, 264
Palatinate, in colonial Maryland, 38-39
Panic of 1837, generated by land speculation, 183
Patroons: and land system in New York, 30-32; manorial privileges abolished, 61
Peasants' Revolt, in England, 14
Pejepscut Co., 48, 192
Pelham Manor, N.Y., 32
Penn, William: and development of Philadelphia, 37-38, 230-31; and land deals in New Jersey, 36, 37; and Wyoming (Pa.) land dispute, 57
Pennsylvania: early land history of, 37-38; and dispute over Wyoming region, 57; Dutch holdings in after Revolution, 72; exploitation of coal land in, 211-12; exploitation of oil lands in, 214; land politics in, 195-96; land speculation in after Revolution, 76-77; method of land taxation in early federal period, 253; primogeniture modified in, 61
Pennsylvania Railroad, 158
Peralta Reavis Grant, N. Mex., 146
Petroleum: Congress curbs rapid exploitation of, 210; production of, an important mineral industry, 214
Phelps, Oliver, land purchases of in N.Y., 71, 72, 73
Phelps and Gorham Purchase, 71-73
Philadelphia: development of, 37-38; and Girard's Louisiana grant to, 40, 116; land-warrant business in, 76; rise of real estate values in, 230-31; sale of public domain in, 85
Philipsburg Manor, N.Y., 32
Philipse Manor, N.Y., 32
Phillips, W. A.: advocates land reform, 181; on failure of pre-emption and homestead laws, 140; on land speculation, 46; on Northwest Ordinance, 85
Pickering, Timothy, 77
Pico, Andre and Pio, 144
Pilgrims, type of settlement formed by, 22-23

Pinckney, Charles, 65
Pittsburgh: sale of public domain in, 85; and taxation land values, 260
Plymouth Colony, early land systems in, 21
Plymouth Co., nature of, 20-21; and Pilgrims, 23
Pre-emption Land Act (1841), 105, 131
Pre-emption Land Act (1842), labor's influence on passage of, 268; public domain under, 129-33
Primogeniture: abolished in U.S., 60-61; in colonies, 31, 62; a feature of feudal tenure in England, 14, 15, 16
Progress and Poverty (George), influence of, 271-72, 275
Property: ownership of, as a prerequisite for voting, 65; philosophic conceptions of in colonial era, 44-45; personal, decline in as revenue source, 254. *See also* Real estate
Public domain: under Articles of Confederation, 175-76; agitation for reform in policy of, 179-82; and British speculations in, 103-4; bungling administration of, 278-80; in California, 209; changes in policy concerning, 92; classifications of, 208; conflicting opinions about, 176-78; early engrossment of, 98-101; early history of, 82-93; conservation movement, 215-16; disposal of to railroads, 156-64, 165-74; and disposal of timber land, 201-3; effect of "Specie Circular" on sales of, 127-29; efforts to improve administration of, 125; and engrossment of mineral lands, 213-14; a factor in political sectionalism, 125; future of, 142; general tax on, 253-55; and Homestead Act, 136-47; influences in fluctuation in sale of, 183; land offices established, 92; and opening of prairie lands, 101-3; opposing views on, 185-87; and pre-emption acts, 131-33; problems of petroleum on, 210; reason for paucity of sales of, 85-86; rise of speculation in, 124, 126; and "safety-valve" theory, 182-84; and squatters' rights, 129-30; statistics on, 85, 86; and Swamp Land Acts, 130-31; and "town-jobbing," 95-98, 101; use of, as bait to promote economic development, 157; weaknesses in system of disposal, 124, 126. *See also* Forests; Mineral lands

Pueblo Indians, land tenure among, 8
Pullman, George, 244
Pulteney Purchase, N.Y., 72
Putnam, Rufus, and Ohio colonization scheme, 87

Quebec Bill (1774), 51
Quitrents: beneficial result of, 196-97; in colonial Maryland, 38; failure of system in colonies, 41-42, 197; Pennsylvania and Maryland abolish system of, 195, 196

Railroads: eastern and western compared, 163-64; and public domain, 156-64, 165-74; as stimulant to speculation, 165-74
Rantoul, Robert, and speculation in Illinois Central lands, 160
Real estate: as different from land, 259; engrossment of by corporations, 243-46; rapid rise in value of, 230-43
Reavis, James A., and Peralta-Reavis Grant, 146
Reclamation Act (1902), 138
Rensselaerwick Manor, N.Y., 31-32
Rent, economic: difficult to determine, 259-60; and taxation, 62-63, 259-60, 275
Revolutionary War: curbs land-grabbing schemes, 56-57; effect of on status of landownership, 55; and tenure, 59-68
Rhode Island: entails in, 63; method of land taxation in early federal period, 252; proprietaries in, 27
Ricardo, David, and economic law of rent, 265, 266
Riggs, Romulus, land practices of, 132, 133
Rogers, Thorold, on "town settlements," 22
Russel, William, and Spanish grants in Louisiana, 109

Sackett, Nathaniel, 87
St. Clair, Arthur: and selection of site for Dayton, 96; and western land-grabbing, 103
Salem, Mass, land distribution in, 25
San Francisco, land speculation in, 239-41
Santillan Grant, Calif., 144
Scarsdale Manor, N.Y., 32

Scheftel, Yetta, on the taxation of land values in Australasia, 260
Schurz, Carl, recommends reform in timberland disposal, 203
Scioto Project, 88, 89; failure of, 90-91
Scottish Illinois Land Investment Co., 134
Seligman, E. R. A.: on landownership as basis of taxation, 248; on taxation of urban real estate, 256-57; on taxation of unproductive property, 254
Separation Act (1914), 215
Serfdom, decline of in England, 14
Sevier, John, and settlement of Tennessee, 52-53
Seward, William, urges land reform in N.Y., 189
Seybert, Adam: on sale of public domain, 85, 86; survey of government land in Louisiana, 121-22
Show, S. B., on public ownership of forest land, 204-6
Skidmore, Thomas, and views of, 177, 267
Smith, Adam, influence of, 264
Smith, George, and Scottish Illinois Land Co., 134
Smith, Gerrit: against land monopoly, 269; land-reform resolution of, 179-80
Smith, Malancthon, 76
Smith's Hundred, Va., 34
Socage, described, 15
Soulard, Antoine, and Louisiana land claims, 110
South Africa, and taxation of land values, 260
South Carolina: colonial land system in, 61; and land dispute with Georgia, 77; land distribution in, 39; method of land taxation in early federal period, 253; quitrent system in, 197
South Carolina Yazoo Co., 78
Southern Pacific Railroad: and Peralta-Reavis Grant, 146; and rise in Los Angeles real estate boom, 241-42
"Specie Circular," effect of on land sales, 127-29
Spence, Thomas, and land reform in England, 17, 262-63; and *Real Rights of Man,* 178
Spiegel, Henry W., 63; on failure of legislation to improve farm tenant system, 229; on taxation and land tenure, 288
Springfield, Mass., colonial land allotment in, 28

Squatters: in California gold rush, 208-9; in New Hampshire Grants, 191; in Maine, 192-95; rights of, 129-30; in San Francisco, 240
Stubbs, Charles W., on danger of concentration of land, 283
Sub-infeudation, system of in Carolinas, 39
Suffrage, landownership as requisite for, 65, 66-67
Supreme Court: decision in De Bastrop Claim, 116; decision in Myra Gaines' case, 117; and *Fletcher vs. Peck,* 79; and Soulard claim, 110
Susquehanna Co., 57
Sutter, John, and dispute over squatter claims, 208-9
Swamp Land Acts, 130-31
Symmes, John Cleves: and Northwest grants, 83; and Miami Purchase, 91-92, 95; and Ohio purchases, 75; site of Cincinnati selected by, 95; and selection of Dayton site, 96

Taussig, Frank, on special taxation of site values, 247; taxing gains in site value, 247
Taxation, land: in colonial era, 249-51; controversy over in Constitutional Convention, 67-68; in early federal period, 251-53; on economic value of, 62-63, 259-61, 286-87; precedents of, 248-49; incidence of, 256-57; inequitable, origin of, 26; influence of George on, 275-76; on improvements, 255; merges into general property tax, 253-55; suggested by Jefferson, 62; proposals for reform of, 257-58
Tenancy: principal forms of, 217-18; rise of in West, 132-33; statistics on, 227-29. *See also* Land
Tenancy, farm: before and after Civil War, 219-23; European policy on, 226-27; evils of, 223-25; reform measures, 225-26
Tennessee: land taxation in, 252; settlement of, 52-53
Tennessee Yazoo Co., 78
Tenure: among aborigines, 7-8; *ejido,* in Mexico, 9 n.; in England, 23, 35; in New England colonies, 23; feudal aspects of in Maryland palatinate, 38; in primitive Mexico, 8-9; in proprietary colonies, 35; military, 15. *See also* Land
Texas: colonizing projects in, 150-51;

empresario system in, 148, 149, 150, 151, 154; land disposal in, 148-55
Tilden, Samuel J., land-reform recommendations of, 189-90
Timber Culture Act (1873), 137, 201-2; repeal of, 202
Timber Land Act (1878), 202-3
Tobacco, a factor in congregation-type settlement in Virginia, 33
Tobey, Thomas, and land scrip in Texas, 151
Tocqueville, Alexis de, cited, 59, 60, 294
Toledo, O., 97, 134
Town, as basic unit of political organization in New England, 24
Town building, aim of, 96-97
Town-jobbing: and the public domain, 95-98; after Revolution, 231-32. *See also* under cities
Town proprietors, role of in colonies, 27-28
Train, George F., and Crédit Foncier, 166; and Crédit Mobilier, 167
Transylvania Co., and settlement of Kentucky, 52
Trinity Church Corp., 235
Tucker, George, on rising land values, 266-67

Union Pacific Co., railroad project of, 166, 167
United Nations: land-reform resolution of, 281; and progressive land tax in foreign lands, 288-89
United States: and change in national land policy, 94; development of land question in, 26; early history of public domain in, 82-93; land reform in after Revolution, 59-63; origin of inequitable taxation in, 26; as prime mover in U.N. land-reform resolution, 281; progress of land reform in, 262-76; and taxing power of federal government, 67-68; Yazoo lands ceded to, 79
United States Steel Corp., 214; and development of Gary and Morrisville, 244

Vandalia Co., and western land speculation, 55-56
Van Dyke, T. S., on Los Angeles land boom, 242
Van Rensselaer, Killian, patroonship of, 31-32

Van Renssalaer, Stephen, 32
Vermont: dispute over land in, 191; method of land taxation in early federal period, 252. *See also* New Hampshire Grants
Vincennes, Ind., 102
Virginia: early land systems in, 21; land distribution in, 33-35; land speculation in, 76, 77; primogeniture and entail abolished in, 62; and Transylvania claim, 52; western land claims of, 102; and western land grants, 49-51
Virginia (London) Co., 20-21
Virginia Yazoo Co., 78

Wadsworth, James, 73
Wadsworth, Jeremiah, 73-74
Wadsworth, William, 73
Walker, Francis, on theories of George, 273-74
Walker, Thomas, and western land grants, 50
Wallace, Henry A., on reform of farm tenancy, 225
Walpole, Thomas, and Illinois grant, 56
Washington, Augustine, and western land speculation, 53
Washington, George: interest of in western lands, 53-55; opposed to Indian Line, 51; and Yazoo dispute, 78
Washington, Lawrence, and western land speculation, 53
Washington, exploitation of timber lands in, 202
Washington, D.C., town-jobbing in, 232-34
Webster, Daniel: on abolition of primogeniture, 61; and Clamorgan Land Assoc., 112; on cause of land speculation, 128-29; on public-land use, 157
Weiss, Jacob, and exploitation of coal lands, 211-12
Wells, Davis, on opposition to taxation on value of land, 272-73
Wentworth, Benning, and New Hampshire Grants disputes, 29, 191
Western Land Assoc. of Minnesota, 168
Western Reserve, Connecticut's claim to, 93
West Jersey Co., 37
Weyerhaeuser Timber Co., policy of exploitation and conservation, 200, 203-4
Wheeler, John, on merchant adventurers, 19-20
Whitney, Asa, urges railroad to Pacific, 165
Wilkinson, James, and selection of Dayton site, 96
Wilson, James, and Dutch holdings in Pennsylvania, 72
Winthrop, John, 24
Wolcott, Oliver, study of taxation by, 251
World War II, effect of on farm tenancy, 228-29
Wyoming (Pa.) Massacre, 57

"Yankee communism," in New England, 22
Yazoo, dispute over, 77-79
York, Duke of, and New Jersey grant, 36

Zane's Trace, O., 156